C000193631

Ethics and Desire in the Wake of Postmodernism

Continuum Literary Studies Series

Also available in the series

Ethics and Desire in the Wake of Postmodernism

Contemporary Satire

Graham Matthews

Continuum Literary Studies

continuum

Continuum International Publishing Group

The Tower Building	80 Maiden Lane
11 York Road	Suite 704
London SE1 7NX	New York NY 10038

www.continuumbooks.com

© Graham Matthews 2012

All rights reserved. No part of this publication may be reproduced or transmitted in any form or by any means, electronic or mechanical, including photocopying, recording, or any information storage or retrieval system, without prior permission in writing from the publishers.

Graham Matthews has asserted his right under the Copyright, Designs and Patents Act, 1988, to be identified as the Author of this work.

British Library Cataloguing-in-Publication Data
A catalogue record for this book is available from the British Library.

ISBN: HB: 978-1-4411-4007-4

Library of Congress Cataloging-in-Publication Data
Matthews, Graham.
Ethics and desire in the wake of postmodernism: contemporary satire / Graham Matthews.
    p. cm. – (Continuum literary studies)
  Includes bibliographical references and index.
  ISBN 978-1-4411-4007-4 (hardcover: alk. paper) – ISBN 978-1-4411-3439-4 (ebook pdf)
1. Fiction – History and criticism – Theory, etc. 2. Satire. 3. Ethics in literature.
4. Desire in literature. 5. Postmodernism (Literature) I. Title.

PN3347.M27 2012
809.3'9357–dc23   2011047845

Typeset by Newgen Imaging Systems Pvt. Ltd, Chennai, India
Printed and bound in Great Britain

Contents

Acknowledgements

I would like to thank Anthony Fothergill, Peter Boxall, Paul Young, Alex Murray, Kate Hext, Sam Goodman and Christie Smith for all their insights, comments and support. I am also very grateful to the staff at Bloomsbury Academic including Colleen Coalter, David Avital, Rachel Eisenhauer and Laura Murray for all their help in bringing this book to print. I would also like to thank the members of the English department at the University of Exeter for all their advice and encouragement. Finally, I am indebted to Lara Cox – nothing would have been possible without her contributions.

Introduction

Ethics and Desire in the Wake of Postmodernism: Contemporary Satire takes the close of the first decade of the twenty-first century as an opportunity for a reappraisal of postmodernism and its lingering effects. Postmodernism has been the dominant cultural force throughout the second half of the twentieth century and has influenced conceptions of identity across disciplines as diverse as English, Geography, Architecture and Politics. This book offers an intervention into postmodern debates and explores new avenues of radical critique located within contemporary satiric fiction. Within the postmodern era and the accompanying deluge of irony, cynicism and detached enjoyment, critics have bemoaned the loss of real world referents amidst a sea of simulacra. Critics and theorists such as Thomas Docherty, Josh Toth, Jacques Rancière, Timothy Bewes and Zygmunt Bauman have increasingly come to recognize the problems with postmodern forms of critique and the increased difficulty involved in discerning ideological structures. As Linda Hutcheon argues in *The Politics of Postmodernism*, there has always been a tension between postmodern politics and poetics. For some writers and theorists this tension has proved fruitful. However, the unprecedented expansion of postmodern aesthetics into all aspects of contemporary life has led to a cultural hegemony that has in turn hindered the Marxist political rhetoric of emancipation and revolution. In addition to this, the radical thought discussed in the academy has become increasingly divorced from real world praxis, thereby offering itself as an ideological support for the systems of global capitalism. As Thomas Docherty states:

> the successful institutionalisation of theory, modernism and Marxism, has stymied the radical pretensions of their movements and philosophies. What is worse, theory and Marxism have become, doubtless despite themselves, complicit with the institutional imposition of limits upon their revolutionary credentials.[1]

In other words, Marxism situated within the academy today exists as a spectral presence to be discussed in the same register as the nuances of a fictional text. Whereas Marxist theory had previously been predicated upon the denunciation of false consciousness and worked to cut through the illusions of consumer society in order to reveal the machinations of the material economic base, it now constitutes a weakened form of critical praxis that is itself packaged and sold as a consumable object. This was highlighted by the fact that sales of Marx's *Capital* soared in the immediate aftermath of the subprime crisis in 2008 as the population sought out alternatives to the apparent failure of neoliberal economics. Following the devaluation of traditional methods of critique and the celebration of indeterminacy endemic to the postmodern age, it is my contention that satire remains a vibrant mode of critique. Indeed, satire's ability to generate insightful and nuanced debate out of situations seemingly characterized by indeterminacy and indecision has been frequently overlooked. The writers under consideration include Bret Easton Ellis, J. G. Ballard, Chuck Palahniuk, Will Self, Michel Houellebecq and Tama Janowitz. Each author has risen in prominence over the past decade and all have demonstrated a capacity to respond to the problems and doubts that have arisen in the wake of postmodernism. Indeed, I argue that these writers offer a variety of different responses to the problematic relationship between Marxist politics and postmodern aesthetics. Each chapter delivers an intervention into a different aspect of Western society bound up in a single term that has been seemingly emptied of critical content and is increasingly used in everyday speech. These terms are fear, nihilism, revolution, ethics, enjoyment and feminism. By naming the naturalized ideologies of the early twenty-first century, the authors under consideration aim to revitalize radical critique.

While the past decade has witnessed the continued expansion of postmodern aesthetics into all aspects of everyday life, the political efficacy of postmodern approaches to art and literature is in decline. Through an exploration of the work of six contemporary satirists, this book aims to focus critical debate on six crucial issues for our understanding of ethics and desire in the twenty-first century. Rather than adopting the post-structuralist emphasis on plurality and indeterminacy, this volume recognizes that within the era of globalized capitalism and the decline of traditional symbolic authority, this critical approach frequently functions as an ideological support for the status quo. Instead I draw on Lacanian psychoanalysis and contemporary cultural and political theory in order to explore the ways in which satiric fiction contains the potential to cut through the problematic political stance of indecision in order to enact a radical de-centering of the fundamental coordinates of society. Each chapter provides a focus

on one satiric author and the ways in which their work offers fresh insight
into one key issue within the contemporary sociocultural order. In this
introduction, I will begin with a discussion of the nature of critique as it
has developed over the twentieth century. Culminating in the ascendancy
of the postmodern era and concomitant decline of traditional methods of
criticism, this section lays out the strengths and limitations of discourses
of emancipation at the close of the twentieth century. Having explored the
significance of critique in the twentieth century, I trace a selective genealogy of the satiric tradition. In this section, I draw on Lacanian psychoanalytic theory in order to reappraise the often contradictory nature of
satiric critique and suggest ways in which the genre continues to operate
as a vibrant and disruptive form. This is followed by a discussion of the
comic spirit and the ways in which this can be combined with psychoanalytic theory in order to produce an innovative critical methodology that
enables a fresh engagement with the conditions of the present. Finally,
I ask what is significant about writing in the wake of postmodernism. In
this section I lay out the significance of each author and detail the nature
of their particular critical intervention. In this way, I explore the ways in
which contemporary satire offers insight into questions of ethics and desire
in the wake of postmodernism.

Twentieth-Century Critique

In order to understand the proclivities of critique in the present, it is necessary to examine general shifts in theoretical thought over the twentieth
century. Of especial importance is the transition from modernism to postmodernism. In *The Century*, the philosopher Alain Badiou argues that the
term 'modernism' functions as a marker for the two decades between 1890
and 1914 that heralded a period of unbridled invention and creativity:

> in every field of thought these years represent a period of exceptional
> invention, marked by a polymorphous creativity that can only be com-
> pared to the Florentine Renaissance or the century of Pericles. It is a
> prodigious period of excitement and rupture.[2]

This period signalled achievements across a broad range of spheres including the work of many great philosophers such as Wittgenstein and Husserl,
artists including Picasso and Braque, writers such as Joyce, Conrad and
Woolf, scientific achievement in the form of Einstein's theory of general

relativity, mathematicians such as Frege and Poincaré, the birth of psychoanalysis with the publication of *The Interpretation of Dreams*, as well as the flourishing of film-makers such as Griffith and Chaplin. However, as Badiou's statement indicates, this rapid outpouring of creativity across the spheres of human endeavour is not unique. Indeed, it should be noted that there have been many instances of what could be considered to be 'modernist' movements throughout history including the theological critique of magic in the Middle Ages, the European Renaissance and its promotion of individual liberty, as well as the development of Enlightenment philosophy and the triumph of Reason. Rather than referencing a specific historical period, the 'modern' can be understood to be a particular form or gesture that calls into question existing values and posits new ones in their place. In this sense, the 'modern' moment marks a caesura or rupture within the conditions of the present as well as the establishment of new structures and values.

I will discuss the pattern of rupture and establishment of new values in relation to the concerns of psychoanalysis and satire later in the Introduction. For now, the focus of this study is on the development of systems and structures of thought that found their apotheosis at the turn of the twentieth century and continue into the present. Perhaps the most clear-sighted and succinct description of enlightened modernity can be found in the work of Jürgen Habermas:

> The project of modernity formulated in the 18th century by the philosophers of the Enlightenment consisted in their efforts to develop objective science, universal morality and law, and autonomous art according to their inner logic. At the same time, this project intended to release the cognitive potentials of each of these domains from their esoteric forms. The Enlightenment philosophers wanted to utilize this accumulation of specialised culture for the enrichment of everyday life – that is to say, for the rational organisation of everyday social life.[3]

This is the philosophical basis for modernism as classically understood by present day scholars. Modernism is conventionally understood to signal a critique of tradition, the conventions of realism and the omniscience of God in order to reflect the changing demands of the new economic, social and political conditions of the period. Alongside the development of modern politics and aesthetics, came the development of new methods of critique, solidified under the banner of critical theory by the group of Western Marxists who became known as the Frankfurt School. At the same time, this period marked the development of structuralist thought. Habermas' emphasis on objectivity, universality and logic provides an indication that the seeds of structuralist theory were sown in the project of modernity. Structuralism is a continuation and application of the theories of signification developed by Ferdinand de Saussure in the *Course in General Linguistics*, posthumously published in 1916, to the realms of anthropology, sociology and literary study. The focus on the structures and systems that determine lived experience constituted a key moment in the development of theoretical critique. As Stephen Ross states, 'theory's concern with globalization, imperialism, gender and sex roles, race and racism, reason and superstition, enlightenment and benightedness, sovereignty and slavery, margins and peripheries, and ethical complexity continues, albeit in a different register, modernism's already articulated concerns'.[4] In this light, the development of both critical theory and structuralism can be understood to be predicated upon the demands of the incomplete project of modernity.

The traditional concerns of critical theory and structuralist analysis were later challenged by the rise of poststructuralist thought and the deconstruction of normative values across art, culture, politics and society. Against structuralism's desire to produce a method of criticism predicated upon the predictable and scientific study of linguistic structures, post-structuralism constituted a rejection of the conception of structures as fixed and self-regulating systems of control. The transition from structuralism to post-structuralism is rooted in Jacques Derrida's simultaneous development and critique of Saussurean linguistics. The key achievement for Saussure was to recognize that language is arbitrary and differential. It is arbitrary insofar as there is no clear relation between the signifier and the signified and consequently between the sign and its referent. It is differential to the extent that no sign bears positive content in its own right and is defined in relation to the network of other signs. Saussure posited that there must exist a finite number of signifiers in order to ensure sense-making by restricting the free play of signification. This is achieved through the scientific study of language as a grammatical structure (*langue*) separate from everyday speech (*parole*) and as a synchronic structure, held in a fixed position in time. Jacques Derrida's conception of language simultaneously constituted a development and a rejection of Saussure's principles. For Derrida, Saussure's conception of language was restricted by the artificial imposition of scientific parameters. Derrida recognized that language was both arbitrary and differential but instead of binding value to a fixed structure, he instead embraced the free play of signification. Meaning was now understood to be an effect of free play in which the sense of individual units of meaning were produced through the convergence of 'traces' of different signifiers across the chain of signification. This formulation enabled Derrida to recognize the existence of the transcendental signified, which functioned as the (impossible) guarantor of meaning, simultaneously held outside and at the centre of structures of signification. As he argues in *Writing and Difference*:

> Structure – or rather the structurality of structure – although it has always been at work, has always been neutralized or reduced, and this by a process of giving it a centre or referring it to a point of presence, a fixed origin. The function of this centre was not only to orient, balance, and organize the structure – one cannot in fact conceive of an unorganised structure – but above all to make sure that the organizing principle of the structure would limit what we might call the *play* of the structure.[5]

This intervention values indeterminacy and multiplicity over fixed, monolithic structures of sense-making. By displaying the inconsistencies at the centre of the authoritative and hierarchical structures that determine lived experience, Derrida was able to produce a radical new form of critique. The scientific grounding of structuralism was disrupted by deconstructionism's displacement of the very notion of ground and concomitant emphasis on undecideability and multiplicity.

Deconstructionist criticism worked to undermine previously privileged structures of power and control. As such, it constituted a radical critique of the enlightenment project of modernity that presupposed the existence of will and the autonomous self. However, Derrida's emphasis on undecideability results in a 'double bind' consisting of the simultaneous possibility and impossibility of political thought and decision making. Although Derrida claimed that deconstructive approaches could redress real conditions of injustice such as racism, sexism and homophobia, with the deconstruction of metaphysical presence emerged the difficulty of engaging in decisive political action. As Antonio Calcagno asks:

> how do we philosophically account for such a possibility that necessarily comes undone with its own impossibility and the force of its own undecideability? If the double bind truly structures all of reality, then war crimes, holocaust, murder and rape remain ultimately undecideable.[6]

Derrida claims that despite acknowledging the impossibility of justice, one should strive to maintain the possibility of demanding justice. This combination of deconstructive strategies with political fidelity is paradoxical and highly problematic. Putting the question of political engagement to one side for a moment, it is interesting to note that when post-structuralist writers such as Barthes, Kristeva and Lacan engage in literary analysis, they tend to privilege modernist texts as objects of study, to the detriment of postmodern fiction. Indeed, as Josh Toth remarks:

> rarely does poststructuralism bother with postmodern works; it's difficult – if not impossible – to say what, exactly, 'poststructuralists' know about (American) postmodern cultural production. Did Derrida know his Pynchon? Had Barthes read Philip K. Dick? What does Kristeva think of *Pulp Fiction*?[7]

Presumably this is because modernist writers offer grounded epistemological positions that are susceptive to deconstructive critique whereas postmodern fiction already contains within itself the parameters of its own dissolution or critique. As we can see from deconstruction's problematic relationship with both politics and postmodern literature, the unresolved tension between strategies that displace any fixed ground or social formation and the need to make firm political or artistic commitments is highlighted by the problematic relationship between the politics and poetics of postmodernism. In this sense, the rise of post-structuralist criticism alongside postmodern cultural production could be understood to be an 'incomplete' modernist gesture that offered a critique of pre-existing systems and structures but struggled to generate new values and causes of its own. The postmodern era and the critical tools of post-structuralism offer a deconstruction of metaphysical grounding and 'truth' but fail to offer a meaningful ontological structure in its place.

The work of seminal postmodern theorists such as Fredric Jameson, Jean Baudrillard and Jean-François Lyotard offered a new understanding of the social, political and economic conditions emerging in the second half of the twentieth century and delivered new methods of radical critique. Lyotard offered a philosophical study of the postmodern condition that he broadly defines as an attitude of, 'incredulity toward metanarratives'.[8] Metanarratives should be understood as the rules that establish the legitimacy of a particular narrative and produce the effect of sense. As Lyotard notes:

> Languages are not employed haphazardly [. . .] their use is subject to a condition we call pragmatic: each must formulate its own rules and

petition the addressee to accept them. To satisfy this condition, an axiomatic is defined that includes a definition of the symbols used in the proposed language, a description of the form expressions in this language must take in order to gain acceptance (well formed expressions), and an enumeration of the operations that may be performed on the accepted expressions (axioms in the narrow sense). (42)

Consequently, all speech acts require legitimacy from an unspoken structure in order to generate meaning. As such, all metanarratives, which constitute the rules of meaning-making, are bound up with the dominance of totalizing grand narratives, understood as progressive structures that produce a seemingly coherent historical, moral and political view of the world in which we live. According to Lyotard's critique, grand narratives work to obfuscate the narratives constructed through the agency and self-determinacy of the individual. As such, Lyotard's theorization of the postmodern condition offers to emancipate subjective and marginalized narratives from grand totalizing structures, thereby giving voice to previously oppressed groups. However, it is important to note that this thought emerged out of a specific set of historical circumstances. Indeed, it would be wrong-headed to assume that Lyotard's theory remains entirely divorced from the dominant discourses of power, despite its ostensible critique. Jean-Luc Nancy argues that the postmodern condition could only have emerged in the wake of the death and destruction on a mass scale brought about during the twentieth century:

> History can no longer be presented as [. . .] a 'grand narrative', the narrative of some grand, collective destiny of mankind (of Humanity, or Liberty, etc), a narrative that was grand because it was great, and that was great because its ultimate destination was considered good. Our time is the time, when this history at least has been suspended: total war, genocide, the challenge of nuclear powers, implacable technology, hunger, and absolute misery, all these are, at the least, evident signs of self-destroying mankind, of self-annihilating history.[9]

The first half of the twentieth century bore witness to a series of seemingly disastrous events including the birth of Communism and fascism, the decline of European empires and dissolution of the colonial project, two world wars and the Great Depression. These events led to destruction and the loss of life on a grand scale as well as an emerging consciousness of the instability of political causes that had traditionally subsumed the rights and desires of the individual in the pursuit of an ideal. Trust and faith in authoritative structures of power turned to mistrust and disillusionment with the dominant ideologies of progress, rationality and reason. As Badiou states in *The Century*, 'after the war of 1914–18, no longer can anyone trust in History to the point of surrendering to the alleged progress of its movement' (15). Rather than surrendering the individual's subjectivity to the totalizing grand narratives of vast political causes, thought in the second half of the twentieth century celebrated choice, individuality and freedom. In the wake of the death and destruction caused by the imposition of monolithic structures, it was almost inevitable that the artists and theorists of postmodernism would give birth to an ethical stance that celebrated choice, the rights of the individual and freedom.

In contrast to the emancipatory potential promised by Lyotard's celebration of the demise of grand narratives, Jean Baudrillard offered a reading of postmodernity as a period dominated by the endless proliferation of semblances devoid of their referential being or substance. The rise of the simulacrum – roughly glossed as the signifier devoid of its signified – has resulted in the knowledge that truth, reference and objective causality have ceased to exist. For Baudrillard, the explosion of mass media and global communications technology has led to the dissolution of meaning and signification that has in turn resulted in an increasing inability to evoke ethical or affective responses to images of suffering. As he states in *Simulacra and Simulation*: 'we live in a world where there is more and more information, and less and less meaning' (79). Communication has become a circular process of endless replication and simulation in which meaning and value are eroded beneath the influx of images disconnected from their reality. This understanding of postmodernity has significant political effects. In his infamous discussion of the Gulf War, Baudrillard states:

> The victory of the model is more important than victory on the ground. [. . .] War-processing, the transparency of the model in the unfolding of the war, the strategy of relentless execution of a programme, the electrocution of all reaction and any live initiative, including their own: these are more important from the point of view of general deterrence (of friends and foes alike) than the final result on the ground. Clean war, white war, programmed war: more lethal than the war which sacrifices human lives.[10]

Mistaken by many critics as a denial of the suffering and horrors inflicted during the Gulf conflict, Baudrillard's text questions the ethics of representation and argues that the realities of war have been submerged beneath the simulated model of events. In a war presented as being without casualties (on the Allied side), could this clean, white conflict really be called a war? For Baudrillard, this was a hyperreal scenario in which events lost their impact and signifiers referred to one another, devoid of their real-world referent. This scenario reached its apotheosis when CNN in the studio crossed live to reporters in the Gulf, only for them to confess that they were watching CNN in order to find out what was happening around them. In this sense, the Gulf War marked the point when the logic of the simulation replaced reality.

Lyotard's and Baudrillard's reading of the postmodern condition share in common a diagnosis of the late twentieth century as a period of dissolution, fragmentation and the loss of clear ethical measure. This moment of radical indeterminacy and concomitant mistrust of traditional structures of control is reflected in the opening of Bret Easton Ellis' *American Psycho*. This notorious text is shocking not only for its images of transgression and extreme violence but, as Naomi Mandel notes in '"Right Here in Nowheres": *American Psycho* and Violence's Critique', fiction and fact become progressively indistinguishable, causing the reader to lose his or her sense of the real. The opening places a quote from Dante's *Inferno* that reads: 'ABANDON ALL HOPE YE WHO ENTER HERE' in competition for the reader's attention with advertisements for *Les Misérables*, the song 'Be My Baby' on the radio and graffiti that spells out the word 'DYKE' (3). These juxtapositions not only refute conventional distinctions made between high and low culture but more tellingly, replace the conventions of realist description with an onslaught of signs devoid of their real-world referent. In addition, the title highlights the novel's textuality by inviting comparison with Alfred Hitchcock's *Psycho*. However, whereas *Psycho*'s resolution lends itself to a stock psychoanalytic response in which Norman Bates is shown to be grappling with an unresolved Oedipal complex, *American Psycho* refuses to reaffirm the grounds of normative behaviour. Indeed, Ellis' decision to name his protagonist Patrick Bateman in the wake of Hitchcock's Norman Bates generates textual references between Bates and the Everyman plays in which the hero stands as a cipher for mankind in general. As such, the text signals a shift in critical focus from an indictment of individual deviancy to the deconstruction of the surrounding sociocultural order. In *American Psycho* the boundaries between fact and fiction, the literary and the literal, are rendered indistinct. As such the text ably demonstrates the fluidity of both ethics and desire in the postmodern world. At the novel's conclusion, Bateman declares that his confession has meant nothing. Consequently, the text refuses to offer new values or distinctions of its own. As such, the text itself operates as a synonym for the postmodern condition. As Harvie

Ferguson argues, 'in the postmodern world all distinctions become fluid, boundaries dissolve, and everything can just as well appear to be its opposite; irony becomes the perpetual sense that things could be somewhat different, though never fundamentally or radically different'.[11] *American Psycho* offers insight into the postmodern era as one characterized by dissolution, disillusionment and the deconstruction of normative structures, offering in the process the sense that things could be different, but the text resolutely fails to offer a new set of values in their wake. While Lyotard has argued that this is an era of opportunity for previously oppressed and minoritarian groups, it is unclear to what extent we are actually witnessing the construction of new egalitarian or democratic values. The implication is that the post-structuralist valorization of indeterminacy offers us the sense of freedom and choice while obfuscating the possibility of revolutionizing the fundamental coordinates of society.

In summary, whereas modernism could be understood as a movement towards greater 'authenticity' and self-actualization, postmodernism heralded and celebrated the development of a knowing selfhood that weakened the bond between society and the individual. In a similar manner, radical critique throughout the twentieth century can be broadly characterized as inhabiting two stages. This is the transition from a critique of the reality beneath appearances to a critique of the very notion of reality itself. As Jacques Rancière states in *The Emancipated Spectator*:

> Once we could have fun denouncing the dark, solid reality concealed behind the brilliance of appearances. But today there is allegedly no longer any solid reality to counter-pose to the reign of appearances, nor any dark reverse side to be opposed to the triumph of consumer society.[12]

Whereas structuralist writers focused on the structures that determine subjectivity, post-structuralist theorists not only deconstruct the notion of fixed structures but, further to this, insist that these structures never existed in the first place. In the wake of this understanding, how does the subject ensnared within the circuits of global capitalism engage in effective modes of critique? It is useful at this stage to consider the work of the sociologist Zygmunt Bauman. In his seminal text, *Liquid Modernity*, Bauman bypasses debates surrounding the transition from modernism to postmodernism in order to argue that we have moved from a state of 'solid' modernity to a 'liquid' modernism. In the earlier discussion of 'modern' moments, I suggested that these can be understood as ruptures that dissolve the fixed structures that make the world predictable and consequently manageable, thereby providing the impetus for new values to emerge and solidify in their place. Bauman's thesis is that modernism offered just such a rupture in which solids melted into air and new systems of measure were erected in their wake. However, he then proceeds to draw on the metaphor of liquidity in order to describe the present moment as a general engulfment and dissolution of the solid states of the past but one that is tellingly devoid of the concomitant birth of new values:

> Global powers are bent on dismantling such networks for the sake of their continuous and growing fluidity, that principal source of their strength and the warrant of their invincibility. And it is the falling apart, the friability, the brittleness, the transience, the until-further-noticeness of human bonds and networks which allow these powers to do their job in the first place.[13]

Within an era defined by intangibility, flexibility and, indeed, liquidity, what emerges is the difficulty involved in constructing critique. How can the critical tools of post-structuralist thinkers or the self-reflexive narrative devices employed by postmodern authors effectively interrogate the present-day conditions of fluidity and liquidity? Just as post-structuralist theorists failed to engage with postmodern texts that revelled in their instability and self-reflexivity, our current critical tools are ill-equipped to offer insight into the conditions of indeterminacy that characterize the present. This book explores the ways in which contemporary writers and theorists have responded to these concerns and offer new forms of textual practice in order to engage with questions concerning ethics and desire. In an era characterized by fragmentation and the dissolution of totalizing grand narratives, the value of satiric fiction has been overlooked. As a reactive form, satire would appear to necessitate the circulation of fixed normative ideas and common sense. However, as will become apparent in the following discussion, satiric fiction thrives under conditions of uncertainty and indeterminacy. In the next section, I will discuss the value of satiric fiction and highlight the ways in which the genre generates effective modes of critique.

Satiric Critique

Satire is commonly understood to be a literary form that exhibits and examines instances of vice and folly in order to make them appear ridiculous or contemptible. This would suggest that satire is a form that should be defined in wholly moral terms. Indeed, satiric theory from the Renaissance to the mid-twentieth century has remained surprisingly static, concerning itself with establishing the form as a didactic, unified moral discourse. However, from its etymological origins, satire can be perceived as a form that exceeds unified, normative or commonsensical thought. 'Satire' is derived from the Latin *satis* meaning 'mixture', 'medley' or simply 'enough'. In addition, the term *lanx satura* meaning 'mixed' or 'full platter' indicates that satire generates a formless miscellany, with matter no sooner taken up than deserted. This stands in opposition to the theorization of satire as a predominantly moral form directed at a specific person or type as typified by writers such as Dryden and Pope. In addition, although not etymologically linked, the figure of the *satyr* (the half man-half beast) haunts satiric theory with an image of satire as lawless, wild and threatening. As Dustin Griffin argues, 'theorists have long sought to repress or domesticate the shaggy, obscene, and transgressive satyr that ranges through satire's long history, lurking in dark corners, and to make it into the model of a moral citizen'.[14] Griffin's use of terms such as 'repression' and 'morality' immediately speaks to the concerns of psychoanalytic discourse. Consequently, the figure of the *satyr* can be read as emblematic of the unconscious desires of the subject, whereas the unified moral theory of satire bears an affinity with the stable autonomous ego. As this intersection demonstrates, it will prove useful to draw on psychoanalytic theory in order to highlight the productive tensions to be found within narrative satire and unpack the ways in which the genre has responded to the concerns of the twenty-first century.

The consideration of satiric theory must begin with John Dryden's widely influential conceptualization of satire as a predominantly moral form. As Griffin argues, John Dryden's preface to the translation of the satires of Juvenal and Persius, in which he attempts to elevate satire to the level of Art, is the most prominent theoretical document in the great age of English satire. As Griffin points out, for Dryden 'satire should be rigorously unified, attacking a single vice and commending the opposite virtue' (14). This was not an original conception and reiterated the Renaissance ideal. However, Dryden's model was hugely influential for debates over the origins and meaning of 'satire' during the late seventeenth century. Throughout the English satiric tradition there has been the consensus that satire is a lawless form that threatens innocent victims and endangers the State. Against this, Dryden's model stood as an argument for satire's status as fine verse and bearer of didactic moral purpose. This disagreement has a precedent in Horace's satires. Horace is warned by Trebatius that foul verses will result in prosecution. In reply Trebatius states: '*Foul* verses, yes; but what if a party compose / *fine* verses which win a favourable verdict from Caesar? / Or snarl at a public menace when he himself is blameless?'[15] From its inception, it would appear that satire ostensibly follows an imperative to deliver a critique that offers both artistic unity and moral purpose. At the same time, it is worth taking note of Trebatius' answer to Horace's questions: 'The indictment will dissolve in laughter, and you'll go scot free' (76). It would appear that satire functions within a liminal space between transgression and the law. In this example, laughter causes critical judgement to vacillate therefore allowing the satirist to speak that which should normally go unspoken. This play between civilization, repression and jokes can be linked to the Freudian concept of the civilized subject as an ego that must defend its integrity by repressing the dark illicit desires of the id. According to Freud, jokes are an expression of repressed hostility, delivered in a manner that maintains the social relation. This is a theme that will be later explored in greater depth.

For Dryden, satire is bound up within a progressive ideology of increasing refinement and sensibility. He traces a line of reformation and heightened artistic sensibility through Lucilius, Horace, Juvenal, Donne and finally himself. His aim was to sustain the historical transition from 'Nature without Art' or rough vigour and energy, to 'Art Completed' or purposeful discourse. Ultimately, Dryden's theory can be distilled into two key points. Firstly, satire 'ought to treat of one Subject; to be confin'd to one particular Theme; or, at least, to one principally'.[16] Secondly, 'the Poet is bound, and that *ex Officio*, to give his Reader some one Precept of Moral Virtue; and to caution him against some one particular' (4:80). Satire should be a unified artistic form. In addition, it should operate around a central binary opposition, clearly demarcating evil from the good. However, there are more satiric narratives that do not fit with this rule-set than those that do. This is a satiric theory that in seeking wholeness must exclude narrative satire, lampoons and invectives including Horace's satirical odes or libels. This wholeness is predicated upon a process of radical exclusion. Horace in particular, exceeds Dryden's discourse with his rambling, digressive manner and inconsistent morality. Dryden's elevation of satire to the status of Art should be regarded as a fantasy of wholeness or the One. This fantasy of the One was identified by the French psychoanalyst Jacques Lacan and it is for this reason that I turn to psychoanalytic thought in the following section. As we shall see, the fantasy-structure of the One is a structure of thought that has pervaded Western thought since Antiquity.

Satire and Psychoanalysis

Lacan points to the Copernican revolution as an example of man's desire for wholeness. For centuries, mathematicians had argued that the Earth was the centre around which the spheres revolved. By contrast, Copernicus posited that the Sun was the point of origin, around which the spheres turned. This could be read as a decentering of the Earth and subsequently, of man's place in the Universe. However, for Lacan, who emphasizes linguistic structures throughout his work:

> The Copernican revolution was by no means a revolution. If the centre of a sphere is assumed, in a discourse that is merely analogical, to constitute the pivotal point, the fact of changing this pivotal point, of having it occupied by the earth or the sun, involves nothing that in itself subverts what the signifier 'centre' intrinsically preserves.[17]

Rather than disrupting the fantasy of the circle, or the signifier of wholeness, the Copernican revolution ultimately constituted a reinforcement of the categories of centre and periphery. The substitution of the Earth for the Sun retains the belief in a possible harmony and the perfection of the sphere. Consequently, Dryden's demand that satire construct itself as an Artistic moral unity can be read as a Copernican turn that obfuscates satire's link to the *satyr* or the unruly, half man-half beast. Rather than placing satire's disruptive and subversive core at the periphery, Dryden urges his fellow satirists to stand at the centre. This directly contradicts the conception of satire as *lanx satura* or 'mixed platter'; that is, as a diffuse centreless organicity. Lacan goes on to discuss Kepler's introduction of an imperfect shape – the ellipse, into the orbit of the planets, which problematizes the centre. Rather than turning about a centre, the planets are now perceived to fall. In a similar way, satire can be seen to initiate a fall from the fantasy that there can be a single moral purpose. This should be taken in the Biblical sense as a fall from innocence into knowledge.

Satire speaks from a position of knowledge rather than of innocence. It displays vice and folly for critique rather than simply repressing them. Horace's programmatic satires subvert the notion that satire is didactic with a clear moral centre by providing enjoyment and provoking laughter. Until the mid-twentieth century, only the first 28 lines of Book I Satire 2 were published by English commentators due to its bawdy content. Here, Horace depicts immoral behaviour, ostensibly to deliver a normative approach to the sexual relation. However, his depiction of vice leads to ethical inconsistency: 'The sight of a certain aristocrat emerging from a brothel drew / a famous remark from Cato: "Keep up the good work!" he said / "Whenever a young man's veins are swollen by accursed lust / he's right to go down to that sort of place instead of grinding / other men's wives"' (33). Rather than delivering a fixed moral message, Horace's satire generates laughter. The renunciation of one form of enjoyment is shown to produce another. This demonstrates the fluidity of desire and the plasticity of the drives, indicating that moral consistency can never determine enjoyment. As Mladen Dolar states: 'enjoyment appears as the one thing that one can never be rid of [. . .] A and non-A don't cancel each other out but produce more A, or rather a different sort of A, an A1'.[18] All ascetic practices testify to the fact that the imperative 'Stop enjoying!' still constitutes a form of enjoyment, albeit a different kind of enjoyment. Satire as *lanx satura*, presents both transgression and prohibition as sources of enjoyment without contradiction. Rather than presenting satire as a unified moral agency, it should be seen as a fallen form that presents the obscene underside of the social relation for inspection. In doing so, it disrupts the dialectic of margin and centre and constitutes a subversion of the spherical world view.

Humanity has continued to labour under the fantasy of wholeness for centuries. On one hand satire has the potential to stage a significant challenge to this spherical world view, and on the other, it has been upheld by writers such as Dryden as a unified moral discourse. This is indicative of the difficulty involved in sustaining satire in its de-centering role. However, psychoanalytic theory reveals the fruitful tension between ordered moral discourse and the discordant untrammelled energy that marks the genre. In particular, there is a significant parallel in Freud's de-centering of the subject. Freud's project highlighted the radical alterity of the unconscious and indicated the ways in which the subject is not an autonomous spherical entity but is subject to unconscious desires over which he or she has no control. However, psychoanalytic theorists such as Bruce Fink have also been forced to acknowledge the persistence of the fantasy structure of the One: 'despite the Freudian revolution that removes consciousness from the centre of ourselves, it ineluctably slips back to the centre, or a centre is ineluctably established somewhere'.[19] The strength of the psychoanalytic approach lies in its ability to identify and subsequently contend with this fantasy structure. The reason for the tenacity of this fantasy may be found in Scott Wilson's argument that there is, in fact, pleasure to be taken in order. He asserts that pleasure can be likened to an episteme and forms the basis of any discursive formation: 'There is a pleasure in finding resemblances between things, in classifying them, in identifying things and differentiating them with others, in making lists and placing things in a hierarchy'.[20] This can be demonstrated by the fact that subjects frequently do not do the things that they *know* to be in their best interest. Instead, they are guided by pleasure. Indeed, this implicit enjoyment in discourse explains why it is painful to step outside the dominant discourse and the accompanying loss of fantasies of wholeness.

The figure of the *satyr* occupies the liminal space between beast and man, thereby constituting a challenge to the establishment of civilization, classification and order. In a similar way, the *lanx satura* is a mixed platter that represents a refusal of hierarchy. As such, satire has the potential to be the de-centering form *par excellence* and frequently works to actively deny the imposition of boundaries and hierarchies. In particular, satire is notorious for denying closure. As Griffin argues, 'since satirists are not normally interested in narrative wholeness, in character consistency, in drawing that Jamesian circle by which a particular set of human relations appears to be bounded, they will feel no obligation to provide narrative closure' (6). To return to Bret Easton Ellis' *American Psycho*, it is clear that this is a text that refuses narrative closure as demonstrated by the final line: 'THIS IS NOT AN EXIT' (384). Indeed, the closing passage is increasingly fragmented and interspersed with pauses, shrugs, sighs and incomplete thoughts. There is a parallel to be drawn with the interrupted sentences Lacan notices in Judge Schreber's *Memoirs of My Mental Illness*. This text was originally interpreted by Freud who diagnosed the author with paranoid dementia. In *Encore*, Lacan argues that these interrupted sentences, or incomplete thoughts:

leave some sort of substance in abeyance. We perceive here the requirement of a sentence, whatever it may be, which is such that one of its links, when missing, sets all the others free, that is, withdraws from them the One. (128)

The sentence carries with it the demand for wholeness in order to complete meaning. By subtracting unity from the sentence, Schreber and Ellis simultaneously evoke and disrupt the fantasy of the One. *American Psycho*'s active resistance to closure evokes a similar disruption. The text's inexorable, affectless prose is a search for a sense of wholeness in the form of both a coherent self and an ordered world. Following a mugging by a taxi driver, Patrick Bateman murmurs, 'I just want to [. . .] keep the game going' (379).

This game is the drive to create a sociocultural order that explicitly possesses a hierarchy determined by wealth and the latest Zagat guide. This order is perceived to be constantly under threat by the filth and chaos of the city; by some, 'crazy fucking homeless nigger who actually *wants* – listen to me, Bateman – *wants* to be out on the streets, this, *those* streets, see *those*' (5). The incredulity of the speaker highlights the disturbance the tramp's choice makes to a stratified system of norms. At a bar in the closing section, Bateman notes that the yuppies' conversation around him, 'follows its own rolling accord – no real structure or topic or internal logic or feeling; except, of course, for its own hidden conspiratorial one' (380). The lack of a 'real structure' to the conversation parallels the shallow materialism that pervades the novel. However, this materialism, or the semblance of a structure, is supported by a hidden rationale, that is, the fantasy that wholeness is not only achievable but desirable. In short, the word 'one' that concludes the sentence should be capitalized. Lacan suggests that our instinctive reaction is to assume that incomplete sentences constitute nothing of any validity. However, this demonstrates the ineluctable nature of the One (hidden, conspiratorial) against which satire rebels. This indicates that despite the appearance of fragmentation, dissolution and indeterminacy that characterize postmodernity, there is still a fantasy-structure of the One at play that determines the coordinates of lived experience. Like incomplete sentences, satires resist narrative closure and highlight the naturalized state of completion, thereby directing the reader towards a critique. This constitutes a powerful challenge to the dominant discourse that, as a precondition of its efficacy, must always provide a fantasy structure of wholeness. At this stage, it is useful to examine theorizations of the comic spirit and the ways in which this mode intersects with the concerns of the satiric genre to form a distinctive mode of critique.

Comedy as Critique

Against the fantasy of the One, laughter and the comic spirit initiate a destabilization of hierarchy and fixed norms. Indeed, as Horace established, satire is able to subject any individual or institution to critique by producing laughter. Laughter disrupts the fantasy of the One much as Freud's conception of the unconscious decentres the autonomous stable ego. In his much heralded return to Freud, Lacan replaces Descartes' 'I think therefore I am' with 'I think where I am not, therefore I am where I do not think'. This manoeuvre not only places consciousness outside of the centre but also challenges the very notion that there can be fixed coordinates for the self. Henri Bergson understood the comic spirit to possess a logic of its own, much like the unconscious. He states: 'It has a method in its madness. It dreams, I admit, but it conjures up, in its dreams, visions that are at once accepted and understood by the whole of a social group'.[21] This would suggest that the comic spirit is directly linked to the unconscious but simultaneously functions as an unspoken system of social cohesion. Ever since the publication of Freud's 'Jokes and Their Relation to the Unconscious', the comic has inhabited a privileged space in psychoanalysis. However, within the spheres of literature and philosophy, it has traditionally been regarded as a vitiated discourse. It is arguable that the denigration of the comic in philosophical discourse is directly correlative to its position as a vital and transgressive form that subjects mechanisms such as institutionalized academia, state bureaucracy and law to critique. In short, the comic holds the potential to cause a disruption to the fantasy-structure of the One by exposing it to ridicule.

Whilst acknowledging the insufficiency of a single formula, Bergson proposes that the comic effect is generated by 'something mechanical encrusted on the living' (25). By 'life', Bergson means the vitality and fluidity that characterize internal thoughts. In contrast to this, the mechanical signifies automatism, rigidity and repetition. Bergson argues that when the life impulse is overtaken by the mechanical, that is, rigidity is applied to mobility, the effect is comical. However, as Bergson acknowledges, this thesis in itself is reductive. Instead, the mechanism – life binary is positioned as an 'arche-concept' that provides a conceptual matrix for all other theories of the comic. Indeed, 'any form or formula is a ready-made frame into which the comic element may be fitted' (29). In order to illustrate the flexibility of his terms, Bergson uses the example of the body. In relation to clothes, the body appears to be something living and supple. However, one does not ordinarily differentiate between the individual and the clothes they wear. It is only when the individual dresses in an absurd or anachronistic way that the mechanical continuity of custom is dissolved. Subsequently, the living body appears rigid like a machine and provokes laughter. In support of this thesis, Bergson reverses the role of the body through a comparison with spirit or the soul. Now attention is drawn to the materiality of the body:

so far from sharing in the lightness and subtlety of the principle with which it is animated, the body is no more in our eyes than a heavy and cumbersome vesture, a kind of irksome ballast which holds down to earth a soul eager to rise aloft. (31)

The body is perceived to be an unwieldy mechanism encrusted on the soul. This is found in the comic stereotype of the moral, intelligent personality who is obstructed by his machine-like clumsy body. The physical encrusts and undercuts the moral. The reversibility of the body between the two poles succinctly demonstrates that in the comic, the same element can stand on two sides of an opposition. Unlike many formulations of the comic, for Bergson, subject-matter is secondary to form.

Bergson's formulation of the comic as something mechanical encrusted upon the living remains conceptual rather than empirical. Consequently, it forms a structure in which elements such as the body, state and culture can be located on either side of the binary. Indeed, what is comic is the reversibility of these elements. In a development of Bergson's thought, the Lacanian philosopher Alenka Zupančič theorizes comedy as possessing the structure of the Möbius strip: 'comic procedure is a procedure designed to make us see the impossible passage from one side to the other, or to the impossible link between the two'.[22] Rather than tragedy, which through the figure of the hero attempts to stretch the limits of reality, comedy is a sustained encounter between two opposed realities. Its structure allows for the juxtaposition of impossibilities to subversive effect. This can occur through direct, seemingly illogical juxtaposition that obeys the narrative's own internal logic, or through exaggeration whereby the comic subject over-identifies with their surroundings to reveal their obscene underside. The combination of two incompatible elements within one image offers a powerful subversion of the fantasy structure of the One. For Zupančič, the strength of the comic mode lies in its ability to make the viewer:

> perceive a certain duality where we have so far perceived only a (more or less) harmonious One. It makes us perceive this duality simply by reproducing ('imitating') the One as faithfully as possible. This repetition / reproduction has the effect of introducing or 'revealing' a gap in the original itself – a gap that we failed to notice before. (121)

The comic offers an anamorphic perspective that reveals the pre-existing duality and hence the contradiction within the unified whole. Rather than simply thrusting two incompatible elements together, the comic spirit empowers the viewer by revealing the gaps and inconsistencies *within* the fantasy structure of the One. Imitation is a particularly powerful tool that through the repetition of the original renders it mechanical. For this reason, satire often takes the form of parody, imitating the original in such a way as to negate its 'life'.

Bergson's formula of the comic spirit as something mechanical encrusted upon the living is used to great effect in Stewart Home's *Down & Out in Shoreditch and Hoxton*. Home's satires frequently combine insightful and opinionated discourse on literature with detailed depictions of transgressive sex acts and extreme violence. This structure in itself draws together two opposed discourses into a sustained juxtaposition. In a long scene towards the end of the novel the prostitute protagonist, known only as Eve, coerces a punter named Alan Abel into participating in a snuff movie. However, unbeknown to Alan this is, 'a snuff movie of Alan Abel being fucked to death'.[23] What follows is a series of vignettes detailing each prostitute as they 'pleasure' Alan, which extends for nearly 30 pages. Over the course of this series, specific character tropes emerge and are shared across prostitutes. For instance, the phrase, 'was a big girl, so big that when she sat on top of a man he was rendered helpless' appears as a descriptor for Susan Lamb, Angel Lopez and Pandora Underson.[24] The particular becomes a meme and is thereby mechanized. Bergson argues that when something living is imitated, that is repeated, it is rendered mechanical and subject to laughter and ridicule. The imitation of an individual provokes laughter and retroactively causes the 'original' to become funny. In Home's text, the repetitive structure is further emphasized by a brief interlude during which the customary pace of the narrative is temporarily restored. At this point, Eve notes that 'patriarchy and capitalism stratify society with a shameless instrumentalization of identity and difference' (118). This is mirrored by Home's self-conscious instrumentalization of the prostitutes. Accordingly, the narrative constitutes a critique of capitalism and patriarchy, not by writing directly against the dominant discourse, but through the parodic duplication of its effects. Eve's character is an over-identification with the role of woman as determined by capitalist and patriarchal discourse. Consequently, the hegemonic structures of capitalism and patriarchy are satirized through a depiction of prostitution that directly equates sex with financial power. This strategy of mechanization and parodic duplication exposes the fundamental divulgence within naturalized discourses of power, or seemingly harmonious wholes.

Satire is not solely a medium of critique. It also aims to pleasure the reader. Consequently, there must be some complicity or shared intention between the reader and the author. This poses the question, what is pleasurable about revealing the gaps and inconsistencies in the One? We have seen that the comic spirit creatively deconstructs the unity of the One, not with multiplicity but through the exposure of an impossible and sustained link between two constitutively exclusive sides of reality. Rather than disavowing the opposition by deconstructing it into a multiplicity, Zupančič demonstrates the ways in which the mechanical is intrinsic to life and life embedded in the mechanical: 'what is comical is precisely their mutually implying each other – that is to say, the part played by automatism in the very *constitution* of the genuine (revolutionary) spirit' (120). This brings to mind Lacan's classic thesis of the unconscious structured like a language. Although language appears as an external mechanism encrusted upon the spirit, it is actually the matrix constitutive of life. Indeed, Zupančič goes on to argue that speech with all its automatism actually pulls the spirit along: 'the spirit slowly staggers behind the words, until it suddenly comes to life in an idea that has literally emerged with and from speech' (119). Satire represents individuals as mechanized, imitative and predictable entities by disavowing psychological depth and notions of closure. Through the jux-taposition of two opposed realities, it reveals the mechanism to be found within the living. Satire mechanically repeats and imitates because it is only through this mechanical repetition that comic pleasure and the vivac-ity of life appear. By reducing life to mechanism, satire's wild, revolution-ary spirit bursts forth. It is this shared affirmation of the revolutionary spirit which generates enjoyment in the reader. As Northrop Frye argues, 'almost any denunciation, if vigorous enough, is followed by a reader with the kind of pleasure that soon breaks into a smile'.[25] Through its repeti-tive negativity, satire produces a negative excess that results in enjoyment. Following Home, it could be said that satire 'fucks' the reader to death. It reduces individuals to their base instincts but simultaneously enables a pleasure to be taken from the satisfaction of fundamental drives. It is now useful to examine further the ways in which psychoanalytic theories of the comic offer a distinctive critique of civilized norms.

Psychoanalytic Critique

In order to draw out the source of the pleasure that satire brings, it is use-ful to turn to Freud's essay, 'Jokes and Their Relation to the Unconscious'. Here, he argues that tendentious jokes deliver pleasure by enabling the subject to circumvent the decorum that prohibits their hostile and aggres-sive instincts. Consequently, jokes should be seen as a 'safe' means with which to exhibit hostile or uncivilized behaviour. As Freud states, the pleas-urable effect of purposeful jokes is a result of *'economy in expenditure on inhibition or suppression'*.[26] By this, Freud is referring to the psychic effort required to maintain the semblance of unity. The pleasure of jokes is not to be found simply from the satisfaction of the drive but in the reduction of the psychic effort required to conform to prohibition, be it internal or external. Although Freud was yet to introduce the concept of the super-ego, its effect as a moral agency that judges and censures the ego is apparent here. The superego represses desire and regulates subjectivity. It is the 'portion of the ego which sets itself over against the rest of the ego [. . .] and in the form of conscience, puts into action against the ego the same harsh aggressiveness it would like to exert on others'.[27] It forces the subject to maintain the fantasy-structure of him or herself as an autonomous stable ego in the face of unpleasant realities. Through the sustained linkage of two impossibilities, the comic spirit temporarily disrupts the boundary between inside and outside, therefore frustrating the efforts of the super-ego, which in turn reduces psychical expenditure. Indeed, the appearance of unity or wholeness in the subject, 'is deceptive, and on the contrary the ego is continued inwards, without any sharp delimitation, into an unconscious mental entity which we designate as the id and for which it serves as a kind of façade'.[28] The purpose of this façade that structures the boundaries of the ego is to maintain the semblance of a state of civilization, itself dependent upon the imposition of strict boundaries.

Boundaries, both internal and external, are the necessary precondition of civilization. The irony is that the superego that maintains the boundary line between the ego and the external world is itself described by Freud as an internalized external authority that traverses the boundary it seeks to enforce. This structure continues to have significance in the present, most notably in the work of the political theorist Giorgio Agamben and his formulation of the sovereign exception, in whose person the law is suspended but not abnegated. Satire is a transgressive form that disrupts boundaries as well as the notion of boundary itself. This lends it its threatening aspect and indicates why traditionally it has either been denigrated as a low or base form, or reconciled with a direct (and often reductive) moral purpose. Satire employs the structure of jokes in order to confront civilization with its obscene underside. In doing so, it demonstrates that the obscene is not simply the opposite of civilized values, to be kept outside the gates. Instead, it functions as a support for civilization. This structure can be readily understood in the relationship between Lacan's registers of the Symbolic and the Real. The Symbolic order is language and the entire realm of culture conceived as a symbol system structured on the model of language. The Real should be differentiated from 'reality', which can be understood only through and by language. Instead, the Lacanian Real is 'the domain of that which subsists outside of symbolisation'.[29] The Real is resistant to symbolization and is therefore impossible to integrate into the Symbolic order. For this reason, it appears as something horrific or traumatic, which intrudes upon reality. As the Lacanian philosopher Slavoj Žižek notes: '"Reality" is a fantasy-construction that enables us to mask the Real of our desire'.[30] The Real is always a missed encounter that expresses the truth of desire that the dream envelopes and hides from the subject: 'this is the real that governs our activities more than any other and it is psychoanalysis that designates it for us'.[31] Accordingly, the Real is a concept of central importance to Lacanian psychoanalysis because it functions as an invisible support for 'reality'. Freud understood civilization to be predicated upon the fantasy that it functions as a coherent whole while base and obscene instincts are repressed and removed from the social fabric. There is a parallel to be drawn between these obscene instincts and the Lacanian Real that appears as a traumatic incursion into 'reality' while simultaneously functioning as the condition of its existence. Satire functions as a mode of critique that presents civilization with its obverse in order to challenge the established order. Consequently, satire can be theorized as a form that stages an (always missed) encounter with the traumatic Real.

In a lecture delivered on 20 April 1967, Lacan discusses excrement in relation to civilization. He states:

> Talking about this is always shocking, even though it has always been a part of what we call civilization. A great civilization is first and foremost a civilization that has a waste-disposal system. So long as we do not take that as our starting point, we will not be able to say anything serious.[32]

Like comedy, satire should be regarded as a serious form. What may appear to be facile, sensationalist or simply in 'bad taste' carries with it a serious need to examine the obscene underside of civilization. By presenting the waste of human endeavour for inspection, it confronts humanity with the intricate set of pipes that remove waste from 'everyday life'. The presentation of the obscene brings with it the re-examination of the structures and mechanisms of the community and the status quo. Michel Houellebecq's *The Possibility of an Island* offers a portrayal of hedonistic consumption, misogyny and unbridled promiscuity within a cloning cult at the beginning of the twenty-first century. This narrative is interspersed with depictions of a potential future for humanity whereby the human race does indeed develop cloning technology that enables it to plot out its own evolutionary trajectory. Inevitably, the key modifications concern energy and waste. As the aptly named modern day scientist Knowall argues:

For a long time animal nutrition had seemed to him to be a primitive system, of mediocre energy efficiency, producing a clearly excessive quantity of waste, waste that not only had to be evacuated, but which in the
process provoked a far from negligible wear and tear of the organism.[33]

He proposes to equip the neo-humans with a photosynthetic system that
would enable the human subject to subsist purely on solar energy, water and
mineral salts. As a consequence, the digestive and excretory systems would
disappear. However, as the chapters set in the distant future demonstrate, the
subject who does not defecate does not desire. The neo-humans live alone in
sealed-off shelters, serenely contemplating the barren and apocalyptic world
outside. Waste becomes a metaphor for lack and the subject who does not
lack, does not desire. Consequently, civilization, waste and decorum should
be seen as interlinked themes for both psychoanalysis and satire.

The removal of waste in civilization is the external counterpart to the
phenomenon of repression. As Lacan points out, both phenomena are
related to the issue of decorum. Decorum establishes codes of behaviour
and propriety in order to avoid anything unseemly or offensive in manner.
By presenting the waste of human industry for inspection, satire reveals
the intricate series of pipes and mechanisms that conceal the obscene, or
'other scene', thereby exposing them to critique. In this way, satire could
be said to stage a return of the repressed. However, it is unclear whether
this constitutes a genuine subversion of civilized norms. Civilizational
boundaries are dependent upon the binary division of the decorous and
the obscene. By displaying the obscene, satire reveals the decorous to be
an empty term, dependent upon its obscene underside for its meaning. As
a linguistic entity, civilization is modelled on the structure of the Symbolic
order composed of signifiers that have no positive existence in themselves
but are constituted purely by virtue of their mutual differences. As Lacan
notes, the Symbolic is characterized by the fundamental binary opposition between absence and presence and their mutual implication of one
another. This leads Lacan to assert that absence can be said to have an
equally positive existence in the Symbolic as presence. As Houellebecq's
text indicates, the absent (repressed) waste of human endeavour impacts
upon civilization as an absent presence to the same extent as (decorous)
presence. The socio-symbolic presents itself as a unified whole and it is into
this fantasy structure that the Real intrudes, exposing the gaps or fissures
within the Symbolic. These gaps are swiftly papered over by the retroactive
effects of language. For this reason, the Real is always experienced as a
missed encounter. There is a structural homology with satire's subversive

function. Despite exposing the gaps and inconsistencies in the sociocultural order, its radical potential is often swiftly contained or repressed.

The containment of satire's radical potential is symptomatic of the ineluctability of the fantasy-structure of the One. As Lacan notes in *Encore*:

> a certain number of biases are your daily fare and limit the import of
> your insurrections to the shortest term, to the term, quite precisely, that
> gives you no discomfort – they certainly don't change your world view, for
> that remains perfectly spherical. (42)

Despite challenges to the semblance of wholeness, fantasy ineluctably returns to the centre. The key revolution for psychoanalysis was Freud's removal of consciousness from the centre of the subject. Indeed, the radical alterity of the unconscious lies at the heart of Freud's psychoanalytic theories. Nevertheless, despite psychoanalysis' de-centering of the subject, the fantasy that the individual is a unified whole ineluctably returns to the centre. This is reflected by cognitive development psychology in which the formation of the subject is presented as a finite process resulting in a positive knowledge of truth and reality. By contrast, Lacan interprets the formation of the subject as a series of alienating identifications, inaugurated by the mirror stage. When the infant first encounters his or her image in the mirror, he or she greets it with jubilation and excitement: 'The image appears to the infant as a gestalt – the complete figure is more than its parts added up.'[34] The child encounters the image of him or herself as a unified whole in contrast to the myriad drives and desires that the subject feels are animating him. As Lacan notes in *Écrits*, the gestalt 'symbolizes the I's mental permanence, at the same time as it prefigures its alienating destination' (76). The mirror stage inaugurates the ego's disabling illusions of permanence and stability. The external representation of the subject as a unified whole causes the subject to perceive itself as a subject of lack and to aggressively attempt to take the place of the gestalt. Desire is generated by the subject's lack. The dialectical structure of wholeness and lack is demonstrated by the 1980 videogame, *Pac Man*. The eponymous character is a circle with a segment removed, which functions as a mouth. This should be interpreted as the perfect shape that symbolizes wholeness with an absence signifying lack. It is apt that the lack functions as the object of consumption, or the mouth. Progression from one level to the next is determined by Pac Man's consumption of the dots that litter the maze. The dots signify the object as well as the cause of Pac Man's desire. Pac Man is a subject of lack who desires the dots because they appear as the missing object that will fill in his lack. The levels of *Pac Man* continue on in a repetitive loop until the 256th level. At this point an error in the coding causes the right-hand side of the screen to display an unintelligible series of code. Turning again to Lacan, this can be read as an irruption of the Real into Symbolic reality. Binary code, like the Symbolic order, is a series of ones and zeroes or absences and presences. The 'error' in the code is a traumatic intrusion of the Real that exposes and disrupts the structures of signification. As this example indicates, desire operates as a double bind. On the one hand, it can be seen as a liberating and excessive force that exceeds structure and rule. On the other hand, it is predicated upon a system of structural lack that now forms the basis for consumer capitalism. In a similar manner, satiric critique can be seen to offer the potential for radical critique but can equally function as a support for conservative norms. In the next section, I will explore the ways in which satiric critique treads on a knife-edge between discourses of subversion and containment.

Subversion and Containment

The containment of satire's radical potential can take one of two forms. First, it can be recuperated as a predominantly aesthetic form, resulting in its radical potential being contained by the established sociocultural order. This is visible in Dryden's polemical attempt to define satire along strict moral and artistic aims. Secondly, it can hit its target but make little to no impact with the subject continuing as before. Each reception can be explained through reference to the psychoanalytic terms of sublimation and disavowal. As previously discussed, the majority of commentators on satire through to the mid-twentieth century have sought to present it as an aesthetic form by refining it into a form acceptable to civilized tastes. This can be understood as a sublimation of the wild, aggressive and libidinous instincts associated with the figure of the half man-half beast *satyr*. Sublimation is a process whereby excess libidinous energy is channelled into socially acceptable, apparently non-sexual activities such as artistic creation and intellectual work. As Lacan notes in *Seminar XI*:

Sublimation is nonetheless satisfaction of the drive, without repression. In other words – for the moment, I am not fucking, I am talking to you. Well! I can have exactly the same satisfaction as if I were fucking. That's what it means. Indeed, it raises the question of whether in fact I am not fucking at this moment. (165–6)

Sublimation demonstrates that the drives are plastic by altering the equation of satisfaction with sexual pleasure to more decorous aims. This is a form of self-protection insofar as the trauma of non-satisfaction is reduced if the instincts are directed to other aims rather than simply inhibited. However, as Freud points out in *Civilisation and Its Discontents*, 'the feeling of happiness derived from satisfaction of a wild instinctual impulse untamed by the ego is incomparably more intense than that derived from sating an instinct that has been tamed' (79). This is indicative of the appeal of transgressive enjoyment and, as explored above, offers the basis for an explanation of the pleasure of satire. Like jokes, satire offers an opportunity to temporarily suspend the taboos instigated by the superego and indulge in aggressive and instinctual behaviour by proxy. Sublimation is a civilizational protection against the wild, untamed enjoyment of the *satyr*. As such, the sublimation of satire raises it up to the level of the aesthetic object and in the process redirects aggressive and subversive instincts.

In *Mythologies*, Roland Barthes comments on Charlie Chaplin's satiric film *Modern Times*. He locates the strength of Chaplin's figure of the Tramp, in the role of the factory worker, in the presentation of the working man as blind, mystified and alienated. This is in opposition to socialist works which, 'in showing the worker already engaged in a conscious fight, subsumed under the Cause and the Party, give an account of a political reality which is necessary, but lacks aesthetic force'.[35] The strength of Chaplin's character resides in his presentation of the poor, lost in a world of strikes and machinery and unable to attain a broader knowledge of political causes beyond the need for daily sustenance. Rather than becoming a transgressive or politically active character, the instincts of the Tramp are sublimated, or blinded by, the demands of his hunger. Indeed, by demonstrating industrial capitalism's manipulation of the Tramp's instinctual demands away from the Cause and the Party, the viewer is empowered to recognize the machinations of the sublimated response. As Barthes points out:

> To see someone who does not see is the best way to be intensely aware of *what* he does not see: thus, at a Punch and Judy show, it is the children who announce to Punch what he pretends not to see (40).

The presentation of the Tramp as a subject who does not know reveals to the audience the daily sublimation of the instincts. Sublimation ensures that the subject does not experience dissatisfaction but is instead redirected in his or her aims. Indeed, according to Lacan, 'the operations of sublimation are always ethically, culturally and socially valorised'.[36] This dynamic can be discerned within the contemporary ideology of 'choice' and free market economy. In *Invisible Monsters*, Chuck Palahniuk depicts a supermarket: 'except for that name-brand product rainbow, there's nothing else to look at'.[37] This rainbow of choice obfuscates the subject's inability to choose and impact on the fundamental structure of society. Indeed, Slavoj Žižek differentiates between two forms of freedom: 'formal freedom is the freedom of choice within the coordinates of the existing power relations, while actual freedom designates the site of an intervention that undermines these very coordinates'.[38] Formal freedom is a sublimation of the drives that reinvests transgressive behaviour within the structure of late capitalist society. The reduction of political parties to brand names delivers a formal freedom in the place of actual freedom. Satire is a form that brings the decorous and the obscene into a sustained juxtaposition in order to undermine the structure and boundaries imposed by civilization. However, following Dryden's ideals, it is often sublimated into a formal freedom that offers the illusion of choice while obfuscating the possibility of genuine revolutionary change.

The second form in which satire's revolutionary practice can be contained by the dominant sociocultural order is related to the psychoanalytic concept of disavowal. Disavowal is the necessary precondition for interpersonal relationships. As Žižek notes, in our most 'intimate relationship to our neighbours: we behave *as if* we do not know that they also smell bad, secrete excrement, and so on – a minimum of idealization, of fetishizing disavowal, is the basis of our coexistence'.[39] Disavowal is frequently characterized by an attitude of 'I know well, but all the same . . . .' The subject is conscious of the refutability of their beliefs but chooses to continue under the illusion provided by reality. The reader of satire may well recognize themselves to be the target or complicit with the target of the satire but continues with his or her actions anyway. This should be linked to the phenomenon of religious belief in the face of a contradictory reality. Religion imposes obsessional restrictions that are justified with a system of illusions and a disavowal of reality. The concept of disavowal emerges from Freud's discussion of fetishism. For Freud, the fetish is a substitute for the woman's (castrated) penis that the child once believed in. Freud notes that the discovery that woman lacks the phallus does not simply negate the former belief. Instead, the child is seen to have 'retained that belief, but he has also given it up. In the conflict between the weight of the unwelcome perception and the force of the counter-wish, a compromise has been reached'.[40] Freud cites the example of a young man who had disavowed the death of his beloved father. One part of him did not recognize his father's death, while another part took full account of the fact. This constitutes a simultaneous acknowledgement and displacement of unwelcome knowledge. In the same way, the target of satire will recognize their complicity with vice and folly but fail to alter their actions. This is clear in the cultural icon, Homer Simpson, who simultaneously takes cognizance of the stupidity of his actions while continuing to be lazy, overweight and incompetent. His frequent misdemeanours and subsequent subversive potential is offset however, by his recognition of the necessity of work and consistent adherence to the ideological structure of the nuclear family. One particular comic trope is for Homer to debate with his own mind, expressed through voice-over. His mind frequently gives reasoned advice that is not followed through by the character himself. This is the model of disavowal *par excellence* by which the subject is split between their knowledge of reality and their adherence to the fantasy-structure that sustains the ego in the face of unpleasant truths. In disavowing reality, Homer is able to believe there is no reason to fear, thereby retaining the satisfaction of the drives.

The psychic structures of sublimation and disavowal limit the subversive elements of satiric critique. Sublimation functions as a socially acceptable escape-valve while disavowal enables the subject to maintain belief in the face of unpleasant or even traumatic knowledge. It is significant that within totalitarian regimes, satire is often censored, which can be read as a form of repression. The repression of the satiric impulse renders it transgressive, thereby lending it greater efficacy. By contrast, liberal democracies frequently sublimate the satiric impulse, resulting in the vitiation of its potency. This is supported by the subject's disavowal of the unpleasant truths presented by satire. Within liberal democracy, criticism is not simply a disruptive force to be contained but functions as a structural support for the Established Order. As Barthes notes:

> take the established value which you want to restore or develop, and first lavishly display its pettiness, the injustices which it produces, the vexations to which it gives rise, and plunge it into its natural imperfection; then, at the last moment, save it *in spite of*, or rather *by* the heavy curse of its blemishes. (40)

In this way, the presentation of unpleasant truths as a mode of critique functions as a structural support for the dominant sociocultural order. Disavowal is a psychic structure that sustains the status quo. Indeed, Barthes concludes that, 'a little "confessed" evil saves one from acknowledging a lot of hidden evil' (42). Through the criticism of a partial object, the whole achieves the status of a transcendental good. The workings of sublimation as a form of containment indicates that genuinely subversive satire must not merely target partial objects but the structural base of the social fabric in the form of the fantasy-structure of the One.

Concluding Remarks

As the preceding discussion has established, there is an urgent need to explore new forms of critique. Despite the conditions of liquidity and indeterminacy that have become the norm within the postmodern era, satire continues to offer new and vital forms of resistance. Rather than celebrating the free play of desire that functions as an ideological support for the conditions of late capitalism, contemporary satirists have worked to re-establish points from which ethical interventions can take place. Drawing on the concerns of Lacanian psychoanalysis, I argue that Bauman's description of the transition from 'solid' to 'liquid' modernism can be read in relation to Lacan's formulation of the fantasy-structure of the One. Although the postmodern moment appears to be characterized by conditions of indecision and uncertainty, Lacan's understanding of the ineluctable nature of the One indicates that beneath the liquidity of the present moment lie pernicious ideologies and discourses of power. Their submergence, in an effort to sustain Bauman's metaphor, renders them invisible and therefore naturalized and resistant to critique. On the one hand, Marxist theory is unable to offer a sustainable ground from which to launch critique. On the other hand, deconstructive strategies are blinded by the multiplicity of signs and continue to generate and sustain the conditions of indeterminacy. However, as we have seen, formulations of the comic spirit by Bergson and Zupančič offer fresh insight into new potentialities for resistance and critique. Rather than the post-structuralist celebration of diffusion and multiplicity, this method operates through the sustained juxtaposition of two incompatible elements. This approach has the dual effect of revealing the fantasy structure of the One that sustains the status quo as well as locating a split or point of non-coincidence that displays its inconsistencies without fragmenting it into endless multiplicities. At this point it is useful to further examine the significance of this critical methodology for literary analysis.

The fantasy structure of the One has haunted the academic study of literature for decades although the closest it came to be being theorized as such was by the liberal humanist F. R. Leavis. In his search for a 'great tradition' of English literature, Leavis considers a number of widely respected novelists. Often, the reasons for his exclusion of one author are more interesting than his reasons for including another. For instance, in his discussion and eventual dismissal of D. H. Lawrence for canonization, Leavis states: 'but it seems plain to me that there is no organic principle determining, informing, and controlling into a vital whole, the elaborate analogical structure, the extraordinary variety of technical devices, the attempt at an exhaustive rendering of consciousness'.[41] Leavis is concerned with the creation of Art as a unified moral whole. Art for him is born out of the chaos of life and given unity through form and composition. As such, satirists such as Dickens and Fielding were (initially) excluded from the great tradition because of their meandering narrative structure and lack of a clearly definable moral core. Leavis' exclusion of Dickens on the basis of his ramshackle, dishevelled style is especially significant when considered in relation to his great satire on the law, *Bleak House*. This novel lacks any discernable centre with its vast number of minor characters and intricate subplots. The closest thing the novel has to a centre is the High Court of Chancery. However, as the name implies, this is a place of chance in which fortune and success are rooted in an utterly opaque system of laws, bills and bureaucracy. This is highlighted by the opening to the novel that depicts the fog that engulfs everyone from all walks of life: 'Fog everywhere. Fog up the river, where it flows among green aits and meadows; fog down the river, where it rolls defiled among the tiers of shipping, and the waterside pollutions of a great (and dirty) city.'[42] The novel's various characters and scenes are all linked but only by being thrust into a dense, obscuring medium. Just as the fog obfuscates every detail, the authoritative discourse of the law courts is depicted as an utterly opaque structure. Consequently, *Bleak House* can be read as a pre-emptive retort to Leavis' demand for artistic unity. The satire offers a depiction of the conditions of indeterminacy and moral confusion in nineteenth-century London, while simultaneously displaying the British judiciary system as a fantasy-structure of the One that determines the fates of all of the characters. As such, Dickens' novel offers an insistent critique out of conditions that were previously understood to be formless, contradictory and indeterminate.

At the start of the twenty-first century, literary criticism is dominated by the post-structuralist emphasis on plurality and multiplicity. However, critics such as Alain-Philippe Durand and Naomi Mandel have recently detected a trend in recent literature that they have dubbed the 'contemporary extreme'. This label is for texts from all over the world that are, 'set in a world both similar to and different from our own: a hyperreal, often apocalyptic world progressively invaded by popular culture, permeated with technology and dominated by destruction'.[43] These texts each display a form, subject matter and aesthetic that is inextricably linked to forms of violence. These texts not only depict violence but enact it in a variety of imaginative ways. As such they offer a more aggressive form of satiric critique influenced by among other sources 'In-yer-face' theatre and the work of the New Brutalists. Consequently, in a reversion of Leavis' emphasis on artistic unity, the contemporary extreme can be seen to be an aesthetic that 'does not strive for harmony or unity but, instead, forces the confrontation between irreconcilable differences' (1). This structural thematic can be productively linked with Alenka Zupančič's Lacanian-inflected theory of comedy as the sustained juxtaposition of two incompatible elements. Consequently, the texts selected by Durand and Mandel ostensibly appear to offer critiques of the fantasy-structures of the One located at the start of the twenty-first century.

Durand and Mandel argue that the term 'extreme' was 'deliberately chosen for its connotations with political extremity and a fascination with transgression' (2). However, transgression does not in itself necessarily constitute a subversive act. Whereas subversion offers the opportunity of radical critique, transgression is simply a movement outside of the norm. Indeed, it is by crossing a boundary that a boundary's position is reaffirmed. As Georges Bataille states, 'the transgression does not deny the taboo but transcends it and completes it'.[44] For example, transgression of the law is met with retribution that thereby re-inscribes the law. By contrast, the sustained juxtaposition of two incompatible elements forces antagonism to rise to the surface, rendering the familiar unfamiliar in the process. This focus on antagonisms or gaps *within* the social fabric, as opposed to 'extreme' discourses of transgression or the emphasis on marginality favoured by contemporary identity politics, stages a disruption to the normative rhythms of 'everyday life'. Rather than simply transgressing or crossing boundaries, I argue that the satires under discussion in this volume disrupt the notion of boundary itself. Rather than searching for limits, these writers represent the conditions of indeterminacy and seek ways to subject the fantasy-structures that condition everyday experience to critique. Durand and Mandel's concept of the contemporary extreme provides a useful category with which to highlight the response of a number of contemporary writers to the problems and challenges of the twenty-first century. However, I argue that satire works to combine the energy of the comic spirit with effective political critique. Although the work of many of the writers under consideration may be conventionally understood as transgressive or 'underground' literature, I argue that in order to break free from the indeterminacy of the postmodern age, it is imperative that we examine these texts as satirical exhibitions of vice and folly.

Ethics and Desire in the Wake of Postmodernism: Contemporary Satire is composed of six chapters, which each focus on a single author and examine the ways in which they offer insight into a theme of particular importance for the twenty-first century. Rather than being strictly theoretical terms, they are commonly deployed in everyday speech. In this book, I work to defamiliarize and reconfigure them in order to both explicate and critique the dominant ideologies that structure the contemporary moment. When these terms are used in everyday speech, the enunciator is often unaware of their ideological significance. However, as the writers under consideration demonstrate, within the supposedly post-ideological era of the twenty-first century it is more important than ever to reassess naturalized forms of praxis and speech. Consequently, this book delivers critical analyses of Bret Easton Ellis on fear, Chuck Palahniuk on nihilism, J. G. Ballard on revolution, Will Self on ethics, Michel Houellebecq on enjoyment and Tama Janowitz on feminism. These authors were chosen because they conflict with commonsensical discourse, resist intellectual elitism and foster the motto that there is greater profundity to be found in absurdity. It is significant that critical responses to these authors have been muted to date. It is likely that this is because the *de facto* deconstructionist critical framework has been challenged by these authors' shifts between metaphysical truth and absolute indeterminacy. Irony is not a binarized system but works in degrees. These authors deploy multiple levels of irony in order to problematize any reading that attempts to either sublimate their artistic energy in an aesthetic unity or alternatively, deconstruct their texts into endless and indeterminate complexity.

This book comprises an examination of the fantasy-structures that continue to structure our lives. The texts under consideration present the cultural dominants of the twenty-first century that lie concealed beneath the indeterminacy of everyday life. Individuals are depicted as masters who are actually slaves and the sociocultural order is represented as being in a continuous state of flux. The first half consists of readings of novels by Bret Easton Ellis, Chuck Palahniuk and J. G. Ballard. Bret Easton Ellis' *Lunar Park* is ostensibly a horror fiction set within the domestic sphere. However, this chapter draws out the ways in which the private and the personal are intrinsically linked. The text deploys numerous uncanny tropes in order to satirize the contemporary culture of fear. The uncanny is a problematic concept that disrupts the boundary between the familiar and the unfamiliar. Consequently, the text refuses to accept clear divisions between the known and the unknown, the self and the Other. As such, the pervading atmosphere of fear that has captivated America in the years following the attack on the World Trade Centre is linked to the decline of traditional models of authority. In particular, this analysis examines the decline of the paternal function and the loss of security that marks the millennial *fin de siècle*. The sense of a millennial *fin de siècle* is continued in the analysis of violence in Chuck Palahniuk's *Fight Club*. This chapter develops a close reading of the politics manifested by the fight clubs and later Project Mayhem. Like *Lunar Park*, this text deconstructs the coordinates of the autonomous stable ego. Its critique of consumer culture is reflected by the main characters' conscious reduction of self and absorption into an excessive asceticism. This chapter builds on the insights developed in the previous chapter on the relationship between the subject and the socio-symbolic by positing that the Lacanian Real stands as a terrifying, traumatic gap that offers the possibility of radical change. The alienation and atomization depicted as endemic to the era of late capitalism in *Lunar Park* is here converted into an empowering affirmation. In addition, the theme of the uncanny returns in the form of the double. However, in this instance, the theme of the double is linked to the sublime, understood as an aesthetic that causes critical judgement to vacillate. These two chapters draw on conceptions of the double and relate them to fear and violence in order to examine the status of politics at the start of the twenty-first century.

The following chapter solidifies some of the key concepts explored in the discussion of *Fight Club*. J. G. Ballard's *Millennium People* explores and satirizes the revolutionary spirit that increasingly appears to be a necessary component of neoliberal culture. Ballard is highly influenced by the surrealist tradition that produces an alternately defamiliarizing and comic effect through the sustained juxtaposition of two incompatible elements. By depicting the traditionally docile middle classes in revolt, Ballard draws out the interstices between the systemic violence of globalized capitalism and the naturalizing ideologies of suburban life. This chapter charts a shift in Ballard's work from a concern with the apocalyptic scenarios depicted by Jean Baudrillard to the possibility of emancipation through the work of Antonio Negri. His concepts of Empire and 'the multitude' help position the middle-class revolution depicted in the novel as a visible element of a centreless and fragmented globalized resistance to the ideologies of late capitalism. Drawing on a major theme in the *Fight Club* chapter, this discussion will examine the role of nihilist philosophy in the development and growth of radical political expressions of dissent. In this instance, the absence of meaning paradoxically comes to signify as a gap or limitation embedded within the socio-symbolic fabric.

The second half of this book examines issues of ethics, enjoyment and feminism in Will Self's *Dorian: An Imitation*, Michel Houellebecq's *Platform* and the fiction of Tama Janowitz. As discussed above, the postmodern era is characterized by radical indeterminacy and the fluidity of previously solid concepts. In my reading of Will Self's *Dorian: An Imitation*, I question the place of ethics at the turn of the twenty-first century. This novel empha-sizes the fluidity of previously fixed values and suggests that within the postmodern era ethics has been replaced with aesthetic concerns. Drawing on the work of the contemporary French philosopher Alain Badiou, this chapter re-examines concepts such as being, fidelity and truth in order to debate the possibility of forming a consistent ground for critique. Badiou's reading of ethics as an ideology is productively linked to Self's criticism of false philanthropy and cynical reason. As a re-visioning of Oscar Wilde's *The Portrait of Dorian Gray* in which the eponymous character switches his soul with a painting, I argue that an ethical reading of Dorian's position can be understood in relation to Badiou's conception of the subject bound in fidelity to the event. I argue that Dorian's eventual betrayal of this fidel-ity empowers the reader to make an ethical critique of his subject position. In a development of Badiou's critique of ethics as a naturalized discourse that sustains the status quo, the following chapter delivers an analysis of Michel Houellebecq's *Platform* that explores the concept of enjoyment as an unquestioned ideology. This novel's depictions of sex, tourism and one man's quest for enjoyment, develops into a strident critique of globalized capitalism. Through a psychoanalytic reading of the unary trait that stands as a marker of shared pleasure that binds together otherwise diffuse socio-cultural groups, I argue that enjoyment is a principle motive for hostility, conflict and violence.

In the concluding chapter of the volume, I discuss the satiric fiction of Tama Janowitz and question the apparent ubiquity of male authors in the satiric tradition. Against the cultural consensus that satire is a male-dominated form, I argue that women have consistently engaged in satiric critique but are frequently undervalued and overlooked. Indeed, Janowitz's fiction engages with the ongoing concerns of feminism at the turn of the twenty-first century and indicates that political solidarity has been lost in the wake of postmodernism. I argue that patriarchal logic operates as a fantasy-structure of the One that appears increasingly fragmented and dif-fuse yet ineluctably continues to have pernicious and far-reaching effects.

Unlike the other authors under consideration, this chapter provides insight into a range of Janowitz's work. This is because one of the key strengths of Janowitz's satiric critique is located in the ways in which she explores the oppression of women from all walks of life, thereby countering accusations of the women's movement's exclusive focus on white, middle-class individuals. Accordingly, this chapter discusses the role of working-class women in *The Male Cross-Dresser Support Group*, the significance of ageing in *A Certain Age*, and the theme of marriage and adultery in *Peyton Amberg*. Collectively, these novels demonstrate that the twin effects of patriarchy and capitalism continue to influence and oppress women across every strata of society. Through these novels' depictions of the apparatus of patriarchal bias that continues to function at the turn of the twenty-first century, I argue that Janowitz indicates ways in which feminism remains an issue of vital importance in the wake of postmodernism.

Overall, this selection of novels identifies and exposes to critique the cultural dominants that have helped define the first decade of the twenty-first century. By combining absurd scenarios with biting satiric techniques, these authors cut through the indeterminacy of the present in order to expose the ineluctable fantasy-structures of the One to critique. Collectively, these texts reveal that the time of ideologies is far from over. Indeed, far from being diffuse or fragmented, ideological structures continue to play a dominant role in support of global capital, gender inequalities, racial prejudice and the obscene underside of the seemingly liberal status quo. Consequently, the need for compelling satiric criticism is more timely and urgent than ever.

Chapter 1

Fear and Uncertainty in Bret Easton Ellis' *Lunar Park*

Bret Easton Ellis is a self-proclaimed satirist whose writing career began with the publication of *Less Than Zero* (1985). This novel about disaffected and nihilistic youth in Los Angeles was later followed by *The Rules of Attraction* (1987) and *American Psycho* (1991). Whilst these earlier novels are renowned for their transgressive subject matter and flat affectless prose, Ellis' later novels such as *Glamorama* (1998) and *Imperial Bedrooms* (2010) increasingly draw on metafictional devices that problematize the relationship between reality and representation. Indeed, *Lunar Park* self-consciously reflects upon the rest of Ellis' oeuvre by combining the conventions of a celebrity memoir with a horror narrative. Ellis has been known to deliver misleading and contradictory statements about his personal life and the genesis of his novels in interview, consequently representing himself as an indeterminate persona. This strategy has the effect of displacing received notions about the intentionality and authority of the author figure. This confusion is reflected by the varied reception of his novels, which ranges from condemnation and censorship to praise for his scathing critiques of vacuous hedonism and proclamations that the novels in fact evince a strong moral core. He was named as a member of the literary Brat Pack in the 1980s alongside Jay McInerney and Tama Janowitz. Notable for their minimalist prose style, these authors successfully chronicled the vacuity and nihilism of urban life at the close of the twentieth century. Indeed, I will further discuss the work of Tama Janowitz in the final chapter and her significance for ongoing gender debates.

In this chapter, I engage in a reading of Bret Easton Ellis' *Lunar Park* in order to argue that fear has become a cultural dominant at the start of the twenty-first century. Indeed, it is significant that Ellis' first novel written in the twenty-first century is a horror story that, due to its metafictional elements, is able to comment obliquely on the construction of horror. Traditionally, societies have associated fear with a clearly formulated threat such as plague, famine or war. However, at the start of the twenty-first century, fear has become a cultural dominant devoid of the solidity of a perceived threat. As the sociologist Frank Furedi argues: 'today we frequently represent the act of fearing as a threat itself. A striking illustration of this development is the fear of crime as a problem in its own right'.[1] Fear is simultaneously a symptom and a cause of indeterminacy. In this chapter I argue that fear generates indecision and conservative attitudes in the population. As such, the conditions of indeterminacy it promotes function as an ideological support for the status quo. In what follows, I engage in a psychoanalytic reading of *Lunar Park* in order to explore the ways in which the text depicts a self-perpetuating culture of fear while in the process offering the possibility of critique.

Although *Lunar Park* contains the key characteristics of the gothic horror story, the use of a variety of metafictional devices allows the text to simultaneously construct its tale and highlight that construction. As such, it simultaneously constructs a fear narrative and comments on that construction. The novel begins as an autobiography of Bret Easton Ellis that soon dissolves into fiction thereby thematizing narrative artifice and debunking the association of non-fiction with truth. This is highlighted by the assertion that concludes the first chapter: 'Regardless of how horrible the events described here might seem, there's one thing you must remember as you hold this book in your hands: all of it really happened, every word is true.'[2] This ironic statement offers a demonstration of the way 'truth' is constructed through the representation and therefore mediation of fact. Through a series of uncanny tropes such as the ghostly metamorphosis of the family house, the animation of his stepdaughter's doll and the emergence of literary characters from his previous texts into 'real' life, the Bret Easton Ellis depicted within the novel encounters the inexplicable boundary between the familiar and the strange, truth and fiction. Accordingly, the text links the conditions of indeterminacy that characterize the postmodern era to the construction of fear narratives. In this analysis I focus on the uncanny tropes found in *Lunar Park* and argue that the associated characteristics of fear and anxiety are indicative of an underlying fantasy-structure that generates conditions of uncertainty. Consequently, I draw upon Lacanian formulations of subjectivity, the paternal function and 'extimacy', a neologism that simultaneously embodies and combines the most intimate experience with the outermost. By reading the text as a colloquium of contemporary sources of the uncanny, a theory concerned with the issue of boundaries, liminality, the strange and the familiar, this chapter offers a critique of the culture of fear and its impact upon the 'everyday life' of the subject.

Of What Evokes Fear and Dread

Lunar Park self-consciously reworks the conventions of the horror genre in order to expose the construction of fear narratives at the turn of the twenty-first century. Throughout this analysis, I draw on the psychoanalytic concept of the uncanny in order to explore the apparent substitution of rationality, order and traditional symbols of authority with conditions of fear and anxiety. The uncanny is the sense of things out of place, of uncertainty, the unnatural, strangeness and alienation. The uncanny or *unheimlich* in German, derives from the word *heimlich* or familiar and homely. In his essay on the uncanny, Freud states that '*heimlich* is a word the meaning of which develops in the direction of ambivalence, until it finally coincides with its opposite, *unheimlich*'.[3] Consequently, the uncanny occupies the point of minimal difference between the sensation of familiarity, belonging and homeliness and the frightening, unknown and unfamiliar. Accordingly, there is a strong connection between the uncanny and Kant's general notion of an antinomy. An antinomy is the simultaneous expression of two propositions that are 'mutually exclusive and collectively exhaustive, i.e. such that both of them cannot be true and both of them cannot be false'.[4] For Kant, the antinomies can be solved through the application of pure reason. In direct contrast to the logic of pure reason, the sensation of the uncanny is produced through the sustained juxtaposition of two contradictory experiences such as the familiar and unfamiliar, the homely and unhomely, truth and falsity. These themes demarcate the contested borders of experience for a Bret Easton Ellis who finds himself in 'a world that was quickly becoming a place with no boundaries' (10). The structural homology between the uncanny and Kant's antinomies indicates that the prevalence of uncanny tropes is directly correlative to the decline of the category of reason in contemporary society. This is symptomatic of widespread distrust in socio-symbolic apparatus and the accompanying decline of traditional systems of authority.

Freud's notion of the uncanny is indebted to his earlier paper on antithetical meaning.[5] He asserts that antithesis was a constitutive element of all primal languages due to the essential relativity of all knowledge. He cites numerous words that originally had an antithetical structure, containing the experience of two sides, such as 'altus', which signified both 'high' and 'deep'. Another example, memorably employed by Giorgio Agamben is 'sacer', meaning both 'sacred' and 'accursed'. This antithetical structuring principle is also apparent in the words 'history' and 'story', which both derive from the Latin root 'historia' meaning simply narrative.

The distinction between truth and falsity, or narratives based on fact or fiction is only made later. This is especially significant for the quasi-autobiographical premise of *Lunar Park*. Consequently, the uncanny signals a return to primal experience in which clear antithetical boundaries are torn down and the dialectical structure of reason displaced. This forms the structural trope to *Lunar Park* as words and themes frequently appear as antinomies. A key example of this occurs when Ellis first encounters Clayton, a character from his first novel *Less Than Zero*. Here Clayton is described as a sycophant, which conventionally means an abject flatterer but can also be used to signify an impostor or deceiver. Indeed, the reader later discovers that he is Ellis' uncanny double who appears benign but is actually at the heart of the supernatural incursions.

The sense of the uncanny is sustained throughout the novel, primarily due to the fact that the supernatural phenomena are never adequately explained. Instead the reader is faced with two possible solutions, one probable and supernatural, the other impossible and rational. However, even this distinction is blurred by the inconsistency of the narration. Despite the assertion that 'every word is true' the narrator remains extremely unreliable. At the start of the novel, the reader is informed of the (fictional) pre-publication controversy surrounding *Lunar Park* when both Ellis' ex-wife and mother disputed the 'truth' of the narrator's depiction of events. In addition, echoing the divisive issue surrounding Henry James' *The Turn of the Screw*, there is initially some confusion over whether the children or the supernatural are responsible for the uncanny occurrences. As Ellis states, 'the kids were unreliable – their meds were proof of that' (88). However, the reader is repeatedly reminded that Ellis himself is heavily medicated and therefore equally, if not more, unreliable. Indeed, medical discourse is deployed as a recurrent trope to undermine the veracity of Ellis' subjective first person account. For instance, his psychiatrist, 'Dr. Janet Kim, offered the suggestion that I was "not myself" during this period, and has hinted that "perhaps" drugs and alcohol were "key factors" in what was a "delusional state"' (30). In a later passage, during an interview with Detective Kimball, Ellis states: 'I felt like an unreliable narrator, even though I knew I wasn't' (122). Here, Ellis has a sense of his own unreliability but immediately disavows this knowledge. This simultaneously highlights the narrator's opacity to himself and demonstrates the loss of faith in subjective experience in the face of 'expect' or institutionalized knowledge. Unreliability is an essential aspect of the uncanny and Ellis uses this technique to generate uncertainty in the reader thereby denying them rational analysis of the situation. This indeterminacy is symptomatic of the fear and uncertainty that has marked the first decade of the twenty-first century. In the wake of postmodernism, all narratives appear to be fallible, subjective and unreliable. Consequently, institutionalized 'expert' opinion has become the dominant discourse of power. In place of traditional systems of authority such as religion, law or the family, the contemporary sociocultural order is characterized by the institutionalization of knowledge.

The uncanny generates feelings of uncertainty in seemingly secure notions of selfhood and experience. *Lunar Park* specifically evokes this uncertainty when Ellis reunites with his former partner Jayne and becomes the nominal head of a nuclear family. The homely domestic setting provides the stable coordinates for malign supernatural incursions to take place. However, it is possible to read these not as incursions but as manifestations of the repressed family drama. Reversions such as these cloud any straightforward reading of *Lunar Park*. As Slavoj Žižek has noted, stories ostensibly about the conflict between larger social, historical or supernatural forces are often framed by a family drama. In his psychoanalytic readings of Hollywood movies he frequently argues that supernatural phenomena are manifestations of repressed desire. For example, his reading of *The Birds* demonstrates that the titular creatures are in fact manifestations of the mother's repressed incestuous desire.[6] This critical approach reveals that the myth of the stable nuclear family is created and sustained by the culture industry. *Lunar Park* subverts this ideological framework by placing its protagonist in the conventionally legitimate position as the head of the domestic unit, bringing his stepdaughter and previously unacknowledged son in line with the projected social ideal. Whereas the family unit traditionally signifies stability, closure and resolution, in narratives ranging from early medieval literature through to the ubiquitous Hollywood romantic-comedy, Ellis finds himself 'thrust into the role of husband and father – of protector – and my doubts were mountainous' (29). In a reversal of genre conventions in which alienated individuals are united through marriage into the traditional family unit, the supernatural manifestations originate from Ellis' uncomfortable conformity with the dominant social order. As the newly installed father, Ellis is expected to fulfil his symbolic role and bring order, certainty and reason to the domestic sphere. By contrast, over the course of 12 days, his subjectivity becomes increasingly distorted and undermined. In what follows I will discuss three ways in which the novel exhibits aspects of the uncanny and its impact on the family unit. In this way, the novel speaks to concerns about the decline of reason and the concomitant increase in fear at the start of the twenty-first century.

Uncanny Dolls

One of the primary sources of the uncanny is Ellis' stepdaughter's doll – the Terby, a grotesque parody of the popular Furby: 'It was a monstrous-looking but very popular toy that she'd wanted badly yet the thing was so misconceived and grotesque – black and crimson feathers, bulging eyes, a sharp yellow beak with which it continuously gurgled' (42). Although never confirmed by the narrative, the doll appears to carry out attacks on the fabric of the family home; it leaves deep scratches in doors, rips open pillows and leaves trails of slime. In his paper on the uncanny, Freud briefly mentions the uncanny nature of dolls but swiftly rejects or perhaps represses further discussion because it does not fit neatly into the Oedipal schema. However, he does indicate that Jentsch's example of the automaton is an excellent instance of the uncanny at work. Significantly for our previous discussion, the automaton bears an antithetical meaning by signifying as a mechanism which has the power of self-movement like a living being, or alternatively, as a living being whose actions are purely involuntary or mechanical. Both definitions juxtapose the living and the mechanical to evoke 'doubt as to whether an apparently animate object really is alive and, conversely, whether a lifeless object might not perhaps be animate' (135). Although the reader is left in doubt, the Terby is represented as a doll that appears to come to life and therefore has the characteristics of the automaton. It is this doubt evoked by the doll that throws the boundary between life and death into disorder, thereby staging a disruption to the category of reason.

The Terby signifies the intangible point of minimal difference between the living and the dead and this is developed into a recurrent theme throughout the text. During Ellis' first encounter with the doll at a party, he is struck by its juxtaposition of mechanical and living characteristics. One moment 'its movements were so clumsy and mechanical that I giggled at myself for having become so frightened'. However, he soon realizes that, 'the thing was actually warm and something was pumping beneath its feathers' (51). Ellis later wakes up the morning after Halloween to discover the remnants of supernatural activity. The Terby is found lying next to a dead crow and, 'in the morning light it resembled something black and dead' (99). This suggests that rather than being solely mechanical, the doll was previously alive thereby creating an immediate parallel with the dead crow. However, what makes the Terby uncanny rather than the crow is that its lost vitality is found within the mechanical. As discussed in the Introduction, the sense of something mechanical encrusted upon the living conventionally signals the comic spirit. However, in a continuation of the novel's sustained inversion of conventional tropes, here it generates fear and dread. Ellis later discovers a slime trail, presumably left by the Terby, which evokes a sense of 'dead things'. This contrasts with the sounds of children playing, 'their cries of surprise and disappointment associated with something *living*' (100). However, the children come to mirror the uncanny effect of the doll in an unexpected way. Whereas the doll appears alive despite its mechanical nature, the children frequently appear mechanical despite being alive. This is highlighted at a children's party where Ellis notices that 'all the kids were on meds (Zoloft, Luvox, Celexa, Paxil) that caused them to move lethargically and speak in affect-less monotones' (108). This parallel between familiar suburban life and unfamiliar supernatural experience is reinforced when Ellis takes Robby to see *Some Call Him Rebel*, a science fiction film about a rebellious teenage alien that parodies the rebellious alienated teenager. Continuing the novel's inversion of the harmonious marriage trope, the familiar suburban setting is established as uncanny in an antithetical relationship with the unfamiliar supernatural occurrences. As these instances demonstrate, this is a text that replicates the norms of suburban life in inverted form thereby exposing them to ridicule and critique.

Freud ascribes the emergence of the sense of the uncanny to infantile sources. Indeed, uncanny tropes are said to involve, 'a harking back to single phases in the evolution of the sense of self, a regression to times when the ego had not yet clearly set itself off against the world outside and from others' (143). The effect of the uncanny doll is exemplary in this regard because it plays a crucial role in the infantile development of the ego not only for Sarah, Ellis' six-year-old stepdaughter, but for Ellis himself. She frequently expresses herself through the doll, for instance, telling an uninterested Ellis: 'He [the Terby] says you don't like him [. . .] He says you never play with him' (64). This substitution of her voice with the doll is indicative of its role in her developing ego formation. It functions as a transitional object that allows her to gradually separate perception of herself from perception of the external world. At this stage it is useful to draw upon Jacques Lacan's conceptualization of the subject of the Imaginary expounded in his seminars from the early to mid-1950s. Building on Freud's observations in the paper 'On Narcissism'[7], Lacan states in *Écrits* that it is when 'the human individual fixates on an image that alienates him from himself, that we find the energy and the form from which the organization of the passions that he will call his ego originates' (92). Accordingly, the ego should be understood to be an agency foreign to the subject who must be constructed in relation to a series of external images. These external images exercise a (de)formative power over the subject's psyche. The Terby is such an image, initially constructed by Ellis as a child: 'I saw the Terby replicated a hundred times throughout a book I had written thirty years ago' (282). The book is entitled *The Toy Bret*, further blurring the line between the living and the mechanical. In both its 'fictional' and 'real' form, the Terby signifies a specific point in the process of ego formation for both Ellis and his stepdaughter. Whereas for Sarah, it functions as a comforting transitional object in her psychical development, for Ellis it signifies a terrifying return or regression to a state prior to the solidity of the autonomous stable ego.

In the chapter 'The Kids', Ellis voices concerns to his wife, Jayne, that Sarah is unable to differentiate between fantasy and reality. Of course, Ellis himself has the same difficulty and like Sarah this anxiety is also focalized through the Terby. In addition, the teachers at her school express concerns that 'she doesn't know where her personal space ends and someone else's begins and she can't read facial expressions, and she's non-responsive when people are talking directly to her' (165). This confirms the hypothesis that Sarah has not fully integrated with what Lacan termed the Symbolic order, that is, language and the entire realm of culture conceived as a symbol system structured on the model of language. Sarah's developmental difficulties are symbolized by her relationship with the Terby. In a discussion of Rilke and the uncanny, Eva-Maria Simms argues that the doll occupies a privileged site in the ego development of the child. Its function is 'to be an object against which the child must assert its own identity. [The doll] stands at the threshold of narcissism, forcing the child to assume an identity of his own, and to distinguish between I and the world.'[8] It offers a passive receptacle for the child's imagination while at the same time its unresponsiveness symbolizes a lifeless body that refuses to react to the child's emotions. However, rather than forcing her to assume her own autonomous identity, Sarah has an excessive attachment to the doll which holds back her psychical development. She exists in a permanently medicated state in which the doll functions as a receptacle onto which she projects her feelings of hatred and aggression, generated by the loss of her perceived unity with the world. It is for this reason that Ellis encounters the doll as a monstrous and aggressive entity.

Lacan argues in *Écrits* that the alienating identifications instigated by the mirror-stage generate both narcissism and aggression in the subject. He states: 'aggressiveness is the tendency correlated with a mode of identification I call narcissistic, which determines the formal structure of man's ego and of the register of entities characteristic of his world' (89). For Lacan, narcissism and aggressivity are directly correlative. As the subject undergoes an alienating identification with their unified, ideal image, they narcissistically desire that image and aggressively aim to take its place. This love–hate relationship is refracted through the Terby. In the chapter 'The Darkness,' Jayne travels to Toronto leaving Ellis in charge of the household. It is at this point when Sarah is completely separated from her mother that the household comes under attack, first by the Terby and then by a second more monstrous manifestation: 'It was three feet high and covered in hair streaked black and blond, and it moved on feet that weren't visible' (235). This creature is a monstrous re-imagining of Ellis' stepdaughter. Her most prominent features are exaggerated and rearranged into a creature characterized by hunger and frustration. Its abstract form composed of hair, mouth and a single eye indicates that it is a direct manifestation of Sarah's undifferentiated and fragmented sense of self. During this scene, the Terby, or the transitional object, is displaced and Sarah's repressed, aggressive emotions, integral to the development of the autonomous stable ego are rendered manifest. Whereas the Terby is an automaton that generates an uncanny effect, this second creature is more straightforwardly aggressive. Ellis is forced to assume the role of the protective father and works to protect the children from the monstrous incursion. This indicates that the father figure plays a highly significant part in restraining aggressive impulses during psychic development. The Terby is terrifying for two reasons. First, it stages an uncanny disruption to the boundary between the living and the dead. Secondly, it highlights that the autonomous ego has an illusory origin. By placing the focus on Sarah's transition through fragmentation, insufficiency and aggression towards an illusory unity, it effectively deconstructs Ellis' illusion of possessing a stable, autonomous ego. As such, the novel reflects on the increasingly uncertain coordinates of selfhood and autonomy in contemporary society. The importance of the ego and the figure of the father are further explored through Ellis' encounters with the architectural uncanny.

The Architectural Uncanny

The second form of ghostly manifestation encountered by the fictional Bret Easton Ellis can be broadly categorized as the architectural uncanny. Here the immediate domestic setting is subject to ghostly metamorphoses, including the appearance of large ash footprints, the carpet becoming

darker and shaggier and the rearrangement of the furniture in a manner that appears 'weirdly familiar' to the narrator (53). In his discussion
of the architectural uncanny, Anthony Vidler comments on the apparent
ubiquity of the classic haunted house in gothic literature: 'it's apparent
domesticity, its residue of family history and nostalgia, its role as the last
and most intimate shelter of private comfort sharpened by contrast the
terror of invasion by alien spirits'.[9] Initially, the supernatural incursions in
Lunar Park appear to fit Vidler's thesis. However, the invasion by alien spirits results in a metamorphosis of the furniture, which recreates the site of
his childhood home. There is consequently a doubling of familiar domestic settings with Ellis simultaneously inhabiting the role of both father and
son. The familiar domestic setting acts as the normative contrasting element to the alien intrusions but also generates a deeper sense of unease.
Mirroring the significance of the automaton, which juxtaposes the living
and the dead, these uncanny metamorphoses place two opposing domestic
sites into an impossible and sustained juxtaposition. The uncovering of
one house within the other indicates that the uncanny alien intruder is
found within.

In a manner homologous to 'the green world' of Shakespearean com-
edies, the party at the start of *Lunar Park* is the moment where hierarchy,
critical judgement and 'normal' expectation wildly vacillate. Traditionally
the carnival was established as a moment of transgressive enjoyment that
ultimately reaffirmed boundaries and the dominant ideology. However,
Ellis insists that the carnivalesque atmosphere of the party is for him the
norm: 'parties seemed frivolous and random and formless but in fact were
intricately patterned, highly choreographed events. In the world in which
I came of age the Party was the surface on which daily life took place' (33).
This reflects concerns with the systems and structures of control to be found
beneath surfaces characterized by indeterminacy and flux. However, this
description also continues the text's sustained inversion of the coordinates
of everyday life, disrupting the distinction between the universal, rational
'real' world and particularized situations of transgression and disruption.
Ellis' memory of being a college student also evokes limitless and therefore
ineffectual subversion: 'there were no boundaries, everything was acceptable, transgression was legitimate' (129). In a similar way, the party inverts
the postmodern substitution of the 'real' with the simulation. Initially,
'though this was most decidedly an adult party there was nothing too
frightening going down at 307 Elsinore Lane – just something playful and
innocent to amuse the guests' (34). At this stage the boundary between the
elaborately decorated house and the safe domestic environment is clear.

However, this is the point when the house metamorphoses from *seeming* to be the ubiquitous haunted house, to *becoming* haunted. Echoing the post-modern substitution of the simulacrum in place of the 'real', this is the moment when Ellis' fictions start to become real.

The boundary between performance and reality is further deconstructed the morning after when the now hung-over Bret Easton Ellis wraps himself in a sheet and is subsequently referred to by the narrator as a ghost. In this scene, his inability to connect with the children in any meaningful way is analogous to his portrayal as a ghostly presence. This link between the paternal figure and the alien intruder is reinforced when Ellis discovers that the ash footprints and metamorphosis of the furniture are ghostly demarcations of his own deceased father. Despite being a new building, the paintwork on the house steadily peels away to reveal his childhood home: 'in my memories it was all there – the pink stucco house, the green shag carpeting' (170). In addition, a gravestone bearing his father's name, his father's bathing shorts and his old car – a cream coloured 450 SL – all appear at different moments. Ellis is simultaneously portrayed as haunting his children and haunted by his father. This ambivalent position is echoed by the house, which alternately signifies as either shelter or entrapment. At times it is a defence against the unknown forces that Ellis senses are amass-ing outside. At other times, it becomes a confining space from which Ellis struggles to escape. These conditions of ambivalence and indeterminacy are generated by fear and result in circularity and stasis. In this way, the narrative presents conditions of indeterminacy in order to highlight the ways in which the culture of fear sustains the status quo.

The house functions as a reflection of Ellis' deteriorating psyche. Rather than a unified architectural form, the house's rapidly peeling walls and internal metamorphosis to the site of his childhood reflects Ellis' increas-ingly fragmented identity and accompanying regression to a childlike state of insufficiency. The house itself is located on Elsinore Street although Ellis is 'semivague about the setting itself because it doesn't matter, it's a place like any other' (30). Consequently, Ellis' experience is universalized. As well as echoing the name Ellis, and thereby reinforcing the novel's spa-tial representation of his psyche, Elsinore is the setting of *Hamlet*, another text centred on the haunting of a son by the father. Like *Hamlet*, the novel focuses on existential malaise and fears that are not acted upon. However, the transition from an aristocratic setting to a blandly suburban milieu indicates that the fear that restricts action and sustains the status quo has become a cultural dominant. For this reason it is significant that the 9/11 attacks were the initial motivation for Jayne to move her family out of the city and into the suburbs. The uncanny can (and is most likely to) erupt in the most sanitized environment, meaning that no place is safe. This constitutes an unsettling echo of the political assertion that no place is safe from terror in the wake of 9/11. Even within the apparent safety of the anonymous suburbs, Jayne is depicted as 'fearful of just about everything: the threat of paedophiles, bacteria, SUVs (we owned one), guns, pornography and rap music, refined sugar, ultraviolet rays, terrorists, ourselves' (28).

The 9/11 attacks on the World Trade Centre and the Pentagon function as a vanishing mediator to the uncanny experiences in the novel. In his preface to *The Uncanny*, Nicholas Royle states that the twin towers of the World Trade Centre were already uncanny. One was the uncanny double of the other, 'weirdly close yet far away'.[10] Early in the novel, Ellis enters the World Trade Centre to contend his son's parentage when he realizes that Jayne has named their son after his father, constituting an uncanny doubling across the generations. He states: 'I am certain [naming the son after Ellis' father] is the reason that the following events in *Lunar Park* happened – it was a catalyst' (16). The use of the World Trade Centre in this scene is not incidental. As Royle notes, 9/11 was an uncanny event that has become a catalyst for widespread uncertainty and fear: 'On September 11 the familiar, so-called domestic security of the United States was evidently wiped out forever' (viii). Consequently, *Lunar Park* can be seen as a politico-social allegory in which the familiar, domestic space is invaded by an unknown enemy: 'There were so many faceless enemies – from within the country and abroad – that no one was certain who we were fighting and why' (27). In the face of these perceived threats the nuclear family represents a return to stable boundaries, traditionalism and normality. Within this social environment, Jayne desires a father figure who embodies certainty, domestic authority and community cohesion. In what follows, I will discuss the significance of the decline of the paternal function at the start of the twenty-first century.

The Paternal Function

Ellis' father is the focal point of many of the disparate supernatural incursions, mirroring Ellis' troubled position as the newly installed father figure. Across the generations, the father is depicted as a haunting presence for the son. The doubling of the father figure indicates that the pervasive sense of the uncanny is not caused by a particular father but with the very role of the father and its changing significance within the contemporary sociocultural order. The father figure plays a central role in psychoanalysis, most notably in Freud's exposition of the Oedipus Complex. During natural psycho-sexual development the (male) infant experiences sexual desire for the mother. The father intervenes and prohibits that desire, redirecting it down socially acceptable pathways. However, Freud's emphasis on the real father proves problematic because the monstrous and prohibitive father of the Oedipus Complex generally fails to coincide with the often ineffectual and sometimes absent, biological father. As compensation, Freud invented the myth of the primal father whose power and significance is passed down through phylogenetic memory.[11] However, neither myth is convincingly developed nor are the questions surrounding the issue of phylogenetic inheritance fully answered. Lacan's subsequent reinterpretation of the Oedipus Complex circumvents these problems by raising the status of the father to the level of the signifier, which generates the term the Name-of-the-Father. This indicates that 'the real father is nothing other than an effect of language and has no other real'.[12] Consequently the symbolic paternal function can operate without the presence of the father and can even be embodied by the mother.

The paternal function inaugurates the subject's entry into the Symbolic order. Lacan puns on the homophony between the *Nom-du-père* (Name-of-the-Father) and the *Non-du-père* (No-of-the-Father) to indicate that the paternal function operates as a prohibition that directly restricts the infant's desire. This process is experienced by Ellis when his sustained encounter with the uncanny causes his symbolic identity to fragment:

> The denial of everything would pull me gently from reality, but only for a moment, because lines started connecting with other lines, and gradually an entire grid was forming and it became coherent, with a specific meaning, and finally emerging from the void was an image of my father. (170)

This passage represents Ellis' regression from the Symbolic and its subsequent re-formation focalized through the paternal function. The lines represent signifying chains that are bound up into a grid representing the Symbolic order. The image of the father signifies the paternal function that re-inaugurates Ellis within the reality of the Symbolic. This indicates the importance of the paternal function for maintaining symbolic efficacy while simultaneously demonstrating the regressive effects of the uncanny. Throughout the text, the sustained juxtaposition of Ellis' family with the uncanny and the uncertainty it engenders serves as an indication that the symbolic efficacy of the paternal function is in decline. As Paul Verhaeghe states: 'today, in spite of Freud's allegedly real myth, we are witnessing a very strange phenomenon: the massive collapse of the father figure'.[13] Rather than shifts in the real or biological father, Verhaeghe claims that it is belief in the symbolic father that is in decline. This is symptomatic of the rise of conditions of cultural indeterminacy and the accompanying lack of belief in any symbolic function.

Throughout the text Ellis experiences difficulty making emotional connections with the rest of his family. In the chapter 'Couples Counselling' he attempts to enunciate and come to terms with the contemporary decline of the parental function. During this emotionally charged passage, Ellis argues that fatherhood 'is a process [. . .] It's not intuitive. It's something you learn.' Jayne replies: 'No, Bret, it's something you *feel.* You don't *learn* how to connect with your own son from a fucking manual' (197). This exchange is indicative of the extent to which the nuclear family unit has become a naturalized cultural dominant. For Jayne, fatherhood is a natural and instinctive subject position. By contrast, Ellis argues that it is a construct. Lacan's re-visioning of the Oedipus Complex supports Ellis' view by indicating that the paternal function, or the Name-of-the-Father, is a symbolic role or construct rather than an essence. Ellis' difficulty engaging with his children stems from his failure to coincide with the symbolic paternal function. Indeed, his entry into the family unit can be interpreted as a reversal of the original Freudian primal myth. Rather than the real father being replaced by the symbolic function, the children are suddenly confronted with the real father, who lacks authority and therefore symbolic efficacy. As Verhaeghe states, 'contemporary sons have great difficulties in regarding their fathers as representatives of ancient patriarchal authority' (138). Significantly, Robby is known as Robby Dennis, after Jayne. He literally lacks the Name-of-the-Father and is marked instead by his matrilineal parentage. This constitutes the most significant psycho-drama in the text as both Ellis and his son attempt to integrate with social norms and conventions in the wake of traditional models of patriarchal authority.

The decline of the paternal function has resulted in the development of what Alain Badiou describes as 'atonal' worlds.[14] These are worlds devoid of the certainty of grounded positions, binary logic and order. Instead they are composed of endless multiplicities. In response to this loss of certainty and structure, the families depicted in *Lunar Park* rely on scientific and institutionalized forms of knowledge to negotiate 'everyday' life. In the chapter titled 'The Dinner Party', Ellis and Jayne meet couples from their neighbourhood. Here the conversation revolves around their children who all attend the same school. The school is the institutional embodiment of the discourse of education that continually interpellates their speech. This highlights the decline of power grounded in traditional symbolic authority and its replacement with knowledge based in 'expert' opinion. As they discuss the multitude of disorders, pathologies and obstacles that their children encounter, Ellis observes that: 'These parents were scientists and were no longer raising their kids instinctually' (133). The paternal function is being replaced with scientific knowledge. Paternal authority is irreducibly based on faith; we never know with certainty who the father is. The act of faith that would ground fatherhood within a naturalizing discourse has been eroded by the contemporary hegemony of scientific discourse that enables biological parentage to be systematically (dis)proved. The decline of trust and power grounded in traditional symbolic authority correlates with the rise of indeterminacy and fear. Instead, the parents in the novel rely upon scientific discourse and institutional advice to raise their children, resulting in affectless relationships. As Slavoj Žižek states in *In Defense of Lost Causes*: 'the language of science is not the language of subjective engagement, but the language deprived of its performative dimension, desubjectivized language' (32). In the first decade of the twenty-first century, belief in symbolic authority has been replaced with positive scientific knowledge. As Žižek suggests, this in turn may lead to the suspension of the symbolic laws and functions constitutive of human subjectivity.

In a reversal of the notable lack of parents in *Less Than Zero*, *Lunar Park* depicts the disappearance of children, culminating in Robby's removal from the plot. These disappearances are frequently pre-empted by the fathers' attitudes to their children: 'It wasn't that they were concerned about their kids, but they wanted something back, they wanted a return on their investment – this need was almost religious' (133). This indicates that economic imperatives have replaced religion and systems of belief. This utilitarian ethic is reflected by a series of parenting games that include the deaf-daddy routine: 'When he starts whining just pretend you don't understand what he's saying,' and 'hide-and-get-lost' (135–6). In the novel, the fathers' symbolic function has been effectively replaced by computer screens that function as portals to vast amounts of positive knowledge. This contributes to the sense that the sons exist in an atonal world. As the fathers complain: 'They have no idea how to put things into context [. . .] they're fragment junkies' (136). With the decline of the paternal function, the sons are coerced by fear to enter into a sea of simulacra, increasingly removed from real world referents.

The psychoanalytic readings delivered so far bring degrees of under-standing to a narrative structure that is rooted in hesitation, uncertainty and duplicity. This uncertainty is centred about the figure of the Other that, in Lacan's schema, signifies in relation to the subject in a number of ways. As Lorenzo Chiesa explains: 'the big Other may be equated with: (a) *language* as a structure; (b) *the symbolic order* as the legal fabric of human culture; (c) *the Freudian unconscious*'.[15] Ellis' stepdaughter and the supernat-ural animation of her uncanny doll highlight the relation between the ego and the subject's entry into the Other of language. Robby and the missing boys symbolize the decline of the paternal function and the accompany-ing vitiation of the Symbolic Other. The final form of Otherness in *Lunar Park* is that of the unconscious. The Other of Lacanian discourse operates in a cyclical relationship with the subject. For example, the subject of the unconscious is both the unconscious of the subject and the subject sub-jected to the unconscious. This parallels the subject's relationship with lan-guage or the Symbolic order. The subject is able to signify using language but is simultaneously subjected to or constrained by language. It is for this reason that Lacan states in *Seminar XI*: '*the unconscious is structured like a language*'. This is not to say that the unconscious *is* a language but that it is structured *like* one. This indicates that the seeming flux of language and unconscious thought has a structure, thereby opening them up to analysis and formal critique. *Lunar Park* is an exploration of the structure of Ellis' psyche through language and the process of writing. It self-consciously references the boundary between autobiography and imaginative fiction, and employs a number of metafictional devices that subvert 'common-sense' interpretations. Lacan's thesis makes a valuable connection between language and the unconscious and this provides us with insight into the impact of fear narratives on the subject's psyche.

Writing the Uncanny

Lunar Park utilizes a variety of metafictional devices with which to thema-tize narrative artifice. The most instantly recognizable is the inclusion of the author as the central character. The second is the intrusion of charac-ters from Bret Easton Ellis' previous novels into the narrative. This is not a new technique; the use of recurring characters and settings is a key char-acteristic of Bret Easton Ellis' oeuvre. Each instance of intertextuality has the effect of debunking the notion that a novel exists as an autonomous fictional universe. The third metafictional device is the emergence of 'the writer' who delivers a different version of events to Ellis. The first instance of an autonomous writer delivering a second narrative is found towards the end of the first chapter and is attributable to a journalist interviewing the newly married Bret and Jayne. They seek to present themselves as a stable, married couple. However, 'the writer had his own pop-psychology take on matters' (26). Consequently, there is a clear disparity between the way Bret and Jayne attempt to present themselves to the world and the way in which the writer *re*presents them. Neither version is entirely true or entirely false but by presenting these views, Ellis highlights the diegesis that mediates the dissemination of knowledge.

The most immediate metafictional device is the quasi-autobiographical beginning. The author is ostensibly writing about himself and delivering a personal but 'truthful' account of his life and writing career. However, the intrusion of the supernatural causes the reader to question the veracity of the narrative. By presenting fiction as truth, the text parodies the performativity of both authorial and authoritative discourse, indicating that all structures must be supported by some artifice. The fictional Ellis initially saw a clear distinction between truth and falsity, symbolized in terms of life and death. For Ellis, his writing persona is a separate 'dead' sphere of consciousness, generating untruths that 'flow onto the whiteness of a blank screen – into the part of me that was tactile and alive' (147). The blank screen is the page or computer screen on which he is writing but also represents that part of him that is subject to impulses from the unconscious. When Ellis recounts how he wrote *American Psycho*, he describes how a force beyond his control completed the novel: 'I would often black out for hours at a time only to realize that another ten pages had been scrawled out. My point is that the book *wanted* to be written by someone else. It wrote itself and didn't care how I felt about it' (13). This can be explained by Lacan's thesis that the unconscious is structured like a language; Ellis' unconscious psychic agency is directly writing itself in opposition to the narrator or the conscious ego.

Eventually the writer emerges from Ellis' interior psychic space to become an external personification and begins to deliver an alternative supernatural yet probable narrative. Again, Ellis' first person narration represents the perspective of the ego while the writer represents the unconscious or the id. Whereas Ellis ostensibly attempts to deliver a straightforward and linear account, the writer operates around a different logic. Mirroring the relation between the subject and the unconscious, the writer is a part of Ellis but Ellis is simultaneously subjected to the writer. This dynamic is explored in the chapter 'The Cat' when Ellis discovers the tortured body of a dead cat. On the one hand, the writer forces Ellis to look closer, mirroring the subject's instinctual (unconscious) fascination with the grotesque. On the other, Ellis is able to disavow knowledge in order to retain his sanity: 'I did not tell this to the writer because the scenario he would have come up with – the obstacles he would solve and the world he would make me believe in – was more than I could bear' (207). This conflict with the writer continues as Ellis becomes increasingly caught between the two possible solutions to the uncanny events, one probable and supernatural, the other impossible and rational. He eventually reaches the point, 'at which I believed the two had merged and I could not tell one from the other' (147). As Ellis' fictions enter into external reality, so do his innermost psychic thoughts and fears. This represents the dissolution of the boundary between inside and outside as well as the private and the public.

As explored above, Freud's conception of the uncanny deals with the sensation of strangeness and otherness found both externally in the unfamiliar but also within the familiar itself. The positive German term *heimlich* already contains within it, its antonym, the negative *unheimlich*. Because *unheimlich* has no equivalent in French, Lacan produced the neologism 'extimacy' that Jacques-Alain Miller glosses to mean 'the exterior is present in the interior'.[16] Significantly, this is a word with an antithetical meaning; it simultaneously signifies the most intimate and the outermost experience. Just as Freud's uncanny stages a disruption to the dialectic between the familiar and the unfamiliar, Lacan's formulation of extimacy subverts the division within conceptions of the Other to render the unconscious as both interior psychic structure and intersubjective structure. This enables a reading of *Lunar Park* that conceives of internal psychic apparatus on the same level as the socio-symbolic, thereby equating Ellis' experience of fear and psychic turmoil with the broader society outside.

Lacan's formulation of extimacy suggests that the supernatural incursions are actually manifestations of Ellis' unconscious. This is confirmed by the paranormal investigator who Ellis hires: '"But if the house is not the source [. . .] what is the source of the haunting?" Miller finally said it. "You are"' (264). As the course of the novel demonstrates, the ego is an alien intruder that occupies the most intimate part of the subject. Lacan states in *Seminar VII* that the Other is 'something strange to me, although it is at the heart of me' (71). In other words, the most intimate experience is often the most opaque. Extimacy problematizes the opposition between inside and outside to demonstrate first that the unconscious is the discourse of the Other, and secondly, that the centre of the subject is outside

or ex-centric. This is represented within *Lunar Park* by the external manifestation of Ellis' unconscious in the form of the writer and his fictional
creations. Accordingly, the disruption, fragmentation and insecurity of
Ellis' ego should be read not only as the inconsistency of subjective experience but as the inconsistency and even inexistence of the external socio-
symbolic Other.

   Lacan is clear that the mythical, complete Other does not exist. However,
as Ellis' experience demonstrates, although something may not exist, it
can still function *as if* it does. Even if the supernatural incursions do not
exist in physical reality, their impact upon Ellis' psychic reality is such that
the issue of their (in)existence becomes mute. In the same manner, the
external Other functions symbolically as psychic reality *as if* it exists. Miller
demonstrates this with the example of a bomb scare that had interrupted
one of his classes. Although the bomb did not exist, the signifier, 'Bomb!'
had the same psychic impact a bomb would have. There is a clear analogy
with the 9/11 attacks, which function as the catalyst for the plot. This event
constituted a puncture or a wound in the American myth of wholeness
and self-sufficiency. The image of the planes and the destruction of the
(phallic) twin towers resulted in the revelation that the Symbolic Other is
not complete, that there is a *lack* in the Other. Accordingly, these attacks
can be read as having a castrating effect on the American people's belief
in their nation's exceptional status. Consequently, reading the attacks in
relation to Lacan's formulation of extimacy, we see that they constitute a
challenge to the efficacy of traditional symbolic forms of authority and
their guarantor in the form of the paternal function. As Jerry Flieger states:
'embedding "the other" in "the Other" figures a new parity in the status
of other and Other. In this formulation, the locus of the Other can no
longer be simply equated with a paternal Law imposed from above, as symbolic authority.'[17] The 9/11 attacks constituted a blurring of the division
between individual and national identity. Here, the small other became
interchangeable with the big Other, revealing the lack in both.[18] Just as the
efficacy of the paternal function has entered into decline in the domestic
sphere, so the power and authority invested in the signifier 'America' has
been effectively vitiated.

   Bret Easton Ellis' *Lunar Park* provides insight into the culture of fear that
thrives under conditions of indeterminacy yet functions as an ideological
support for the status quo. The novel indicates that the culture of fear has
become increasingly prevalent in the first decade of the twenty-first century
and is bound in a mutually constitutive relationship with the decline of faith,
symbolic authority and the paternal function. However, commentators were

first to recognize that fear was becoming an ideological structure in the wake of the Second World War. As Camus argued in 1946:

> The seventeenth century was the century of mathematics, the eighteenth, of the physical sciences, and the nineteenth, of biology. *Our twentieth century is the century of fear.* Fear isn't a science, you may be thinking. Well, to begin with, science is no stranger to fear, since the latest theoretical advances have led science to repudiate itself, and since its practical applications threaten the entire earth with destruction. Furthermore, even if fear can't be considered a science in itself, there is no question that it is a method.[19]

As Camus recognizes, fear was increasingly being used as a tool or technique with which to manipulate public consensus. As *Lunar Park* demonstrates, cultures of fear infect the psyche and the unconscious, thereby destabilizing the ego and consequently leading to indeterminacy and inertia. Camus' equation of fear with science should be historicized in relation to the threat of nuclear war in which there was both a clearly identified external enemy, in the form of Soviet Russia, coupled with the fear of Communist spies or the enemy within. The 9/11 terror attacks mark the further disintegration of internal and external categories. The terrorist threat that has marked the first decade of the twenty-first century is simultaneously abroad and at home. As such, fear has become a cultural dominant and works to contain the potential for radical change to the fundamental coordinates of society.

Concluding Remarks

The theme of the fantasy-structure of the One and its subversive split is found in each of the novels under examination. Bret Easton Ellis' *Lunar Park* presents the contemporary sociocultural order as characterized by indeterminacy, the decline of traditional symbolic modes of authority and grounded instead in an ideological grand narrative of fear. However, the sense of the uncanny that pervades the text also offers the possibility of resistance. By disrupting any clear divisions between the familiar and the unfamiliar, the self and the Other, Lacanian psychoanalysis delivers a direct challenge to American ego psychology that emphasizes the sufficiency of the will in the face of the demands of the unconscious. As such, ego psychology constitutes a return to the fantasy-structure of the One, directly contradicting Freud's emphasis on the radical alterity of the unconscious. The emphasis on the will has a societal impact as reflected by the contemporary desire to erect clearly demarcated boundaries and the valorization of scientific and 'expert' knowledge. This theme is reflected throughout *Lunar Park*, which depicts the decline of traditional symbolic authority, focalized through the paternal function. This analogy is extended by the use of an unreliable narrator, the quasi-autobiography premise and the self-conscious vitiation of the authority of the author. These examples are indicative of a millennial *fin de siècle* marked by the confusion of boundaries and a loss of security. It is significant then, that the uncanny operates within the liminal point of minimal difference. The uncanny is not simply the experience of the Other but confuses boundaries to display the Other within the self. Rather than a unified whole, the ego is revealed to be an alien intruder within subjectivity. Jerry Flieger comments on the way scientific discoveries frequently increase the sense of alienation from naturalized states of being. In particular, she notes the strangely doubled nature of the human:

> They also evolved a stereoscopic seeing apparatus, providing the parallax (sight 'beside itself') that combines two points of view to provide depth vision. This biaxial disposition of limbs and senses means that we humans always situate ourselves thanks to an exterior point of reference, the third point 'out there' where our vision focuses. (224)

Sight and the human subject are thus seen to be divided. The subject always makes use of paranoid knowledge, which Lacan defines as the attempt to perceive the self through the Other's eyes. This external examination of the self defamiliarizes the subject and renders him or her as Other. As such, there is always a troubling part of the self that is opaque to both the subject and to others. For this reason it is within the contemporary sociocultural order in which the subject insists upon his or her unity and selfhood that he or she feels increasingly haunted by the spectre of a sinister Other within. This in turn offers the possibility of critique of fantasy-structures of wholeness. Paradoxically, the closer the subject comes to achieving wholeness or satisfaction, the more they feel alienated from themselves. The theme of doubling as a form of criticism of wholeness is continued in the next chapter, which examines Chuck Palahniuk's *Fight Club* in relation to the significance of nihilism in the twenty-first century.

Chapter 2

Nihilism and the Sublime in Chuck Palahniuk's *Fight Club*

Chuck Palahniuk is the author of a series of satires written at the turn of the twenty-first century including *Choke* (2001), *Lullaby* (2002), *Rant* (2007) and *Pygmy* (2009). Palahniuk is renowned for the transgressive qualities of his writing that depicts the obscene underside of everyday life. In particular, *Haunted* (2005) has become infamous for its graphic depiction of bodily horror and the frequency with which audience members have fainted during live readings by the author. Palahniuk's work is notable for its combination of nihilism with the comic spirit and the resulting depiction of a distorted world that obeys its own internal logic. His aphoristic style mimics the short, punchy prose employed by advertisements in inverted form, thereby offering a critique of capitalist discourse. This approach defamiliarizes the reader and opens up critical debate on otherwise naturalized or commonsensical discourse. This chapter focuses on *Fight Club* (1996), which – following the release of David Fincher's film adaptation in 1999 – has become Palahniuk's most popular novel and a cult classic. The novel and the film depict the workings of an underground group led by the charismatic Tyler Durden as they attempt to disrupt the smooth functioning of the capitalist system that dominates their lived experience. Critics such as Bülent Diken and Carsten Bagge Lausten have argued that the novel presents a cautionary tale that, despite its seeming celebration of rebellion and violence, ultimately works to shore up the functioning of globalized systems of capital.[1] While mindful of this sceptical approach, this chapter seeks to re-engage with the radical potentiality contained within the text through an exploration of the text's depiction of nihilism through a psychoanalytic lens. This fruitful combination offers a fresh understanding of the significance of nihilism in the wake of postmodernism.

Fight Club is first and foremost a satiric critique of contemporary consumer culture. Thanks in no small part to the film adaptation directed by David Fincher, *Fight Club* accrued a vast degree of cultural resonance at the close of the twentieth century. Indeed, the depiction of banal corporate culture coupled with undertones of decay and decline evokes the sense of a twentieth century *fin de siècle*. Importantly for the themes addressed in the novel, the phrase *fin de siècle* connotes the decadence and degeneration of an era as well as the sense of an ending or unavoidable radical change. *Fight Club* offers a scathing critique of what Ernest Mandel has dubbed late capitalism by following the unnamed narrator and his double, the charismatic Tyler Durden as they self-consciously attempt to strip away the accoutrements of consumer culture. Through a conscious reduction of the self, Tyler and the narrator attempt to evade the ideologies of late capitalism and radically change the world around them. This chapter places the nihilistic philosophy that drives Tyler Durden into dialogue with Lacanian psychoanalysis. This theoretical model achieves two things. Both positions effectively counteract the mythology of the will or the autonomous stable ego that serves as an ideological support for neoliberal capitalism. In addition, while acknowledging the limitations of radical thought, Lacan's formulation of 'a circular causality between the Symbolic and the Real also makes it possible to account for the fact that individual subjects are produced by discourse and yet manage to retain some capacity for resistance'.[2] As explored in the preceding chapter, the Symbolic order is comprised of the laws and languages that constitute the dominant sociocultural order. As such, it functions as a support for the hegemonic capitalist system. By contrast, the Real is experienced as a terrifying, traumatic gap in the social fabric that offers the possibility of radical change. In their rejection of and retreat from contemporary society, Tyler and the narrator, referred to only as 'I', create and sustain a morbid cult of violence in which identities are reduced down to their carnal state. In embracing a separatist politics, the participants temporarily suspend the demands of the hegemonic sociocultural order in a manner that stages an encounter with the Real. Consequently, the alienation experienced within the everyday is transformed from a position of subordination into an affirmation. By reading the fight club as a caesura embedded within the social fabric of late capitalism, this chapter works to displace cynicism in order to explore the possibilities for revolution offered by the link between militant nihilism and the Lacanian Real.

Desire and loss are highly significant themes throughout *Fight Club*. When depicting the banal consumer culture of which he is a part, the unnamed narrator describes his living environment as a 'condominium on the fifteenth floor of a high-rise, a sort of filing cabinet for widows and young professionals'.[3] This imagery is indicative of the spread of bureaucratic and mercantile discourse into all aspects of everyday life. Traditional Marxist critics view capitalism as a repressive force that positions subjects as objects in order to increase productivity. Against this background, desire can be seen to be a potentially subversive force, antagonistic to the mechanizing ideologies of industrial capitalism. However, as Fredric Jameson points out, 'it is not hard to show that the force of desire alleged to undermine the rigidities of late capitalism is, in fact, very precisely what keeps the consumer system going in the first place'.[4] *Fight Club* expresses desire as an ideology of late capitalism through the juxtaposition of the commodity-form with the quotidian: 'I wasn't the only slave to my nesting instinct. The people I know who used to sit in the bathroom with pornography, now they sit in the bathroom with their IKEA catalogue' (43). Here, sexual desire is redirected towards the commodity-form. In the film, the narrator's environment is superimposed with captions and prices that render the flat as if it were contained within an IKEA catalogue. This overlay signifies capitalism's colonization of the private sphere through the medium of the sign. Rather than a system of control imposed by visible power structures, the discourse of consumer culture is naturalized through a series of signs. Indeed, the culture of novelty, desirability and instant gratification obfuscates or conceals the absence of real choice regarding the fundamental structure of society.

As Jacques Lacan indicates, desire is not a relation to any object but a relation to lack. Desire is a social product constituted in relation to the perceived desires of other subjects. As such, the trope of the intrusive IKEA catalogue demonstrates the ways in which the desire of the subject is subjected to perceived sociocultural ideals. As discussed in the Introduction, desire is born out of the subject's entry into the Symbolic order, inaugurated by the mirror-stage. The image reflected in the mirror is an external representation of the subject as a unified whole, which causes the subject to perceive him or herself as a subject of lack. The subject is driven to fill their lack under the belief that possession of the object of desire will deliver satisfaction. However, desire is characterized by a process of continual deferral since desire is always desire for something the subject does not possess. For this reason, Lacan states that desire has a metonymic structure insofar as it is a movement from one signifier to another, along the signifying chain, in a constant deferral of meaning. The nihilistic philosophy spread by the narrator's double Tyler Durden constitutes a radical break with this constant deferral. It is through an outright refusal to participate in the desiring economy that the agency of the subject is restored. This chapter will investigate three ways in which Tyler subverts the ideologies of late capitalism. First, I will examine the significance of the sublime in the fight clubs and the gap between active and passive nihilism. This is followed by a discussion of cultural terrorism. Finally, I examine Project Mayhem and the different forms that active nihilism can take.

The Shortest Shadow

Fight Club dramatizes the conflict between a subject, identified only as 'I', and his uncanny double, the deviant and charismatic Tyler Durden. The narrator's 'I' conveniently stands in as a marker for the stable autonomous ego. However, the existence of the double throws this fantasy-structure of wholeness into confusion. Indeed, the division between the narrator and his double is emblematic of the division between the subject and his gestalt. Lacan states in *Écrits* that the primary function of the mirror stage is 'to establish a relationship between an organism and its reality- or, as they say, between the *Innenwelt* and the *Umwelt*' (78). In Lacan's early work it is clear that the subject's specular self-identification is the first of many and that many other external images can and do perform this role. Consequently, the primordial ego is constituted through a series of alienating identifications caused by the redoubling of external images through which the individual recognizes him or herself as an autonomous ego. This identification is alienating because the subject can no longer conceive of him or herself as a unified whole. As discussed in the previous chapter, the ego is an imaginary construction and should be differentiated from the subject of the unconscious. As Lacan states: 'If the *ego* is an imaginary function, it is not to be confused with the subject.'[5] The instability of the 'I' can also be located in Nietzsche's philosophy. When discussing the metaphysics of language and the presuppositions of reason, Nietzsche argues that the belief that the will has causal efficacy is the great fallacy of Western civilization:

> It believes in the 'I', in the I as being, in the I as substance, and it *projects* this belief in the I-substance onto all things – this is how it *creates* the concept of 'thing' in the first place [. . .] Being is imagined into everything – *pushed under everything* – as a cause; the concept of 'being' is only derived from the concept of 'I'.[6]

Consumer culture is predicated upon the belief in the autonomy and self-determination of the individual. Each subject is constituted as an 'I' who, secure in their being, is able to sustain the subject-object relation between themselves and the commodity-forms they purchase and consume. However, the narrator of *Fight Club* succinctly reverses this relationship: 'you're trapped in your lovely nest, and the things you used to own, now they own you' (44). Nietzsche's philosophy challenges the causal efficacy of the will and this finds resonance in the nihilistic philosophy espoused by Tyler Durden throughout *Fight Club*.

Fight Club repeatedly reverses the commonsensical power relation between the subject and the object. The initial stages of the text follow the narrator as he becomes increasingly disillusioned with his life, career and living environment before his encounter with Tyler Durden. However, the insistence that everyday reality is an illusion problematically suggests that there is a 'true' or 'real' world that stands in opposition to it. For this reason, the figure of the double is important because it throws the categories of truth and illusion into confusion. The double is not simply an illusion or fantasy but as Mladen Dolar points out, signifies all three constitutive elements of the psyche: 'he constitutes the essential part of the ego; he carries out the repressed desires springing from the Id; and he also, with a malevolence typical of the superego, prevents the subject from carrying out his desires'.[7] Tyler Durden embodies all three of these elements. He acts as the unconscious, carrying out acts unbeknown to the narrator. He engages in the narrator's repressed, illicit desires such as murdering his boss and sleeping with Marla Singer. Towards the narrative's conclusion, he increasingly prevents the narrator from following his desire. This final aspect is crucial to the novel's critique of consumer culture. Upon discovering that he and Tyler Durden are the same person, the narrator's identity is thrown into uncertainty. He attempts to retain the boundary between truth and illusion and thereby retain his sense of being a coherent self: 'Oh, this is bullshit. This is a dream. Tyler is a projection. He's a disassociative personality disorder. A psychogenic fugue state. Tyler Durden is my hallucination. / "Fuck that shit," Tyler says. "Maybe you're *my* schizophrenic hallucination"' (168). Neither Tyler nor the narrator are 'real' insofar as each are illusory semblances of wholeness. The narrator believes that his ego is a coherent self while Tyler functions as a gestalt or an image that is perceived as a unity incapable of expression simply in terms of its parts. The double functions as a radically destabilizing agency. Rather than presenting a clear division between the self and the other, *Fight Club* insists on the illusory character of the autonomous stable ego.

Psychoanalysis teaches us that, 'the ego might give a feeling of permanence and stability to the subject, but this is an illusion'.[8] The double is an effective means of subverting the codified social norms that construct the illusions that sustain the subject. Palahniuk extends this destabilizing technique by refusing to name the narrator. The narrator's lack of identity reveals the power structure at play in the authorial voice. This in turn, places the essence or being of the author in doubt. These disruptive strategies open up the individualist ideology of neoliberal capitalism to critique: 'You are not a beautiful and unique snowflake. You are the same decaying organic matter as everyone else, and we are all part of the same compost pile' (134). *Fight Club* is full of dualities contained within a singularity. This is immediately demonstrated by the narrator and Tyler Durden who exist within the same body. However, there are similar points of coincidence between the narrator and the authorial voice, the novel and the film adaptation, as well as within the two central rules of fight club: 'The first rule about fight club is you don't talk about fight club [. . .] The second rule of fight club is you don't talk about fight club' (48). These dualisms are repetitions that indicate points of minimal and irreducible difference within the same. Close examination of the non-coincidence of the same marks the theoretical intersection between Nietzschean philosophy and Lacanian psychoanalysis.

Although the plot of the film closely mirrors that of the novel, there are occasional differences that highlight the permanent and inherent tension that drives the ethos behind fight club and indicates why the text accrued such cultural resonance at the close of the twentieth century. In the novel, the initial split in the narrator occurs when he first meets Tyler on a nude beach after a lengthy period of non-stop travelling between places and time zones. This disruption to the stable coordinates of time and space is a physical enactment of the narrator's increasingly decentered self within an alienating and atomized society. On the beach Tyler plants logs into the sand so that they cast the shadow of a giant hand: 'At exactly four-thirty the hand was perfect. The great shadow was perfect for one minute, and for one perfect minute Tyler had sat in the palm of a perfection he'd created himself' (33). In contrast to the flux experienced by the narrator on his incessant business trips, Tyler creates an aesthetically and structurally 'perfect' point of spatial unity in a fixed period of time. This 'perfect' image is constructed through a series of doubles and representations, which is further complicated by the fact that Tyler is himself the narrator's shadow or double. As Tyler places the logs, it is the shadow cast by the logs that creates the sublime image of the 'perfect' hand. Like Tyler, the shadow is a gestalt that forms a specific whole or unity incapable of expression in terms of its parts. This scenario highlights the fundamental gap or disjunction between the individual and the image of their ideal, namely, the illusion that they exist as an autonomous stable ego. As Philip Shaw states: 'Just as in language, the "I" who speaks and the "I" that is spoken of fail to coincide, so in the mirror stage we cannot both "see", as subjective experience, and "be seen", as object.'[9] This impossible gap or point of non-coincidence of the same is succinctly dramatized through the formal devices of the double and the hand-shadow. It is significant that they are perceived to be perfect yet inexpressible. As such, they convey a sense of the sublime, which Shaw describes as, 'a descriptive failure [which] raises a negative, even painful, presentation of the ineffable' (3). *Fight Club* presents sublime objects that exist beyond the limits of language and thought. These are always momentary and inexpressible: 'a moment was the most you could ever expect from perfection' (33). As such, they exist as glimpses of, or missed encounters with, the Real that remains situated beyond the Symbolic.

The sublime is an experience that lies beyond conventional understanding so that the power of an object or moment is such that words and points of comparison evaporate. As discussed in the Introduction, for Freud, sublimation is the redirection of libidinal energies towards an object that is beneficial to civilization and its norms. However, Lacan reverses this formula so that libidinal energy is redirected from the transcendent void to an object that assumes a sublime quality. In *Seminar VII*, he argues that the sublime object points to the 'beyond-of-the-signified' (54). It indicates the void at the heart of symbolization without which signification could not take place. In his reading of Sophocles' *Antigone*, Lacan sets to one side the moral question found in the conflict between Antigone's demand for her traitorous brother's death rites and the prohibitive law of the state embodied by Creon. Instead, he focuses on the effect of Antigone's sublime beauty. The Chorus that conventionally provides the audience's emotional commentary loses its head in the face of Antigone's beauty so that the just appears unjust. This causes the Chorus to transgress the limits of the law. With this in mind, Lacan argues that the sublime 'causes all critical judgement to vacillate, stops analysis, and plunges the different forms involved into a certain confusion or, rather, an essential blindness' (281). The sublime object is a blinding force that stands beyond self-legitimating discourses of power. Instead it points to the void or the nothing beyond symbolization. As demonstrated by *Antigone*, the sublime opens up a space that challenges conventional morality while also providing a space from which it is possible to construct values other than the recognized and established common good.

It is significant that throughout *Fight Club*, the sublime object emerges at a point *between* two semblances that are almost entirely the same. This is achieved through the reduction of one object to zero. Throughout the text, Tyler Durden repeatedly proclaims that man must return to zero. This manifesto echoes one of Nietzsche's aphorisms in *Twilight of the Idols*: 'You are looking for something? You want to multiply yourself by ten, by a hundred? You are looking for disciples? – Look for *zeros!*' (157). Nietzsche's aphorisms frequently have something of a manifesto-style ring to them and like Tyler's pronouncements stand against commonsensical discourse. Tyler's reduction of man to zero is antithetical to the dominant ideologies of progress and reason. His formal style echoes that of Nietzsche's, and like Nietzsche, he calls for, 'a *revaluation of all values*' (155). In order to achieve this, both Tyler and Nietzsche point to the void or vacuum that operates as, 'the privileged place from which it becomes possible to create, as well as to see or perceive what has been created'.[10] This vacuum is located at the inner limit or inherent impossibility of a given discourse and can be activated as the potential locus of creation. As Tyler states, the ultimate aim of fight club is to, 'break up civilization so that we can make something better out of the world' (125). The fight clubs direct the reader towards an experience of the sublime, otherwise understood as an encounter with the Real, which in turn, causes a revaluation of all perceived values. It is out of this subtraction that cynical reason can be evaded and new values can emerge.

To return to the narrator's initial encounter with Tyler in the novel, it is significant that Tyler constructs a sublime object from shadows and semblances. This mirrors the relationship between Tyler and the narrator, who are themselves semblances. This encounter also reflects the image of noon deployed by Nietzsche. Nietzsche invents the theme of midday in order to symbolize the idea of a break or a new beginning following on from the dark night of nihilism. Ordinarily, one would assign such a meaning to the break of day but Nietzsche is insistent that morning acts only as the prelude to midday: 'This is *my* morning, *my* day begins: *rise up now, rise up, great noontide!*'[11] Why does Nietzsche emphasize noon? The answer to this lies with the fact that daylight brings with it not only light but the shadow cast by the subject. As the sun rises, this shadow becomes shorter and shorter until midday when the sun is directly overhead. However, rather than being the point at which the shadow disappears, noon marks the point when the shadow splits into two. Noon is the moment of the shortest shadow. However, this does not mark a point of unity among things beneath the sun, but the moment of splitting: 'Mid-day; moment of the shortest shadow; end of the longest error; zenith of mankind' (*Twilight of the Idols*, 155). As Zupančič argues, rather than creating and sustaining the fantasy-structure of the One, midday is the moment of the splitting of One into Two: 'the thing (as one) no longer throws its shadow upon another thing; instead, it throws its shadow upon itself, thus becoming, at the same time, the thing and its shadow' (27). This figure of the two is found throughout *Fight Club*, most notably in the relation between Tyler and the narrator. Despite occurring at 4:30, the perfect hand constructed by Tyler is emblematic of Nietzsche's figurative concept of noon. The logs throw a shadow that, rather than representing the world, creates something new. This is a sublime object that exists only for a moment and inaugurates the split between Tyler and the narrator. Nietzsche's figure of noon and the Lacanian Real share a comparable structure. They both appear as the point of minimal difference between two semblances. A piece of paper has two opposing faces or semblances. Both the Lacanian Real and the figure of noon can be likened to the edge that simultaneously structures and separates these semblances. *Fight Club* contains multiple figures of the two. These splits herald the emergence of the Real that as a disruptive force beyond the Symbolic order exposes the gaps and inconsistencies in the social fabric. As we shall see, the relationship between representation and the Real is of crucial importance for *Fight Club*'s critique of the cynical reason endemic at the close of the twentieth century.

Active and Passive Nihilism

As indicated by the image of the shortest shadow, 'the moment when "one becomes what one is" is not a moment of unification but, on the contrary, the moment of a pure split' (*The Shortest Shadow*, 25). This split or event is said by Nietzsche to articulate the gap between a discourse of affirmation and a discourse of negation, otherwise understood as the gap between active and reactive forces. This split between activity and passivity is a recurrent theme throughout *Fight Club* that warrants further investigation in relation to the Lacanian Real. Throughout the text, the narrator appears as a passive vessel, highlighted by his insomnia, which makes him feel increasingly detached from reality: 'three weeks without sleep, and everything becomes an out-of-body experience' (19). This distancing of the self from the body is symptomatic of an alienating consumer culture and indicative of the reactionary and deadening conditions it engenders. These are caused in part by the pervasive spread of images throughout

society. In *Simulacra and Simulation*, Jean Baudrillard discusses the proliferation of second order simulations or images so graphic that they blur
the boundary between representation and reality. This has resulted in
what Baudrillard terms a third order simulation, or a reality of its own
removed from reality: the hyperreal. The proliferation of semblances is
commented on by the narrator who experiences the 'insomnia distance
of everything, a copy of a copy of a copy. You can't touch anything and
nothing can touch you' (97). The proliferation of simulacra, or signifiers
devoid of their signified, has increasingly alienated the subject from his
or her own body. In an attempt to awaken from his insomnia, the narrator
attempts to re-connect with himself by experiencing 'real' pain at numerous patient support groups. At the cancer group he encounters Big Bob
who has been castrated in order to combat the spread of his testicular cancer. As a reactionary response to the testosterone Bob takes as part of his
reparatory hormone programme, his body has grown breasts. It is here,
surrounded by Bob's feminized, impotent body that the narrator finds
release from the demand to function as a stable autonomous ego and is
able to cry: 'crying is right at hand in the smothering dark, closed inside
someone else, when you see how everything you can ever accomplish will
end up as trash' (17). Like the narrator, Bob is alienated from his diseased
and feminized body. By bringing their alienated bodies into contact, the
two characters undergo mutual recognition and are subsequently empowered to express their lack.

The narrator finds the patient support groups to be an effective means
of reconnecting with his emotions. However, it is significant that Bob's recognition of the narrator is actually a form of misrecognition: 'Bob loves
me because he thinks my testicles were removed, too' (17). Lacan discusses
the necessity of misrecognition in the construction of the stable autonomous ego. As the refusal to recognize wishes and desires as they impact
upon the external world, misrecognition enables the ego to sustain its
sense of singularity in the face of its actual conditions of existence, namely,
it's reliance upon external symbolic structures for legitimation and support. For the narrator, the therapeutic benefit of the support groups is
founded upon the adoption of victimhood. In order to escape their pain,
the patients are induced into guided meditation: 'Eyes closed, we imag-
ined our pain as a ball of white healing light floating around our feet and
rising to our knees, our waist, our chest. Our chakras opening. The heart
chakra. The head chakra' (20). This meditation is intended as a means of
negotiating the pain of disease and alienation. However, this is a fallacious

state of being that narcotizes the will. This serves as an ideological reduction of the agency of the subject that coerces him or her to accept the
status quo. There is an analogy to be drawn between the patient support
groups and religion. The New Age philosophy expounded by the groups
is legitimated through their association with medicinal discourse. Freud
argued in 'Civilization and Its Discontents' that religious belief functions
as a means for the subject to attempt to inure itself against suffering by
deploying 'a delusional remoulding of reality' and subsequently concluded
that they 'must be classed among the mass-delusions' of mankind' (81).
Rather than bringing the narrator back in touch with his body, the support
groups further distance him from genuine emotion. His alienation from
everyday life is subdued but at the cost of assuming the passive role of the
victim.

Against the backdrop of the narrator's passive assumption of victimhood,
Tyler pursues an actively provocative path. The conflict between the narrator's passive acceptance and Tyler's active resistance is forcefully dramatized during the lye episode. Here, Tyler kisses the back of the narrator's
hand and then pours lye over it, causing an extremely painful chemical
burn. The narrator resorts to his taught meditation techniques in order to
block out the pain in contrast to Tyler who exhorts the narrator to embrace
the sensation:

'Come back to the pain,' Tyler says. / This is the kind of guided meditation they use at support groups. / Don't even think of the word *pain*. /
Guided meditation works for cancer, it can work for this. / 'Look at your
hand,' Tyler says. / Don't look at your hand. / Don't think of the word
searing or *flesh* or *tissue* or *charred*. (75)

The narrator attempts to disavow the bodily trauma by distancing himself
from it and avoiding its associated signifiers. However, this is a fallacious
attempt to empty the mind of thought. Not thinking is still thinking of
nothingness. As he retreats within himself in an attempt to shut out the
pain, the narrator finds himself, 'on a platform in a castle in Ireland with
bottomless darkness all around the edge of the platform' (76). The castle is
a standard psychoanalytic trope denoting the ego comprised of defensive
boundaries. The bottomless darkness signifies the traumatic appearance
of the Real that appears as an alien intruder into the narrator's coherent sense of self. This passage indicates that the ego is an imaginary construct that seeks to preserve the individual myth of the neurotic, that is, an

illusory ideal of wholeness that can never be attained because the subject is essentially split. Against this retreat into a fantasized wholeness, Tyler actively assaults the fantasy structures of the ego:

> 'You can cry,' Tyler says. 'You can go to the sink and run water over your hand, but first you have to know that you're stupid and you will die' [. . .] 'We can use vinegar,' Tyler says, 'to neutralize the burning, but first you have to give up'. (76)

Whereas the narrator attempts to evade bodily trauma by seeking refuge in fantasy-structures that support the ego-construct, Tyler strips away the illusions and semblances that sustain the autonomous stable ego. Whereas the narrator attempts to foreclose the Real in order to retain the semblance of a rational reality, Tyler actively seeks the Real beyond semblances.

This moment is once again analogous to Nietzsche's figure of noon. Like the edge of a piece of paper, this event takes place between two semblances: '"Because everything up to now is a story," Tyler says, "and everything after now is a story." / This is the greatest moment of our life' (75). Like the perfect hand, the lye episode is an instantaneous moment that takes place in-between symbolically inscribed acts. The illusory character of the ego is dependent upon the production of a coherently unified narrative or story. The lye episode marks the non-coincidence of the narrator's supporting fictions. His moment of pain is the point of minimal difference between stories, which exists beyond signification and points to the void at the heart of symbolization. The kiss burnt on to the narrator's hand is raised to the level of the sublime object. As such it causes a revaluation of all values. This is an initiation sequence that disrupts the function of misrecognition that makes reality appear only through fictions, montages and masks. Instead, like Tyler, the narrator comes to actively search for the real beyond semblances. This movement to a search for reality beyond the appearances and illusions generated by the ego is of critical importance for the text's critique of consumer culture. Not content with stripping away the ideological trappings of everyday life, the text continues to strip away the individual ideologies that sustain the subject.

The Real of the narrator's identity structures the space between Tyler and the narrator. The point of minimal difference between the two is characterized by the division between Tyler's active and the narrator's passive nihilism. Zupančič argues that 'active nihilism could be described as a fight against semblance, as an attitude of exposing and unmasking the "illusions," "lies," and imaginary formations *in the name of the Real*' (63).

The philosopher Alain Badiou refers to active nihilism as the passion for the Real. For Nietzsche, this is a form of militant atheism, in which the semblances or delusions of religious belief are stripped away. Accordingly, Tyler seeks to strip away the semblances, illusions and fantasy-structures generated by the positivist ideologies of progress, success, technology, rationality and morality. Tyler's imperatives are internalized by the narrator: 'I shouldn't just abandon money and property and knowledge. This isn't just a weekend retreat. I should run from self-improvement, and I should be running toward disaster' (70). By contrast, the narrator's existence prior to his encounter with Tyler should be regarded as an example of passive nihilism that is defined by Zupančič as, 'the name of the configuration where *men will not to will rather than will nothingness*' (64). The guided meditation techniques deployed at the patient support groups exemplify this notion. However, it would be inaccurate to suggest that passive nihilism is simply the disappearance of the will. Rather, it should be understood as a form of scepticism, in which the subject exhaustively practises self-restraint and self-regulation. Whereas active nihilism is characterized by a passion for the Real beyond semblances, passive nihilism is a sedative defence against the radical and destructive character of active nihilism.

Tyler's passion for the Real expresses itself through his drive to unveil the fantasy-structures and illusions that structure everyday life. By stripping away the efficacy of the Symbolic order's fictions and structures that mediate the subject's relation to reality, Tyler highlights the pain and antagonism located within the very structure of late capitalist consumer culture. This is a passion for the Real that counteracts cynical reason by accepting its own worst excesses. In his reading of André Breton's *Arcanum 17* in *The Century*, Alain Badiou posits that 'a creative disposition, be it vital or artistic, must be the conversion of a negative excess into an affirmative excess; of an unfathomable pain into an infinite rebellion' (142). By engaging in fist fights with the narrator and other alienated white-collar workers, Tyler literalizes the oppressive bindings of consumer culture and thereby converts a negative force into one of affirmation. This is demonstrated by the famous scene in which the narrator assaults himself in front of his manager: 'without flinching, still looking at the manager, I roundhouse the fist at the centrifugal force end of my arm and slam fresh blood out of the cracked scabs in my nose' (116). At this moment, the narrator is rendering overt the systemic violence that appears natural and therefore invisible. This scene results in the security guards reaching the office just as the narrator lies bleeding on the floor with the manager standing over him. Although it would be untrue to say that the manager assaulted the narrator, the scene reveals a deeper truth about the exploitative practices that pervade capitalist society. This is an example of Tyler's passion for the Real that expresses itself as a literal tearing apart of the semblances that sustain codified social norms in order to reveal the violent, obscene underside of civilized existence.

Just as Tyler and the narrator express the antagonisms that remain a naturalized and invisible structuring principle of the contemporary sociocultural order, the fight club itself incorporates pain and violence into its very structure in order to give voice to oppression. The text frequently depicts the grotesque, unacknowledged underside of reality and in doing so exposes the unspoken rules that support the Symbolic order's drive to appear as a closed 'natural' order. There is a parallel to be drawn with the psychoanalytic concept of disavowal as discussed in the Introduction. Although subjects within the contemporary sociocultural order have some awareness, albeit often limited, of their oppression, they act as though they do not. As Slavoj Žižek states in *The Parallax View*, 'a minimum of idealization, fetishizing disavowal, is the basis of our coexistence' (347). As the narrator points out, subjects know of the existence of 'dirt and hair and shit and bone and blood', but in order to achieve legitimacy within the sociocultural order they act as if they do not (136). The efficacy of the Symbolic order relies upon the disavowal of the grotesque and unknowable basis of human existence; it operates through the disavowal of the Real. As the harbinger of the Real, Tyler challenges the Symbolic hegemony by using violence as a means of breaking through the population's collective disavowal. The violence depicted at fight club renders visible the gaps and antagonisms found throughout the social fabric. As such, it functions as a separatist underground movement that challenges the language and norms that sustain consumer culture: 'What happens at fight club doesn't happen in words' (51). As such it touches upon the Real. The rules of fight club sustain this: 'The first rule about fight club is you don't talk about fight club [. . .] The second rule of fight club is you don't talk about fight club' (48). These two rules are ostensibly the same and separated purely by virtue of their iteration. This structuring principle inscribes the club with the non-coincidence of the same, which also marks the gap between Tyler and the narrator and points to the radically destabilizing potential of the sublime. You do not talk about fight club because to do so would return it to the domain of the laws and languages of the Symbolic. Instead, the inscription of the figure of noon generates a permanent and inherent tension within the group. This is further developed through the secondary rules that emphasize the two within the one: 'two men per fight, one fight at a time, no shoes no shirts, fights go on as long as they have to' (50). The repeated motif of two within one disrupts the appearance of seamless unity and indicates that there is a central antagonism to be found within every perceived whole. Passion for the Real is expressed as a violent spectacle of binary conflict that breaks through the hyperreality of consumer culture to engage with action rather than representation: 'after you've been to fight club, watching football on television is watching pornography when you could be having great sex' (50). Passive nihilism becomes active nihilism; the simulation becomes passion for the Real.

Culture Industry

The fight club produces a spectacle of perverse enjoyment that conflicts with both repressive and ideological state apparatus. The participants embrace pain as a means of turning the alienation engendered by consumer culture into an affirmative antagonism. This antagonism is sustained through the non-dialectical juxtaposition of two combatants. Nothing at fight club is geared towards synthesis. The focus on the fight brings the antagonism that sustains the fantasy-structure of the One into sharp relief. As the fight club grows in popularity, it increasingly begins to mimic the structure of neoliberal, globalized capitalism. Fight clubs spring up like fast food chains across the United States; each able to operate as autonomous units devoid of a centralized system of operations. As such they operate in a manner analogous to multinational corporations. However, instead of controlling and regulating the flow of financial capital, they function as nodes in a network of libidinal energy sublimated into aggression. By mimicking the diffuse structure of globalized capitalist institutions the fight clubs function as the obscene underside to the system of systemic violence that sustains the status quo. In this way, the fight clubs negate the repressive state apparatus such as the army, police, courts and prisons that function by way of violence directed at the individual. By directing violence against each other, the combatants at fight club convert the threat of violence posed by repressive state apparatus into an affirmation, thereby diffusing its power. The active nihilism or passion for the Real that sustains the fight clubs is also directed towards the ideological state apparatus that support the social formation. In particular, Tyler Durden targets the culture industry as the primary distributor of the ideology that sustains the authority and legitimacy of the dominant social order.

The passion for the Real is concerned with stripping away the semblances, illusions and false consciousness that situate the individual within the social fabric. Louis Althusser argued that the goal of the ruling ideology is the reproduction of the relations of production. As such, Tyler subverts the production processes within the film and catering industries. This constitutes a challenge to the culture industry that operates as a key ideological state apparatus that interpellates the masses and obfuscates the potential for emancipation. Indeed, as Adorno states: 'The customer is not king, as the culture industry would have us believe, not its subject but its object.'[12] Cultural entities are now first and foremost commodities that parade the semblance of newness while concealing the fundamental lack of change to the alienating system propagated through the division of labour. Social networking sites frequently invite users to list their favourite cultural products, thereby expressing their individuality through the medium of the commodity-form. Indeed, it is a common misconception that cultural products provide escapism that temporarily removes the subject from the material conditions of their existence. Instead, this escapism reinforces the subject's oppression. As Adorno states: 'Each product affects an individual air; individuality itself serves to reinforce ideology, in so far as the illusion is conjured up that the completely reified and mediated is a sanctuary from immediacy and life' (101). The comforting illusions presented by the culture industry distance the subject from an awareness of their material conditions. In what follows, I will discuss three instances of cultural subversion initiated by Tyler.

Tyler's cultural terrorism initially targets the production process of the film industry. He splices single-frame flashes of pornography into feature-length family films so that the audience is subliminally confronted with 'a lunging red penis or a yawning wet vagina close-up' (30). Broken down into its component parts, the cinema experience takes place in darkness while images are projected onto a screen before the viewer who lacks conscious control over the images. Consequently, the cinema could be interpreted by a psychoanalytic critic as a cultural dream experienced en masse. Tyler disrupts the efficacy of the cultural unconscious, or the audience's 'movie dream,' by sending out an obscene subliminal message at the point of mass consumption (28). These images are grotesquely magnified and projected on to the cinema screen in order to stage the Real of the audience's desire. As discussed above, desire has a metonymic structure and accordingly takes place in a system of endless deferral. In a similar manner, seduction stimulates and sustains desire through the play and gradual unveiling of semblances. Desire is maintained through deferral because it sustains the illusion that satisfaction can be achieved. The stark magnification of the sexual organs effectively desexualizes them by presenting them as matter devoid of semblance. Direct confrontation strips away the fantasy-structures and illusions that surround seduction, laying bare the 'goal' of sexual desire. This image of the Real is unconsciously received by the audience but has real effects: 'People ate and drank, but the evening wasn't the same. People feel sick or start to cry and don't know why' (31). By staging this encounter with the Real, Tyler demonstrates that the effects of the Real, although invisible, have real repercussions on the socio-symbolic fabric.

Tyler and the narrator highlight the cyclical nature of human industry when they turn 'into the guerrilla terrorists of the service industry' (81). Employing the same method as at the cinema, they subvert the commodity-form at the production stage; in this instance, by urinating into food at a hotel before it is served. The narrator works as a banquet waiter solely because 'the job will stoke [his] class hatred' (65). The narrator depicts wealth from the perspective of the producers and labourers: 'from here at cockroach level the green corridor stretches towards the vanishing point, past half-open doors where titans and their gigantic wives drink barrels of champagne and bellow at each other wearing diamonds bigger than I feel' (80). Ostentatious consumption is contrasted with the modes of production thereby disrupting the illusion that Western civilization maintains a classless society. The juxtaposition of cockroaches with titans signifies the insurmountable gap between the stratified extremes of the class system. Most importantly however, urinating into the food highlights the cyclical nature of human industry. As Lacan points out in *My Teaching*, waste:

> goes through pipes and is collected in fantastic places you have no idea of, and then there are factories that take it in, transform it and make all sorts of things that go back into circulation through the intermediary of human industry, and human industry is a completely circular industry. (64)

As discussed in the Introduction, for Lacan, the waste-disposal systems that sustain civilization operate as an analogy for repression. The insertion of waste prior to serving is a subversive strategy that reveals the truth of human industry. Matter is cycled through civilization and returns as a cultural product that then enters into and sustains social hierarchies. This is neatly encapsulated when Tyler steals fat from a liposuction clinic and uses it to make soap, which is then sold on to the wealthy. Mirroring the insertion of obscene images into the cultural unconscious, Tyler presents the shit of civilization as a return of the repressed that throws the inequalities embedded within the service industry into sharp relief.

The third key incidence of subversion occurs in a passage that is absent from the film adaptation. Perhaps this is because unlike the catering and film industries, it does not tap into an easily universalized experience of oppression. While working as a waiter at a private dinner party, Tyler discovers the hostess' bathroom, which contains about a hundred bottles of expensive perfume. Without tampering with the product, Tyler leaves a note that reads: 'I have passed an amount of urine into at least one of your many elegant fragrances' (82). As the discussion of fear in the preceding chapter demonstrates, even if something does not exist, it can still function as if it does. The note conspicuously lacks any unit of measurement and it is this that causes the host's critical judgement to vacillate. Tyler's note functions as an absent presence that signals an intrusion of the Real, tearing a rent in the hostess' socio-symbolic fabric. She accuses her husband of, 'trying to drive her crazy by having an affair with one of the women guests, tonight, and she's tired, tired of all the people they call their friends' (83). The note is not in itself true. Nevertheless, it reveals to the hostess the artificiality of the social relation.

These three examples demonstrate the ways in which individuals are integrated into late capitalist society. Each time, Tyler's actions invisibly disrupt the smooth operation of a system that appears to be 'natural'. The culture industry is a powerful ideological supplement to capitalism because of its ability to incorporate and homogenize almost any form of difference. As Tyler states: 'our culture has made us all the same. No one is truly white or black or rich, anymore. We all want the same. Individually, we are nothing' (134). Divisions between gender, race and class have been stripped away as subjects become a series of target markets. This is supported by Lacan's reading of culture:

> The function of what we call a cultural trend is to mix and homogenize. Something emerges and has a certain quality, a certain freshness, a certain tip. It's a bud. The said cultural trend kneads it until it becomes completely reduced, despicable, and communicates with everything. (69)

Lacan argues that innovative artistic forms are assimilated by culture and their freshness is reformed into an ideological support for the status quo. The fight club's links to the sublime is an example of a fresh counter-cultural movement that inexorably comes to reflect rather than subvert the structural coordinates of the social order surrounding it. In order to avoid incorporation into consumer society and thereby nullify the active nihilism that stands at its centre, Tyler constructs Project Mayhem that parodies and combats both repressive and ideological state apparatus. This is the point at which the fight clubs appear to enter into a fascistic discourse. In what follows, I will discuss the ways in which this movement can be understood as a politics of purification distinct from the fight club's politics of subtraction.

Politics of Subtraction and Purification

The passion for the Real is concerned with stripping away the structures, semblances and fictions that contain the subject within the Symbolic order. However, this raises questions of authenticity. As the growth and expansion of the fight club indicates, the violence of the Real must eventually enter into representation. Although they ostensibly provide access to the Real beyond language, there is no certainty or guarantee that this is absolutely untainted by the Symbolic order. As Badiou states in *The Century*:

> the real, conceived in its contingent absoluteness, is never real enough not to be suspected of semblance. The passion for the real is also, of necessity, suspicion. Nothing can attest that the real is the real, nothing but the system of fictions wherein it plays the role of the real. (52)

There is no guarantee that the encounter with the Real experienced by the combatants is authentic. Indeed, the fight clubs themselves provide a series of semblances and a social structure that while ostensibly directing members to the rawness of the Real nevertheless maintain a set of illusions. In response to this, Tyler produces Project Mayhem which seeks to purify the fight club schema and insist upon the Real. Project Mayhem is a parody of state bureaucracy comprised of the committees of Arson, Assault, Mischief and Misinformation. This is the embodiment of Tyler's active nihilism that empowers its members to participate in acts of class warfare and cultural terrorism on a large scale. It is initially characterized by a stringent initiation ritual that demands that candidates display their unquestioning belief in the cause: 'You tell the applicant to go away, and if his resolve is so strong that he waits at the entrance without food or shelter or encouragement for three days, then and only then can he enter and begin the training' (129). By demanding unquestioning belief, Project Mayhem effectively purges the semblances that have grown up around the fight clubs in an impossible attempt to guarantee the authenticity of the Real.

Alain Badiou highlights two particular orientations in the passion for the Real: 'The first assumes destruction as such and undertakes the indefinite task of purification. The second attempts to *measure* the ineluctable negativity; this is what I call the "subtractive" orientation' (54). A politics of purification embodies the blind imperative of destruction. This is exemplified by Project Mayhem that directs violence against the state apparatus. By contrast, the politics of subtraction thinks negativity through a self-reduction to zero. This brings the point of minimal difference to the fore. As Slavoj Žižek states:

> Unlike purification, which endeavours to isolate the kernel of the Real through a violent peeling-off, subtraction starts from the Void, from the reduction ('subtraction') of all determinate content, then tries to establish a minimal difference between this Void and an element which functions as its stand-in.[13]

Kazimir Malevich's *White on White* symbolizes this crucial distinction. The painting has traditionally been interpreted as a symbol of purification in which, 'colour and form are eliminated and only a geometrical allusion is retained' (*The Century*, 55). However, as Badiou suggests, it is more useful to perceive this painting as a display of minimal difference between white and white. This is the non-coincidence of the same that marks Nietzsche's figure of noon and the Lacanian Real. This is a subtractive rather than destructive reading that pinpoints the crucial difference between the philosophies behind the fight club and Project Mayhem respectively. Instead of seeking the Real as a substance, subtraction treats it as a gap or antagonism. Whereas purification seeks to separate, contain and possess the Real, subtraction acknowledges this separation to be the Real itself. Whereas Project Mayhem is characterized by a search for authenticity through the destruction of all known semblances, subtraction highlights the Real between semblances. As such, a politics of purification can never be complete. It is for this reason that the members of Project Mayhem engage in increasingly violent terrorist attacks in a desperate attempt to lay claim to the Real. In the film, this culminates in the destruction of the city around them.

Project Mayhem's initiation ritual marks the beginnings of the rift that develops between Tyler and the narrator. This is indicative of the suspicion that marks the passion for the Real. How genuine or authentic is the experience of the Real? The initiation rite demands unquestioning loyalty and the complete rejection of the demands of the ego. As such, there is a strong parallel with Buddhist philosophy in which the state of '"no-self" (*anatta*) in Buddhism – is one's true nature, and in becoming aware of it one is said to become aware of the true nature of everything else'.[14] Total immersion in the selfless 'now' of instant enlightenment is accompanied by the loss of all reflexive distance. This is reflected by the narrator's conflict-ual embrace of a karmic existence: 'until today, it really pissed me off that I'd become this totally centred Zen Master and nobody had noticed [. . .] when I pass people in the hall at work, I got totally ZEN right in everyone's hostile little FACE' (63). This seeming contradiction between benevolent Zen philosophy and outright hostility is actually no conflict at all. Spiritual enlightenment marks the subject's subjection to a fantasy-structure of the One in which desires are sublimated to a transcendent absolute. This loss of self interlinks precisely with the demands of militaristic fidelity because it produces mindless subordination. Consequently, the nameless soldiers of Project Mayhem do not take any reflexive distance towards the condi-tions of their existence: 'nobody asked anything. You don't ask questions is the first rule in Project Mayhem' (122). Complete subordination to the cause results in desubjectivization. On the one hand, the subject is freed from the demands of desire and is directly told what to desire. On the other, the subject loses all reflexive distance through his rejection of the will. As Žižek notes in *For They Know Not What They Do*, 'the subject avoids his constitutive splitting by positing himself directly as the Other's Will' (xlv). The subject is no longer a split subject defined by his lack. Instead, he is reduced to the level of an instrument, subject to Tyler's will. The politics of purification is one orientation of the passion for the Real that destroys illusory semblances. However, this is to purge the subject of all positive content.

Project Mayhem begins a project of purification along the lines of milita-ristic Zen whereby enlightenment is delivered through violent coercion. As Tyler states: 'We have to show these men and women freedom by enslaving them, and show them courage by frightening them' (149). The members of Project Mayhem discover that their lack has been foreclosed. They are no longer desiring subjects and are therefore freed from the demands of the desiring economy instated by the system of late capitalism. Instead, they are entirely subsumed to the cause. This is taken to its logical extreme when the narrator begins to rebel against Tyler's imperatives. In response, the Project Mayhem followers attempt to castrate and thereby purge their founding member: 'You said it yourself. You said, if anyone ever tries to shut down the club, even you, then we have to get him by the nuts' (187). At the same time, the members continue to engage in pleasantries: 'Nothing personal, Mr Durden. It's a pleasure to finally meet you' (188). This is indicative of the extent to which they are emancipated from responsibility for their actions. Rather than subjects of lack who are assailed by doubt and uncertainty, the 'space monkeys', as the narrator refers to them, simply obey the rules.

Concluding Remarks

Over a decade has passed since the publication of Chuck Palahniuk's *Fight Club* and the dynamic between the Real and the Symbolic order presented by the novel continues to have relevance into the twenty-first century. In particular, the combination of Nietzsche's figure of noon and the Lacanian Real demonstrates the need for an active nihilism in the face of a passively nihilistic populace. *Fight Club* demonstrates that in order to revolt against contemporary consumer culture, the subject must strip away the semblances that sustain their position within the sociocultural order in an open embrace of an active nihilism. By stripping down to zero, the subject is empowered to reconstitute the social fabric on the principles of that subtraction. However, as Project Mayhem demonstrates, it is easy to slide into a politics of purification rather than one of subtraction. Whereas subtractive politics offers the possibility of radical change, purification results in indiscriminate destruction. In this way, *Fight Club* presents the reader with a glimpse into the revolutionary psyche but offers stern warnings about the form such an event could take. Active nihilism highlights the fragility of the dominant sociocultural order as well as the dangers implicit in the blind pursuit of the Real. *Fight Club* demonstrates the need for a sublime object to stand at the heart of the revolutionary movement, which, as Lacan formalizes it, causes critical judgement to vacillate.

Fight Club posits the need for an active response to the deadening effects of late capitalism. The fight clubs present a new form of community that converts symptoms of alienation from a form of subordination into an affirmative politics. This cuts through the psychic structures of sublimation and disavowal that confine the subject within a normative position and sustain the status quo. However, this conversion of active nihilism into an affirmative politics is reliant upon the discovery of a position that is not simply found beyond civilized norms but instead resides in the non-coincidence of a whole. Satiric fiction in the wake of postmodernism does not simply search beyond appearances for a concrete, material reality. Instead, it seeks to unveil the hidden gaps and fissures that structure and sustain the Symbolic order. This is the principle that guides Tyler's terroristic assault on the culture industry. However, *Fight Club* also delivers a cautionary warning when this active passion for the Real ultimately results in a politics of purification rather than subtraction. Rather than reducing semblances to their point of minimal difference, Project Mayhem brutally strips away semblance in order to confront the 'false' consciousness disseminated throughout the sociocultural order with the Real. By contrast, satire is a genre that subverts the system of codified norms by revealing this structure to be predicated upon an integral split. Building on this discussion of nihilism and the sublime, the next chapter delivers an analysis of J. G. Ballard's *Millennium People* that focuses on the significance of revolution in the wake of postmodernism.

Chapter 3

Revolution and the Multitude in J. G. Ballard's *Millennium People*

J. G. Ballard is renowned for a lifetime's work of compelling and provocative fiction influenced by surrealist art and experimental literature. His fiction refuses easy categorization and incorporates elements from a variety of genres including science fiction, detective fiction and the experimental novel. His work can be read as inhabiting three distinct periods. The novels written during the 1960s can be broadly characterized as science fiction and include texts such as *The Drowned World* (1962) and *The Crystal World* (1966). These speculative novels, dubbed 'extinction fantasies' by Fredric Jameson, depict the dissolution of civilization from a variety of imaginative causes and this apocalyptic theme was informed by his boyhood experiences in Shanghai during the Second World War.[1] Indeed, Ballard's childhood was later depicted in fictional form in *Empire of the Sun* (1984) and *The Kindness of Women* (1991) and as a more conventional biography in *Miracles of Life* (2008). Ballard's 'science fiction' period was followed by what Martin Amis dubbed Ballard's 'concrete and steel' period in the 1970s, which includes novels such as *Crash* (1973), *Concrete Island* (1974) and *High-Rise* (1975). These novels evince an ongoing concern with psychology and the fragility of the human body alongside the increasingly central role of technology in a period characterized by the increasingly affectless nature of human relations. Ballard's later work is preoccupied with an increased focus on conditions of affluence, boredom and psychopathic social environments. *Running Wild* (1988) is the precursor to a series of novels ranging from *Cocaine Nights* (1996) to *Kingdom Come* (2006) that can be understood as variants on the detective novel in which the protagonist investigates seemingly quotidian communities in which the veneer of normalcy is supported by an undercurrent of criminality, violence and madness. Consequently, Ballard's later fiction develops his concerns with technology and social alienation in order to focus on the construction of civilized norms and the potential for radical political change. Indeed, these texts evince a keen focus on the social impact of neoliberal economics and the ambivalent possibilities offered by the promise of revolution. This chapter draws on the work of a series of post-Marxist theorists including Slavoj Žižek, Jean Baudrillard, Michael Hardt and Antonio Negri in order to explore the late-period Ballard's representation of revolution in *Millennium People* (2003).

Millennium People is distinctive for its depiction of revolutionary struggle emerging from the middle classes rather than presenting dissatisfaction and alienation as the exclusive preserve of either the working classes or the intellectual elite. Indeed, the strength of this text is found in its portrayal of a hypothetical shift in radical politics from the margins to the centre: 'the revolution of the middle class had begun, not the uprising of a desperate proletariat, but the rebellion of the educated professional class who were society's keel and anchor'.[2] Avoiding straightforward leftist readings that would assimilate the protagonists' concerns into the traditional Marxist emphasis on class struggle and the rights of the proletariat, or alternatively, aligning the novel's concerns with the post-structuralist valorization of marginalized communities and the Other, I argue that Ballard's fiction calls for a reassessment of the aims and concerns of radical politics in the twenty-first century. Ballard constructs 'what if . . .?' scenarios in which microcosms of contemporary or near-future societies experience collective insanity. These groups commit ostensibly meaningless acts of violence that draw out and expose the antagonisms that structure 'everyday' life. In *Millennium People*, the dialectic of subversion and containment within contemporary British society is explored through the absurd juxtaposition of sedentary middle-class life with seemingly meaningless acts of terrorism and violence. The central protagonist is a corporate psychologist named David Markham who is inexorably drawn into a shadowy protest group based in the comfortable Chelsea Marina. The quotidian cornerstones of the middle classes are steadily ruptured by a series of terrorist attacks, culminating in a failed suburban revolution. Like Chuck Palahniuk's *Fight Club*, Ballard's text offers a sustained critique of consumer capitalism at the turn of the twenty-first century. However, the message behind Ballard's satire is not always completely clear. Although the reader is compelled to empathize with Markham and the middle classes in revolt, they too are subject to satiric critique. Consequently, the novel depicts the conditions of indeterminacy endemic at the turn of the twenty-first century while searching for a new form of radical politics.

Through a series of satiric techniques, Ballard exposes the naturalizing ideologies that structure 'everyday life' and render subjects complicit with the machinations of neoliberal capitalism. In this chapter, I explore

the ways in which a series of radical discourses conceptualize and challenge the capitalist hegemony at the turn of the twenty-first century. First,
Ballard's depiction of the middle-class revolt is linked to Michael Hardt
and Antonio Negri's post-Marxist concepts of Empire and 'the multitude'.
The second part draws on the work of Jean Baudrillard in order to focus
on the ways in which images of emancipation and freedom, in fact, tend
to further embed the subject within the norms of the dominant sociocultural order. The third area of discussion builds on the theme of nihilism
discussed in the preceding chapter. Like *Fight Club*, Ballard's novel offers
readers the insight that meaningless acts of violence have the potential to
undermine repressive and ideological state apparatus. Drawing on psychoanalytic theory as well as the insight into the paternal function offered by
the first chapter on *Lunar Park*, this section discusses the role of the Father
in both revolutionary and capitalist discourse. Each section explores the
ways in which *Millennium People* points towards potential methods of emancipation from the dominant sociocultural order.

Suburban Revolution

Ballard's satire focuses its critique upon the quotidian middle-class lifestyle that presents the mechanisms of neoliberal capitalism as natural and
therefore invisible. The efficacy of Ballard's satiric technique lies in his
ability to subtly alienate the reader, so that he or she will perceive the everyday in a new light. Ballard initially deploys the tropes of the detective
novel and presents these in realist form. The initial investigatory phase is
then subtly subverted in three ways: first, by the fact that the perpetrator's
identity becomes swiftly apparent; secondly, through the repeated use of
inversions of commonsensical phrases; and thirdly, through the narrator's complicity with the crimes being committed. A brief survey of the
opening chapter, which depicts the aftermath of the middle-class uprising in Chelsea Marina, produces a number of problematic statements. For
instance, as the Home Secretary's visit nears, Markham states that, 'no
armed police would guard us, on the safe assumption that a rebellious
middle class was too well mannered to pose a physical threat. But as I
knew all too well, that was the threat. Appearances proved nothing and
everything' (4). Far from being deliberately obfuscatory or nonsensical
this passage challenges the limits of sense in order to convey the surreal
world produced by the revolutionaries. Although being 'well mannered'

is generally considered to be a positive, for Markham, it reveals the ideological basis of the population's oppression. From the protagonist's ironic stance, it is possible to see that manners constitute a naturalized social relation that sustains the status quo. The seemingly paradoxical phrase that concludes the passage in fact suggests that although appearances are not indicators of 'truth', they continue to offer 'proof' because everyone acts as though they do present the truth. Although the link between appearance and truth is routinely challenged in schools and media, appearances are still commonly received as self-evident. In order to combat this, Ballard draws on the surrealist tradition by repeatedly placing two seemingly incompatible elements into a sustained juxtaposition. Consequently, a recurrent trope for Ballard is that, 'the absurd answer was probably the correct one' (9). This stylistic approach creates an uncanny atmosphere in which the familiar domestic sphere is juxtaposed with violence and revolutionary energy. Indeed, it swiftly becomes clear to the reader that the middle classes are not in revolt against a specific, centralized organization but against themselves: 'Without the slightest regret, they had turned their back on themselves and all that they had once believed in' (5). Just as the residents stand against their own interests, Ballard's aporetic style opposes rational discourse.

As the title suggests, *Millennium People* is set at the close of the twentieth century and in some respects can be said to have anticipated later conditions of civil unrest such as the riots in Paris in 2005 and in London in 2011. As discussed in the Introduction, the first half of the twentieth century can be characterized as a series of world wars, colonial conflicts, dramatic technological advancements and totalitarian politics. Indeed, Alain Badiou's discussion of art and politics in *The Century* can productively inform readings of the revolutionary politics in *Millennium People*. He argues that the twentieth century was characterized by an inexorable drive towards the 'new' and the concomitant dissolution of the superstitions and traditions of the past: 'the century was haunted by the idea of changing man, of creating a new man' (8). However, this belief in a 'Cause' led to totalizing political power structures such as fascism and communism. In their wake, Western civilization has been left bereft of a unified political project beyond the economic imperative. This diagnosis of the twentieth century supports the notion that political conditions in the twenty-first century are clouded by indeterminacy and indecision. In a period characterized by the fluidity and multiplicity celebrated by postmodern writers and theorists, neoliberal economic imperatives have become increasingly naturalized, leading in turn to the subsumption of ethical judgement to the profit motive. As David Hawkes argues:

> While market exchange is obviously present in and necessary to any civilized society, our postmodern society is historically unique in elevating the mercantile principle to a position of complete dominance over the economy and, I argue, over every area of public and private experience.[3]

Playing out the sinister logic described by Hawkes, the *milieu* depicted within *Millennium People* is one in which commodity fetishism and the profit motive dominate all human interaction. In certain respects, the middle-class rebellion is redolent of the belief in a 'Cause' that, for Badiou, characterized the twentieth century. Consequently, the residents' turn to violence can be read as an attempt to cut through the autonomous, non-referential and self-generating character of postmodern capital. Indeed, *Millennium People* reflects a world in which financial capital has become increasingly detached from its real world referent. A brief genealogy of systems of exchange from barter, to coins, to the loss of the gold standard, paper money, electronic money, hedge funds and dealing in debt, demonstrates the increasingly abstract systems of signification utilized in economic practice. In line with this, Jean Baudrillard argues that just as capital has become increasingly free-floating and removed from the conditions of empirical reality, postmodern society has been increasingly characterized by the dislocation of ethical and political values from the touchstones of measure and affect, fostering in turn a spirit of apathy and indifference. In particular, Baudrillard identifies the introduction of university honorary degrees as a symptom of the postmodern severance of value from real-world referents:

> They [honorary degrees] will spiral without referential criteria, completely devalorized in the end, but that is unimportant: their circulation alone is enough to create a social horizon of value, and the ghostly presence of the phantom value will only be greater, even when its reference point [. . .] is lost. Terror of value without equivalence.[4]

According to Baudrillard, the loss of value and material reference has resulted in a politics devoid of conviction. Without measure, circulation generates only the semblance of value. In *Millennium People*, the residents' belief in a new society constitutes a response to the non-stop proliferation and circulation of images, ideas and capital. However, despite their belief in a more equitable society, they are unable to articulate their cause. Instead, they operate under the belief that, 'if the means are desperate enough, they justify the ends' (160). Confronted with the relativism celebrated by postmodern society, they have become a collective of rebels devoid of a coherent political strategy. This example demonstrates that Ballard's satire operates around a double-bind. On one hand, it offers a compelling critique of the contemporary sociocultural order but on the other it highlights the limitations of revolutionary praxis in the wake of postmodernism.

The residents of Chelsea Marina orchestrate a suburban revolution that voices the dissatisfaction of the middle classes. However, the violent methods they deploy such as the building of barricades, the burning of cars and houses and throwing of petrol bombs are oddly constrained: 'The rebels had tidied up after their revolution. Almost all the overturned cars had been righted, keys left in their ignitions, ready for the repossession men' (8). In many respects, this violence constitutes a form of nostalgia for a cause that would cut through the indeterminacy of the postmodern era in order to unite them around a common politics. In a strikingly similar logic, Baudrillard controversially states in *Simulacra and Simulation*:

[there are] still good days left to fascist and authoritarian methods, because they revive something of the violence necessary to life – whether suffered or inflicted [. . .] It is clear, luminous, the relations of force, contradictions, exploitation, repression! This is lacking today, and the need for it makes itself felt. (156)

A comparison between the violent yet impotent actions of the suburban revolutionaries in *Millennium People* and Baudrillard's observations suggests that desire for violence and conflict is sublimated by the pleasures of consumer society. Presented with the anodyne conditions of postmodern culture and concomitant dissolution of fixed values the reader comes to understand why the violence depicted in the novel becomes an attractive and exciting prospect. The middle classes depicted in *Millennium People* are nostalgic for the violence of the 'Cause' but are unable to articulate a coherent aim or indeed, the enemy that they face. Eventually, this lack of focus leads to the formal defeat and reintegration of the suburban classes into the social fabric.

In the first part of this chapter, I have discussed the significance of the revolutionary spirit in the wake of postmodernism. Drawing on the work of

Alain Badiou and Jean Baudrillard, this section has demonstrated that the logic of capitalism in the second half of the twentieth century has resulted in the dissolution of political and ethical certainties. Ballard's dystopian fiction suggests that direct political action is futile in the postmodern age. As the narrative of *Millennium People* illustrates, violence generates visibility but struggles to offer the basis for a sustained political intervention. Consequently, it is instructive to turn to the work of the post-Marxist theorists, Michael Hardt and Antonio Negri, in order to explore the ways in which the conditions of fluidity and indeterminacy experienced in the wake of postmodernism can benefit rather than hinder effective political action.

Empire and the Multitude

It is productive to locate the suburban revolutionaries depicted in Ballard's novel as the visible elements of the concept of the 'multitude' as theorized by Michael Hardt and Antonio Negri. Indeed, this comparison elucidates Ballard's focus on the educated professional classes rather than the working classes. Marx originally located the origins of class conflict in the generation of surplus labour through the exploitation of the proletariat by the bourgeoisie. By contrast, Ballard portrays the working classes as minority elements of society while the middle classes stand at its heart. This shift is reflective of the stance taken by Hardt and Negri in *Empire*. These thinkers conceptualize globalization as a new period of sovereignty for the capitalist economy, to the detriment of the power and autonomy of the traditional nation state. Consequently, the hegemonic reach of global capital is conceptualized as a totalizing Empire governed by the powers of international organizations such as the North Atlantic Treaty Organization (NATO), the World Trade Organisation (WTO) and the International Monetary Fund (IMF). In the sequel, *Multitude*, they focus on the possibilities of resistance implicit within Empire. Sustaining Marx's belief that the capitalist mode of production is a necessary intermediary stage before the emergence of the Communist ideal, Hardt and Negri argue that the plurivocity and fluidity of the globalized Empire offers the possibility of a truly radical democracy. The multitude is composed of a set of singularities or individuals brought together through the new circuits of cooperation and collaboration made possible by the globalized networks of Empire. Hardt and Negri's politics of resistance against the post-industrial capitalist hegemony offers insight into the actions of the residents of Chelsea Marina. Initially, the comfortable

lifestyles of the residents render them proponents of the dominant ideology, unopposed to the logic of capitalism. However, the commentary provided by Markham indicates a shift towards a new mode of collectivization
reminiscent of Hardt and Negri's concept of the multitude:

> I was surprised by the growing number of protest groups. Leaderless and
> uncoordinated, they sprang up at dinner parties and PTS meetings [. . .]
> most of the residents were now set on a far more radical response to the
> social evils that transcended the local problems of the estate. (120)

As this passage indicates, the dissatisfaction expressed by the residents
translates into social unrest. However, at this stage, they lack leadership
and a clearly identifiable target. As was demonstrated in the first part
of this chapter, it is this lack of conviction for an overriding 'Cause' that
undermines political efficacy. However, this undefined sense of discontent
is central to the production of the multitude. The multitude is a concept
that acknowledges the importance of local struggles while elevating them
to combat the broader struggle against Empire. The multitude subsumes
the particular into a universal critique of the ideologies of late capitalism. Consequently, the suburban revolt depicted by Ballard points towards
the same radical possibilities produced through and by the concept of an
organic and disparate multitude.

Ballard's depiction of London in the throes of millennial revolt suggests
that although the nature of capitalism has significantly altered since Marx's
time, the formal principles of oppression and exploitation remain. In *The
Porcelain Workshop*, Negri directly tackles the issue of articulating dissatisfaction and oppression in the twenty-first century. Here Negri lays out the
groundwork for a new grammar of politics, exploring a number of concepts
such as biopolitics, national sovereignty and the common in relation to the
movement from the modern to the postmodern. Negri conceptualizes the
transition from modernity to postmodernity in terms of a caesura or an
abrupt break with the discourses that dominated the political struggles
of the twentieth century. This rupture is necessary, according to Negri, in
order to historicize and subsequently define the specific, singular characteristics of capitalist society at the turn of the twenty-first century. He does so
in three ways. First, industrial labour and Fordist modes of production have
been steadily replaced with social and knowledge-based work, or immaterial labour. Secondly, globalization has led to the demise of the efficacy
and power of the traditional nation state. Finally, sovereignty has become a
form of biopolitics in which power has spread to cover the entire social field.

These points lead Negri to define the postmodern as a period of the '*real subsumption of society under capital*'.[5] This marks the hegemony of capitalist power over social relations and the accompanying homogenization of all forms of production into structures of knowledge. His conclusion is that capital has become parasitic not only upon labour but upon life itself.

Ballard's defamiliarizing satire encapsulates Negri's drive to define and articulate dissatisfaction, sovereignty and the current biopolitical measures of control in the wake of postmodernism. Most of the action of *Millennium People* concerns the charismatic ex-film studies lecturer Kay Churchill, who rouses the docile residents from their ideological stupor to express their dissatisfaction through a series of increasingly violent protests. Mirroring Negri's drive towards a new grammar of politics, Kay repeatedly inverts commonsensical phrases. As touched upon earlier, one key instance of this occurs in the wake of an explosion at the Tate when she states: 'If the means are desperate enough, they justify the ends' (160). This statement inverts the rhetorical commonplace that the ends justify the means. Although the violent revolutionary outbursts can be interpreted as nostalgic retreads of twentieth-century totalitarianism, Kay's statement sidesteps the allure of systematic and authoritarian creeds. According to Alain Badiou, the ideological projects of the twentieth century claimed to change what was seen as corrupt or degenerate about man in order to create a new man in his place. However, as he points out in *The Century*, 'each and every time, the project is so radical that in the course of its realization the singularity of human lives is not taken into account. There is nothing there but *material*' (8). The totalizing grand projects of the past do not consider individuals but reduce them to the status of a raw material. In opposition to this judgement, Negri argues that the resistance of the multitude is generated, not through the establishment of a totalitarian discourse, but through the cooperative convergence of singularities. Rather than utilizing subjects as material, Negri sees the project of the multitude as a collective of individuals defined and expressed through their difference. Kay's movement is born out of nostalgic glimpses of the revolutionary discourses of the past. However, in the light of Hardt and Negri's concept of the multitude, the lack of a clearly definable end can be seen to herald new potentialities within contemporary discourses of social oppression and revolution. In what follows, I will discuss the ways in which the suburban revolutionaries subvert the ideologies of global capitalism at a local level.

Ballard's characters frequently give voice to statements that stand against commonsensical discourse in order to repeatedly astonish the reader, not with the absence of sense but with a sense that is often surprising. This reconfiguration of the coordinates of sense takes place throughout the novel. During a particularly absurd episode, Kay and Markham pose as market researchers from a polling company and interview a number of residents in the prosperous area of Twickenham. Seemingly innocuous questions become absurd and then obscene and the polite bourgeois familiarity assumed with strangers swiftly turns to confusion followed by anger. The first homeowner they encounter is a woman in her forties who works as a doctor. On the one hand, this is indicative of the gains of second-wave feminism through which women have achieved positions of privilege and power. However, for Kay, identity politics do not address deeper social and economic inequalities. She encourages the doctor to turn her medicinal knowledge inwards against herself in order to interrogate the cleanliness of her home: 'How do you feel about the prevalence of toilet taboos among the professional middle class?' (88). This constitutes a critique of the domestic social structure. Kay's implication is that disavowal of excrement, the family's waste, reinforces taboos and social structures: 'the middle classes have to be kept under control. They understand that, and police themselves. Not with guns and gulags, but with social codes [. . .] there are unspoken rules we all have to learn' (89). By articulating these taboos, Kay challenges the hegemony of socio-symbolic structures and commonsensical discourse. From a psychoanalytic perspective, these questions draw out what, in the wake of Freud, might be considered the pathogenic nature of civilized morality. In particular, the emphasis on toilet hygiene is intimately connected with what Freud termed the 'anal object'. During the pre-Oedipal stages of sexual development, the child perceives excrement to be a part of him or herself and presents it as a gift.[6] They soon realize that their 'gift' is worthless and become pathologically conditioned to remove it. This, for Freud, is the model from which all social taboos are formed. As Kay admits, she herself still adheres to socially acceptable levels of personal hygiene. However, the significance of the exercise is to expose the doctor to the contingency of civilized norms, thereby unveiling the potential for social change.

The residents' adherence to unspoken socio-symbolic imperatives is later directly related to the consumer society. Kay encounters a homeowner hosing away the weekend mud on his car. Posing as a market researcher, she asks his opinion of Spray-on Mud: 'a synthetic liquid mud, conveniently packed in an aerosol can [. . .] an effective way of impressing people in the office car park on Monday mornings. A quick spray on the wheels and your colleagues will think of rose pergolas and thatched cottages' (93).

Spray-on Mud indicates that the material base or substance of the commodity-form is unimportant; it is merely mud. Instead, as her reference to the office car park indicates, the commodity-form signifies as a reified expression of relations between people. Kay states: 'We could make a million – it's the product for our age . . .' (94). There is a comparison to be drawn here with the Lacanian philosopher Slavoj Žižek's oft-repeated description of a series of objects deprived of their malignant properties including decaf coffee, beer without alcohol, dessert without sugar and so on: 'Today's hedonism combines pleasure with constraint: it is no longer the old notion of the right balance between pleasure and constraint, but a kind of pseudo-Hegelian immediate coincidence of the opposites: action and reaction should coincide.'[7] Spray-on Mud enters this category as an effortless expression of the social relation. The use-value of status symbols is found in the access to enjoyment they provide. Kay's commodity is the product for our age because it allows the owner to signify their enjoyment of the countryside without going to the effort of enjoying the countryside. This is indicative of the hegemony of the consumer culture, or the point at which Hardt and Negri's *Empire* intersects with 'everyday' life.

Negri defines the postmodern as the period of the real subsumption of society under capital. Under this regime, the spread of the commodity-form into every aspect of everyday life becomes a crucial indicator of the metamorphosis of traditional forms of sovereignty into a biopolitics that encompasses the entirety of the social fabric. Rather than being subject to an authoritarian hierarchy, the subject of late capitalism is interpellated through stratified social norms. The social relation specific to late capitalism is sustained by the signification and circulation of the commodity-form. Similarly, in *The Consumer Society*, Jean Baudrillard argues that consumption is rooted in the purchase of signs ordered according to a social code of values rather than the enjoyment of objects: 'The order of production does not "capture" the order of enjoyment for its own ends. It *denies* the order of enjoyment and supplants it, while reorganizing everything into a system of productive forces.'[8] Likewise, Spray-on Mud represents the signification of enjoyment without enjoying. However, this model presupposes a time before the emergence of the signifier and the social base in which objects were directly consumed and enjoyed. Jacques Lacan's formulation of *jouissance* and the structure of desire indicates that the subject is always already part of the Symbolic order, that is, the subject is always already immersed in language and the entire realm of culture conceived as a symbol system structured on the model of language. As Lacan argues in *Seminar VII*, the satisfaction of *jouissance* cannot be directly achieved: 'If he is to follow the path of his pleasure, man must go around it [. . .] what governs us on the path of our pleasure is no Sovereign Good' (95). There is no 'Sovereign Good' or singular ethic that can directly guide the subject to satisfaction. Instead, the desiring subject is continuously compelled to pursue the object-cause of desire without satisfaction. Spray-on Mud functions as a substitute for the subject's enjoyment. Instead of providing the subject with satisfaction, it sustains the illusion that satisfaction can be attained. Kay's imaginary commodity reveals the systems of production and consumption to be predicated upon the denial of enjoyment. This denial effectively sustains the illusion that enjoyment exists somewhere but is prohibited. Since satisfaction can only be alluded to and not achieved, Lacan argues that: 'there is no ethical rule which acts as a mediator between our pleasure and its real rule' (95). There can be no single ethical law that guides the path of desire. At the same time, there is no such thing as an ethically neutral position. Kay's actions prompt the residents to free themselves from moral constraints. However, she is then confronted with the problematic question as to how the subject should align him or herself in relation to civilized morality. Her answer is simply opposition. Accordingly, the middle-class revolutionaries are increasingly drawn towards the use of violence.

Violence, Culture and Tourism

This section delivers an analysis of the violence employed by the suburban revolutionaries and explores the ways in which resistance to the forces of Empire frequently takes the form of negation rather than positive action. This is most visible in the ways in which the Chelsea residents give voice to their dissatisfaction through acts of cultural terrorism. Although the middle classes are traditionally perceived to be representatives of the established order, they now find themselves in revolt effectively against themselves. Kay and her followers identify, target and disrupt a number of targets that sustain the fabric of the sociocultural order in order to challenge the 'pathology' of civilized morality. These are directly visible signs of what Slavoj Žižek terms 'subjective' violence. In *Violence: Six Sideways Reflections*, Žižek proposes that there are three different types of violence: 'subjective', 'symbolic' and 'systemic' violence. Subjective violence is visible violence that opposes the established order and transgresses the law. Symbolic violence is embodied in language that structures the nature of what can be thought. This is an alternative formulation of the social constraints and taboos that sustain civilized morality. Finally, systemic violence results from the 'often catastrophic consequences of the smooth functioning of our economic and political systems'.[9] Systemic violence is experienced as part of the 'normal' state of things and is therefore invisible. Mapping these modalities of violence on to *Millennium People*, the violence utilized by Kay and her followers can be classified as subjective violence that produces a highly visible spectacle and appears as a completely irrational explosion unless placed in relation to the broader backdrop of symbolic and systemic violence. Kay's revolution fixates upon two zones of symbolic violence and confronts them with a visible subjective violence of its own. Accordingly, this section will first explore the ways in which Kay's group offers a critique of travel and tourism followed by an exploration of their attacks on the culture industry.

In Ballard's fiction, the images presented by the tourism industry act as sites of symbolic violence that conceal the impossibility of direct unmediated experience between the subject and the world. According to David Cunningham, one of the great strengths of Ballard's writing is its direct engagement with 'an everyday world of cars, offices, highways, airlines and supermarkets that we actually lived in, but which was completely missing from almost all serious fiction'.[10] These are spaces that cover vast areas and in which citizens spend large amounts of time but they are almost completely occluded from conscious thought. In this respect, these are 'invisible' spaces that operate in a manner analogous to Žižek's systemic violence. These are not simply negative spaces that fail to register on the psyche in any significant way. Instead, they stand at the heart of 'everyday' life. Consequently, Ballard's perspective may be defined as 'anamorphic'. In this way, the author ensures that the landscape of quotidian space lies exposed as a series of sociocultural nodal points, ripe for subversive practice. Many of these locations relate to the tourist industry, which swiftly becomes one of the key targets for Kay's revolution: 'Tourism is the great soporific [. . .] Travel is the last fantasy the 20th Century left us, the delusion that going somewhere helps you reinvent yourself' (54–5). The tourist industry markets itself on images of landscapes such as seaside or mountain views that enable the traveller to forget the world. These images are presented as 'authentic' representations of the tourist experience and promise viewers an outlet or escape from the demands of everyday life. However, following Baudrillard, these images can be seen to be a parade of simulacra, or signifiers bereft of their signified. This theme is reflected in Ballard's text. Throughout the novel, Heathrow is referred to as the visible centre of the travel and tourism industry. As Markham comes to realize, 'Heathrow was a huge illusion, the centre of a world of signs that pointed to nothing' (251). Like Spray-on Mud, the images displayed by the tourist industry operate as reified significations of enjoyment that sustain the illusion that satisfaction is attainable, only deferred. Kay argues that the tourism industry is predicated upon the production of fantasy in order to conceal the absence of meaning in life. As the centre of a world of signs, the fantasies generated by Heathrow provide a structural support for socio-symbolic reality, not an escape from it.

Heathrow comes to symbolize the power of fictions to sustain relations of enforced domination. Rather than providing access to an essential self, tourism exerts a performative efficiency that directs the gaze of tourists, and in doing so interpellates the bearer of the gaze.[11] Far from finding the subject's 'real self' through an escape from reality and enforced conformity to the dominant sociocultural order, travel and tourism ultimately locate the 'being' of the subject as a socio-symbolic being. By interpreting the globe through a selection of advertising images, tourism determines the very being and social existence of the tourist. This is reflected in Markham's description of the entrance to the airport: 'Acres of car parks stretched around me, areas for airline crews, security personnel, business travellers, an almost planetary expanse of waiting vehicles. They sat patiently in the caged pens as their drivers circled the world' (240). Ballard's focus on waiting and the description of 'caged pens' is reminiscent of the systems of discipline, order and control outlined in Michel Foucault's *Discipline and Punish*. The implication is that the freedom promoted by the travel industry is simply another strategy to sustain the self-disciplining subject. By searching for a new self, supposedly beyond the confines of the Western socio-symbolic order, the subject internalizes the very discourse he or she is trying to escape. In addition, the planetary scale of the car park is suggestive of the imagery deployed in the Borges fable read by Baudrillard in *Simulation and Simulacra*. Here, a set of cartographers draw up a map of an anonymous Empire so detailed that it covers the territory exactly. As the Empire declines, the map frays and falls into ruins. Baudrillard's analysis inverts this myth, thereby rendering it applicable to the postmodern condition:

The territory no longer precedes the map, nor does it survive it. It is nevertheless the map that precedes the territory – *precession of simulacra* – that engenders the territory, and if one must return to the fable, today it is the territory whose shreds slowly rot across the extent of the map. (1)

A similar inversion can be applied to the passage from *Millennium People*. In the wake of postmodernism and the rise of globalization, it is the 'planetary expanse' of the car park that precedes the travellers and their destinations. Ballard's novel depicts the real conditions of travel as the travellers lie in stasis under the illusion of freedom, waiting to return to the orderly ranked rows of cars. The freedom and escape promised by travel is always already preceded by the socio-symbolic ordering of massed car parks.

Millennium People closely identifies the culture industry with symbolic violence. Just as the tourist industry displays images of emancipation while obfuscating the possibility of genuine change, the culture industry is shown to be selling images of liberation and empowerment while rendering the population passive. Accordingly, Kay, Markham and an assorted mix of revolutionaries destroy a suburban video store before targeting the National Film Theatre (NFT).[12] In revolt against her background as a film lecturer, Kay perceives the film industry to be a coercive force that has shaped the formation of a generation. In this passage, the subjective violence of the revolutionaries is depicted through analogies to the films they seek to destroy. Two of the victims, film students moonlighting as guards, are confronted by a sudden subjective violence. When attacked they lie weeping, 'as if shocked to find themselves in a brutal drama straight from the gangster movies they so venerated' (117). The film students lack a language that can convey this violence without recourse to the fictions offered to them by film. This suggests that films do not reflect reality but teach the viewer how to act within society. This relation between film and reality parallels Baudrillard's reading of Disneyland's relationship to America in *Simulacra and Simulation*:

> Disneyland is presented as imaginary in order to make us believe that the rest is real, whereas all of Los Angeles and the America that surrounds it are no longer real, but belong to the hyperreal order and to the order of simulation. (12)

In a similar way, films present a microcosm of social reality but are themselves presented in such a way that the audience recognizes them as mere fictions or illusions. This sustains what Baudrillard terms the 'reality principle', or the illusion that the hegemonic socio-symbolic order (itself a linguistic construct) is more 'real' than fiction. Instead, the 'reality' of the sociocultural order in the wake of postmodernism is characterized by the real subsumption of society under capital and reinforced by the incessant circulation of unreal images. The symbolic violence of the film industry is found in its presentation of adventurous escapes from civilized norms, which, in fact, re-inscribe social norms and values.

Millennium People demonstrates that both the tourist industry and the culture industry generate fictions that sustain the ideology of individualism and the illusion of freedom. After the attack on the NFT, the middle class revolutionaries stage a mass protest outside the British Broadcasting Corporation (BBC):

> For more than sixty years the BBC had played a leading role in brainwashing the middle classes. Its regime of moderation and good sense, its commitment to the Reithian aims of education and enlightenment, had been an elaborate cover behind which it imposed an ideology of passivity and self-restraint. (149–50)

The BBC presents itself as mass culture but is inextricably linked to the machinations of the culture industry. For Kay, it is an elitist establishment that disseminates culture and value from above in order to sustain the ideologies of the State and neoliberal values. It uses broadcasting as a tool for educating the masses. However, this education also constructs and disciplines the subject. At the same time, protests are made at the Victoria and Albert museum (V&A) that Kay denounces as, 'an emporium of cultural delusions', which 'deluded the middle classes that a developed "cultural" sensibility endowed them with a moral superiority denied to football fans or garden gnome enthusiasts' (154). For the revolutionaries depicted in *Millennium People*, institutions such as the BBC and the V&A assign value to cultural artefacts and ways of life that generate a sense of enlightenment and superiority among the middle classes. Consequently, the potential for the middle classes to engage in radical politics is neutered by the precession of otherwise valueless simulacra.

The climax of the revolution comes when the middle-class residents stage a series of massed protests in the normally quiet, suburban streets. They set up a series of barricades down the street, set cars alight and shout and jeer at the orderly ranks of policemen. This is a form of separatism, the dominant form of protest of the twentieth century. Theorists such as Derrida and Agamben valorize marginality as a means of impacting upon the centre. However, Negri mounts a critique of separatism as a mode of resistance that fails to recognize the specific characteristics of the postmodern age. Rather than conceiving of the dominant sociocultural order as a totalitarian and consistent entity that is vulnerable to criticism from the margins, Negri emphasizes the fragmented conditions of contemporary society. As he states in *The Porcelain Workshop*, '*everything occurs on the edge of being* – not on the limit, in the margins of a given ontological totality, but in each moment that makes up the passage from difference to creativity' (97). This theorization draws upon Deleuze's principle that difference is the univocal characteristic of being. That is, all identities are effects of differential relations and this is the single, unitary attribute of being. Negri then induces a move from theory to the actual by placing the Deleuzian subject of difference into discourses of social antagonism and political struggle. When power spreads to encompass all social relations, antagonism also spreads into the social world in its entirety. Accordingly, the global capitalist system of the twenty-first century should be under-stood as a porcelain workshop; a fragile construct with a multiplicity of vulnerabilities, located at every social interaction much like the nodes in a network. Consequently, Derrida's emphasis on marginality can only be limited in scope and is unable to impact upon the social fabric as a whole. As such, the separatist strategy depicted in Ballard's text is doomed to failure.

Rather than leading to a real transformation in living conditions, separa-tism all too often leads to self-destruction. This is borne out by the actions of the residents in the face of the authorities. Initially at least, they appear to be victorious:

> The street was on fire, but Chelsea Marina had begun to transcend itself, its rent arrears and credit-card debts. Already I could see London burn-ing, a bonfire of bank statements as cleansing as the Great Fire [. . .] For the first time I fully believed that Kay was right, that we were on the edge of a social revolution with the power to seize the nation. (228–30)

The middle-class residents destroy their own property to make a stand and abruptly the authorities begin to leave. However, rather than constituting a victorious statement, the spectacle of the resistance is swiftly marginalized and contained. A residents' delegation led by Kay is invited to participate in discussions with the police and the local councils. Despite this apparent dissimulation on the part of the authorities, the compromise reaffirms the hegemony of the capitalist State. The streets swiftly return to normal: 'The single intact meter soon received its first coin' (231). In line with Negri's critique of separatist politics, this detail marks the residents' return to the circuits of capitalist exchange and their recognition of the authority of the liberal and seemingly tolerant State. For a brief time, the residents' separa-tist approach empowers them to transcend the trappings of their sedentary middle-class lifestyles and break the chains of their oppression. However, they are soon reintegrated into the neoliberal capitalist hegemony. The

Chelsea Marina revolt is swiftly flattened into an image for consumption and rapidly subsumed by the culture industry: 'the new guerrilla chic inspired by Chelsea Marina [. . .] had already featured in an *Evening Standard* fashion spread' (234). Although a historically necessary strategy (which has resulted in significant gains being made against oppression), Negri argues that separatism must now be surpassed by a more general, creative movement that harnesses difference as a productive rather than subtractive force. Rather than destroying the apparatus of contemporary suburban life, the residents must create a new set of conditions for their existence.

Negri employs the term 'exodus' with its particular Judao-Christian resonance in order to envision a new world freed from oppression. In *The Porcelain Workshop*, he conceives of it as 'the capacity to reconstruct an entire world from the passionate, personal, social, civil, historical, and political differences that were invented in separatism' (101). As a creative development from separatism, 'exodus' encapsulates not only emancipation but also production. The genesis of this development can be seen in what the Chelsea resistance perceives to be a betrayal. Gradually, but in increasing numbers, several residents pack up their homes and drive off:

> I imagined them endlessly circling the M25 in their muddy Land Rover, locked in a deep trance. Where had they gone? [. . .] Towing their trailers, they were the vanguard of an itinerant middle class, a new tribe of university-trained gypsies who knew their law and would raise hell with local councils. (7)

This retreat is a movement away from the highly artificial, rationalized space of the endlessly sprawling, decentred suburbs. Instead of a betrayal of the revolutionary movement, the exodus is an attempt to escape the strictures of the urban environment and constitutes an embrace of a disparate, spatially fragmented form of political resistance. Indeed, as Markham comes to realize, the residents' exodus can be read as 'a tactical retreat, a principled refusal to accept the rule of police and the bailiffs [. . .] The revolution would continue on a date to be agreed, seeding itself in a hundred other middle-class estates across the land' (269). Following Negri's description of the multitude, this is a resistance that harnesses difference as a productive rather than subtractive force. In the wake of the failure of a strategy of self-directed violence, the residents engage in a politics of exodus and escape from which a new set of conditions for communal living can be established.

Nihilism, Capitalism and Terror

Having explored the significance of the middle-class revolution staged in *Millennium People*, the final section of this chapter will explore the significance of nihilism and the ways in which resistance to Empire is commonly equated with terrorism. Kay's suburban revolution can be understood to be a reconfiguration of classic Marxist doctrine. By contrast, the paediatrician Richard Gould offers a more violent and conceptually ambitious alternative. Markham's first sustained encounter with Gould takes place following his involvement with Kay in their attack on the NFT. Following the night's events, Gould takes Markham to a derelict hospital on the outskirts of London near Heathrow. This derelict building is remarkably similar to the house Tyler takes the narrator to in *Fight Club*. Here, the busy motorways and airport contrast with the surrounding disused buildings: 'This was the architecture of prisons, cotton mills and steel foundries, monuments to the endurance of brick and the Victorian certainties' (129). The setting evokes the transience of seemingly stable structures and reflects the contemporary transition from industrial to immaterial labour as conceptualized by Negri. The operational zone of the airport and motorways is indicative of the acceleration of everyday life, which here has effectively replaced stable boundaries with solely transitional spaces. This functions as a pathetic fallacy that provides a suitable analogy for the loss of moral certainties advocated by Gould. He offers a seductively radical nihilism that confronts the populace with shocking and ultimately meaningless acts that unveil the absurdities of contemporary consumer society.

Gould is initially supportive of the rebellion at Chelsea Marina but later comes to realize that the dissatisfaction and revolutionary energy of the middle classes will eventually be re-subsumed into the hegemonic capitalist state: 'The storm will die down and everything will peter out in a drizzle of television shows and op-ed pieces. We're too polite and frivolous' (170). Instead, Gould posits that highly visible acts of subjective violence are necessary to rouse the population. In particular, he urges Markham to pick targets that do not make sense. This is because meaningless acts paradoxically generate greater meaning than the destruction of political and cultural targets: 'A pointless act has a special meaning of its own. Calmly carried out, untouched by any emotions, a meaningless act is an empty space larger than the universe around it' (176). Like Tyler Durden in *Fight Club*, Richard Gould is confronting a passively nihilistic society with an active nihilism. By committing meaningless acts of violence such as blowing up a car at random or shooting a minor celebrity, Gould insists upon the meaninglessness of the universe. As Philip Tew argues, Gould is following a perverse logic of 'heroic' sacrifice in order to awaken the masses from its communal malaise.[13] As explored in the chapter on *Lunar Park*, the effect of a bomb or a shock reaches out further than its physical effects: 'A terrorist bomb not only killed its victims, but forced a violent rift through time and space, and ruptured the logic that held the world together' (182). The horror of a meaningless, violent attack disrupts the complacencies of the everyday, subsequently defamiliarizing the viewer. Gould's exposition of this violent philosophy is succinctly juxtaposed with the special care and attention he pays to the dying children at a children's hospice. However, there is the intimation that Gould touches the children in a sexual manner: 'Gould had lowered the cot and sat forward, an arm under the blanket. He looked up at me, waiting for me to go, making it clear that I was intruding on a private moment' (173). At one point it is suggested that Gould does this to offer the children a modicum of enjoyment within their brief lives. It is clear that Gould is willing to transgress all societal norms and normative behaviour to provide the children with what he perceives to be brief glimpses of joy. The children are described as 'bedridden, passive little parcels posted to death soon after they were born' (172) and are analogous to the passively nihilistic population. As such, a perverse logic of paternalistic caring through abuse and destruction is at work in Gould's nihilism.

During a psychoanalytically inflected passage in his book on J. G. Ballard, Andrzej Gasiorek argues that Richard Gould is an authority figure who 'replaces Markham's lost father and makes up for his oedipal lack [. . .] but both this figure and that which Markham mimetically constructs out of it end up unleashing a violence so total that it threatens to annihilate the social order altogether'.[14] According to Freud's exposition of the Oedipus Complex, the child, fearful of the recriminations of the father, self-censors against incestuous desire for the mother. The father's prohibition is later internalized as the superego, thereby offering a support for the social order. Consequently, it is problematic to reconcile Gould's position as the powerful and compelling authority figure with the twisted antisocial logic he expounds. Gasiorek's solution is to position Gould as a paternal figure who reverses the role of the father, projecting not the symbol of the superego, but representing instead the illicit desires of the id. However, despite preaching an anarchic form of politics, Gould appears to follow a controlled logic quite unlike that of the id. Both Freud and Lacan are clear that the Oedipal complex has a normative and normalizing function: 'in order for there to be a reality, adequate access to reality, in order for the sense of reality to be a reliable guide, in order for reality not to be what it is in psychosis, the Oedipus complex has to have been lived through'.[15] However, as the concept of the primordial father from Freud's *Totem and Taboo* indicates, there has always been an obscene shadow to 'normal' paternal authority. Here Freud posits the myth of an all-powerful father who kept all women for his own pleasure until his sons rebelled and killed him. However, through his death, the father became a symbolic presence (the superego) that causes guilt and imposes prohibition. In Freud's myth there is simultaneously the father who imposes the Law as well as an obscene father figure who takes incestuous enjoyment. This myth and that of the Oedipus Complex should not be situated as a truth in the normal sense but as a fact of psychic reality. As such, the Oedipus Complex combines in the figure of the father two almost conflicting functions: the protective function and the prohibitive function. Consequently, Richard Gould, like the obscene father in *Totem and Taboo* can be situated as a protective father figure who guards his children against the ideologies and dreams of the outside world, while reserving for himself the right to transgress the barrier at any time.

In his preface to *The Plague of Fantasies*, Slavoj Žižek traces a link between the obscene underside of paternal authority and the Fritzl case. Josef Fritzl incarcerated and sexually abused his two daughters in an underground cellar for 24 years. Fritzl's justification was that he was protecting his children from the dangers of the outside world. There is a direct comparison to be made between this father figure who simultaneously prohibits and protects and the actions of Richard Gould. He simultaneously cares for the populace and seeks to free them from the confines of their false consciousness but does so through acts of violence that invariably result in the death of those he seeks to protect. Rather than seeking to characterize Fritzl as an inhuman monster, Žižek seeks to locate the obscene agency that guided his actions within 'normal' behaviour: 'The attitude in question is neither simply a component of "normal" paternal authority, nor merely a sign of its failure; it is, rather, both simultaneously – a dimension which, under "normal" circumstances, remains virtual, was actualised.'[16] Rather than seeing Fritzl as an inversion of traditional paternal authority, Žižek instead locates Fritzl's grotesque actions as part of the unacknowledged obscene underside of the father figure. In the same way, Gould is compelled to 'protect' his children from themselves, even at the cost of killing them. Consequently, like *Fight Club*, *Millennium People* explores the potential for nihilist strategies to open up new avenues for strategies of resistance while casting a cautionary eye on the excesses that these strategies might generate.

Concluding Remarks

J. G. Ballard's *Millennium People* offers an experimental view that plays out a middle-class rebellion as a 'what if . . .?' scenario. This unveils the ways in which capitalist ideologies in the wake of postmodernism offer the populace the lure of radical change while obfuscating the possibility of impacting on the fundamental coordinates of society. However, by adopting a critical approach to strategies of separatism and nihilism, the novel empowers readers to think through alternative strategies of resistance. By placing Jean Baudrillard's reflections on the loss of value and measure in the wake of the simulacrum into dialogue with the work of the post-Marxist theorist Antonio Negri, it becomes clear that the lack of a politics of resistance at the turn of the twenty-first century is symptomatic of the complete subsumption of society under capital. Baudrillard's diagnosis of the postmodern era as characterized by flux, indeterminacy and shifting semblances indicates the insufficiency of direct political critique. When read through Negri's analysis of Empire's globalized circuits of exchange, *Millennium People* offers a potent critique of the current supposedly post-ideological universe. Despite the apparent decline of traditional models of authority and hierarchy such as the paternal function and the nation-state, Negri's political analysis points to the rise of a new sovereignty in the form of globalized capitalism. The lack of a common measure and concomitant conditions of indeterminacy identified by Baudrillard subsumes all known and named substances into the system of capitalist exchange under the law of general equivalence. Despite the deconstruction of truth, knowledge and authority, capital is raised to the level of an abstract absolute. Consequently, as Ballard's fiction demonstrates, financial growth and the profit motive are two of the most naturalized ideologies of the twenty-first century.

With reference to the work of Jean Baudrillard and Antonio Negri, *Millennium People* reveals the gaps and inconsistencies that are embedded within everyday experience. However, rather than adopting a reactive position that nostalgically conjures up imperialist or patriarchal rhetoric, the revolutionaries depicted by Ballard attempt to find a new form of expression in order to articulate their discontent. In the wake of postmodernism and the rise of global capitalism, the sociocultural landscape appears indeterminate and previously fixed values are in flux. As such, there is no clearly defined proponent of capitalism to be subjected to critique. Consequently, Ballard's novel displays instances of both self-directed and meaningless violence as the population voice their dissatisfaction. However, as Hardt and Negri's concept of the multitude suggests, the conditions of flux and indeterminacy also offer an opportunity to create a new and equitable society. By displaying the directionless movements of would-be revolutionaries, Ballard highlights the inadequacy of traditional forms of political action while continuing to emphasize the inequalities, dissatisfaction and alienation brought about by consumer society. Rather than offering a return to the revolutionary discourses of the past, Ballard demonstrates that new, creative forms of political resistance to capitalist ideologies are needed. In the following chapter, I explore the ways in which the fluidity and indeterminacy that overshadows radical politics in the wake of postmodernism has impacted upon the issue of ethics at the turn of the twenty-first century.

Chapter 4

Ethics and Aesthetics in Will Self's
Dorian: An Imitation

Will Self is best known for novels such as *Cock and Bull* (1992) in which
a woman grows a penis and rapes her husband, while a man develops a
vagina and is raped by his doctor, and *Great Apes* (1997) in which the protagonist wakes up one morning to discover that everyone has been turned
into an chimpanzee. He is swiftly confined to a psychiatric ward for suffering under the bizarre delusion that he is human. As these texts indicate,
Self has a recurrent interest in bodily dysmorphia, metamorphosis and
abrupt shifts in perception. He is highly influenced by a variety of satiric
writers such as Jonathan Swift and Lewis Carroll. In his introduction to a
reissue of *Alice's Adventures in Wonderland* he states:

> the text itself has always been with me, forming some of the fundamen-
> tal antinomies that constitute my imagination: the juxtaposition of the
> quotidian and the fantastic; the transposition of irreconcilable elements;
> the distortion of scale as a means of renouncing the sensible in favour of
> the intelligible.[1]

As this quotation suggests, Self consistently employs defamiliarizing techniques such as surreal juxtapositions and the destabilization of conventional measure and scale in order to subvert the reader's expectations
thereby exposing moral incertitude and corruption to critique. As such,
it is unsurprising that at the turn of the twenty-first century, Self began a
productive engagement with the work of Oscar Wilde that culminated in
the satirical novel, *Dorian: An Imitation*.

Dorian: An Imitation is a satiric text that employs a postmodern aesthetic
in order to question the ethical dimension of this mode of thought. Does
the postmodern emphasis on fluidity, self-reflexivity and pastiche present
new ways with which to deconstruct hegemonic thought, or does it produce
a spirit of apathy and indifference? How can the postmodern aesthetic

present new ethical agendas and what are the limitations of this approach? Self's text is a self-conscious re-inscription of Oscar Wilde's *The Picture of Dorian Gray* that transposes the action from 1891 to 1981. This enables Self to reclaim the contemporary relevance of Wilde's only novel by drawing out the original text's latent content, such as the implicit homosexual elements, in a frank and explicit manner. In particular, the novel functions as 'a satiric demonstration of the synergetic affinity of the two end-of-the-century periods, giving the twentieth century a cyclical aspect'.[2] This aspect of the novel draws out the themes of decadence and decline that marked the two periods and like *Fight Club*, evokes the sense of a twentieth century *fin de siècle*. Also, following *Fight Club*, the social milieu presented by the text is characterized by radical indeterminacy. This is demonstrated by the opening passage:

> Once you were inside the Chelsea home of Henry and Victoria Wotton it was impossible to tell whether it was day or night-time. Not only was there this crucial ambiguity, but the seasons and even the years became indeterminate. Was it this century or that one? Was she wearing this skirt or that suit? Did he take that drug or this drink? Was his preference for that cunt or this arsehole?[3]

This radical indeterminacy is a reflection of postmodern thought in which categories and hierarchies are thrown into disarray. In addition, the passage's temporal ambiguity reflects Self's contemporary re-inscription of Wilde's text. This blurring of temporal boundaries is then extended to issues of gender, sexuality and the images or 'preferences' that construct identity. This opening passage functions not only as a commentary on Self's own narrative technique but presages an underlying concern with the indeterminacy of the postmodern aesthetic and its ethical repercussions for questions of identity. In what follows, I will explore the ways in which Self's re-visionary novel portrays the moral indeterminacy endemic to the postmodern era while highlighting the ways in which it gestures towards the necessity of ethical critique.

The Ethics of Postmodernism

Re-visionary fictions such as Margaret Atwood's *The Penelopiad* and Jeanette Winterson's *Weight* are an increasingly common style of postmodern literature. Peter Widdowson argues that this practice of re-writing canonical texts calls them to account for the formation of narratives that have later been central to the textual construction of hegemonic worldviews. The technique has clear beneficial repercussions for feminist or postcolonial discourses. As Widdowson states, 'what the contemporary text does is to "speak" the unspeakable of the pre-text by very exactly invoking the original and hinting at its silences or fabrications'.[4] One of the most prominent examples of this is Jean Rhys' *Wide Sargasso Sea* that re-writes Charlotte Bronte's *Jane Eyre* in order to expose the patriarchal and imperialist ideologies that invisibly sustained the sociocultural order depicted in the original text. Re-visionary fiction can be understood as a particular form of pastiche, defined by Fredric Jameson as an imitation of pre-existing styles, mannerisms and eccentricities. Self deliberately establishes his text as a pastiche with the titular assertion that the text is not an original but an imitation. Whereas parody is a satiric form that mocks the original, pastiche is a resolutely neutral practice that indiscriminately draws together a multiplicity of forms, styles and narratives. Accordingly, the postmodern shift from parody to pastiche heralds the loss of a normative position that is subject to critique. As Jameson comments: 'in a world in which stylistic innovation is no longer possible, all that is left is to imitate dead styles, to speak through the masks and with the voices of the styles in the imaginary museum'.[5] Indeed, Self's choice to present Wilde's narrative in the form of a postmodern pastiche delivers a comment on art's failure to construct something new beyond aesthetic imitation. This is further supported by Self's emphasis on the cyclical parallels between the birth of the twentieth and twenty-first centuries. Jameson also engages in a discussion of what he dubs the 'nostalgia text' that he separates from the more traditional historical novel with the suggestion that they do not represent the historical past so much as culturally shared assumptions about an era. Self's imitation operates in a similar manner by drawing together cultural memes from the 1980s. As Hayes states: 'A *zeitroman*, or novel of its age, *Dorian* includes a textual soundtrack – pointing perhaps to its genesis as a film script – a way of capturing the aura of its temporal setting' (155). This constitutes a flattening or reduction of history to a series of sound-images.

Re-visionary inscription has met with a variety of critical responses. On the one hand, there are those who unconditionally celebrate the 'procreative abundance of a narrative able to replenish itself ceaselessly out of its own forms and energies'.[6] On the other hand, others bemoan 'the loss of normative stability in a world in which forms seem to slide frictionlessly over each other, proliferating a difference which is really indifference' (124). Implicit to this argument is the fear of the demise of the ethical in the face of the loss of criteria or measure, which are necessary for the creation of moral judgement. These two positions on re-visionary fiction reflect the two dominant modes of thought on the ethics of postmodernism. Since its critical inception, the aesthetics of postmodernism have been questioned with regard to its ethics. As Jameson states in *The Cultural Turn*:

> the political positions which we have found to inform what is most often conducted as an aesthetic debate are in reality moralizing ones that seek to develop final judgments on the phenomenon of postmodernism, whether the latter is stigmatized as corrupt or, on the other hand, saluted as a culturally and aesthetically healthy and positive form of innovation. (29)

The postmodern heralds the collapsing of distinctions between politics, ethics and aesthetics, and denies the possibility of 'final judgements'. Re-visionary fiction should be regarded as the postmodern form *par excellence* because its self-conscious re-inscription of the past equally blurs aesthetics and ethics while on both counts offering something new. The two postmodern theorists who exemplify the radical split between the celebration and denigration of postmodern aesthetics and its ethical efficacy are Jean-François Lyotard and Jean Baudrillard.

Jean-François Lyotard's argument in *The Postmodern Condition* characterizes postmodern thought as a radical questioning of authority, hierarchy and fixed normative structures: 'Simplifying to the extreme, I define *postmodern* as incredulity towards metanarratives.'[7] Postmodernism is a mode of thought that embraces plurality and fluidity over the grand totalizing narratives of history. As such, it gives voice to alternatives to the universal subject, defined as white, male, heterosexual and middle-class. Postmodern aesthetic traits such as metafictional devices, self-reflexivity and magic realism untie narratives from fixed posts of meaning. As Zygmunt Bauman states, the postmodern perspective 'means above all the tearing off of the mask of illusions; the recognition of certain pretensions as false and certain objectives as neither attainable nor, for that matter, desirable'.[8] The postmodern approach to ethics delivers a critical interrogation of identifications and systems of belief by relativizing meanings and morals that have become sedimented over time. This collision of postmodern ethic and aesthetic is found at the close of *Dorian: An Imitation*. Here, a metafictional coda depicts the 'real' Dorian Gray reading the preceding text, now identified as a manuscript left by the recently deceased Henry Wotton. By explicitly naming the preceding text as a fiction, the novel's mimetic foundation is radically destabilized. As elements of the novel seep into the 'real' Dorian's life, the division between fiction and reality is steadily eroded. The ensuing confusion and collapse of characters and authorial voices destabilizes certainty, truth and being, which in turn exposes the everyday perception of quotidian reality to be a construct. This is the postmodern approach *par excellence*, which subverts cultural expectation and destabilizes boundaries between semblances. As such, the postmodern aesthetic offers a powerful critique of hegemonic forms. Conversely however, it can be understood as a reduction of ethical thought to the level of a questioning that does not offer a new set of values or positive content beyond the criticism itself.

The second dominant mode of postmodern ethical thought is represented by Jean Baudrillard. In *Simulacra and Simulation*, he discusses the simulacra that can be glossed as a signifier devoid of its signified. Baudrillard argues that the simulacra precedes reality. It stems from '*the radical negation of the sign as value*, from the sign as the reversion and death sentence of every reference'.[9] The simulacra refers to nothing but the system of signs, thereby negating its real world referent. In *America*, he uses the Californian desert as a metaphor to describe postmodernism: 'culture has to be a desert so that everything can be equal and shine out in the same supernatural form'.[10] The desert represents the flattening of cultural forms into a homogenous mass that eliminates difference and texture. It is the numbing repetition of the same. The figure of Andy Warhol is a recurrent trope throughout *Dorian* and his art reflects the flattening of culture and art into an endless repetition of the same. Art has moved from imitations of reality to a mode of production. This is parodied by a sculpture, 'made from a welded tangle of bent and burnt spoons', which Dorian is encouraged to patronize (113). The artist Baz Hallward argues that, 'the multiple sets the standard for the artefact. Why paint one portrait when you can print a hundred? Why bend one spoon when you can bend a thousand?' (114). This sculpture reflects the capitalist drive towards ever increasing efficiency of production. It does not matter what is produced. The aesthetic is found in the production of multiplicities rather than a singularity. It is significant that the spoons were originally used for substance abuse because it establishes an analogy between compulsive consumption and narcotic addiction. Baudrillard's conception of postmodernity has precedent in Walter Benjamin's criticism of art in the age of mechanical reproduction. Although art works have always been reproducible, mechanical reproduction brings with it vastly increased quantities and accelerated intensity. Benjamin argues that the new techniques of reproduction subsume the 'aura' that renders an art work a unique presence in time and space. Benjamin states: 'By making

many reproductions it substitutes a plurality of copies for a unique existence', which leads to, 'a tremendous shattering of tradition'.[11] The age of
mechanical reproduction brings with it the loss of authenticity and thereby
authority. Baudrillard's desert of the real extrapolates Benjamin's argument and places it in the context of the late twentieth century's explosion of media images. For Baudrillard, the postmodern is characterized by
the hyperreal in which reality is lost beneath a non-stop stream of images
emerging from television, film and the internet. Within this flood of media
imagery it is impossible to deliver value judgements that place one image
in a hierarchical position over another. As Lisa Downing succinctly encapsulates it: 'Images of violence no longer ring the warning bell of any second coming, but create instead the effect of the numbing repetition of the
same. One cannot but lack all conviction.'[12] Within the constant repetition
of the same, ethical judgement is effectively foreclosed.

Self delivers insight into the numbing repetition of the same by sustaining the link between narcotic addiction and consumer capitalism. Early in
the novel, Dorian is introduced to Honey, a drug dealer who buys multiples
of the same item in an effort to dispose of her outrageous profits: 'The
entire room had been crammed full of stuff. On three freestanding Dexion
shelving units reposed irons, televisions, stereo units, tape recorders, ket-
tles, food blenders, and all – as Wotton had said – still in their packaging'
(28). This 'materialistic superfluidity' displaces the commodity-form's use-
value in the face of endless reproductions of the same. Honey's compulsive
consumption mirrors Baudrillard's desert of the real in which items and
images are infinitely substitutable. The only stable referent in the novel is
capital, which sustains the law of general equivalence. This theme is introduced early in the novel:

> combinations of styles, modes, thoughts and orifices were played out
> in the gloom of the Wotton's dusty apartments and the brightness of
> their smeary water-closets, as if artefacts, ideas, even souls were all but
> symbols inscribed upon the reels of the slot machine of Life. Yank the
> arm and up they came: three daggers, three bananas, three pound signs.
> At the Wottons', three of anything paid out generously – in the coin of
> Misfortune. (3)

The slot machine analogy substitutes reality for a series of symbols or images
that reduces every nameable substance to the law of general equivalence.
The indeterminacy of things is related to only one referent – coin. All values aside from capital are placed in flux. As such, Self's novel presents the

postmodern aesthetic as one that naturalizes capitalism. In line with this, Baudrillard's perspective presents a picture of the postmodern as a totalizing and coercive ideological field that is experienced as an unfathomable flow of appearances divorced from their stable points of reference.

Baudrillard's diagnosis of the postmodern era as a hyperreality is one in which entertainment, media, information and communication technologies provide experiences more involving than the scenes of everyday life. As he states in *Simulacra and Simulation*, 'information devours its own content. It devours communication and the social [. . .] Rather than creating communication, *it exhausts itself in the act of staging communication*. Rather than producing meaning, it exhausts itself in the act of staging meaning' (80). Self's characters inhabit this space dominated by the screen: 'Everyone who isn't a pseudo-intellectual loves television – it's so much *realer* than reality' (66). The television screen flattens history to a series of substitutable images that replace any authentic culture. As Wotton notes, in a manner which ominously foreshadows Princess Diana's death, his companions' sense of history:

> was savagely concertinaed, like a speeding limousine that's hit a concrete pillar. Was it any wonder that in place of any real ceremonial or culture of their own, they'd sooner watch the expensive charades invented for a German ruling house by a nineteenth-century popular novelist? Namely: 'The royal-fucking-wedding!' (64)

Rather than producing meaning, the representation stages meaning. Reality is abolished in the face of the vivid ceremonial imagery on the screen. It is significant that Dorian and his sect watch the Royal wedding on a video tape rather than live. Video is a form that produces flattened images of the world removed from their particular time and space. Indeed, Jameson argues that video is an exemplary postmodern art form because, 'it's machinery uniquely dominates and depersonalizes subject and object alike'.[13] It is the technological counterpart to Baudrillard's characterization of the postmodern landscape as a desert or the site of the same. For Baudrillard, the hyperreality of the postmodern condition has resulted in the loss of measure and therefore the dissolution of value. This has severe ethical repercussions. As Wotton quips, 'we are in an age when appearances matter more and more. Only the shallowest of people won't judge by them' (20). The postmodern condition is characterized by the penetration of the image into every aspect of life. The precession of simulacra increasingly removes the subject from the real world referent, leaving them only able to judge and therefore make ethical decisions based on free-floating signifiers. This leads to a world in which, 'violent crimes are in astonishing bad taste, just as bad taste is a violent crime' (180). This formulation renders aesthetics equivocal with ethics. In the following section, I discuss the ways in which the appearance (or aesthetics) of moral engagement frequently conceals a lack of genuine affective or ethical response.

False Philanthropy and Cynical Reason

Dorian: An Imitation portrays two seemingly ethical positions and subjects them to critique, displaying them as ideologies in the process. The first is a Western philanthropy that is concerned with human rights and the ethics of the Other. The second is characterized by Henry Wotton and his sect. The latter is a decadent form of cynical reason that disavows suffering. The conflict between the two positions is dramatized at Wotton's dinner party where two cliques form on either side of the room. At one end, 'their talk was earnest, full of the names of people not personally known to them – Yeltsin, Gorbachev and Rajiv Gandhi – and referring to places they would be disinclined to visit, such as Moscow, Sarajevo and New Delhi' (147). Their discussion is removed from direct experience of violent conflicts, reducing arguments concerning the concrete particularity of the situation to a series of names and images. The seemingly philanthropic discussion of the Balkans conflict contrasts Dorian's cynicism. Echoing Baudrillard, he asserts that, 'the Gulf War didn't happen' (143). Dorian's reasoning is that 'you may be at more than six degrees of separation from this "conflict", and that means it barely exists at all as far as you're concerned' (143). Dorian's argument is that for the Western subject, the experience of the Gulf War was at such a distance from everyday reality that it was completely mediated by the television screen. For Baudrillard, television sets function as second order simulations or images that blur the boundary between reality and representation: 'we are no longer in a logic of the passage from virtual to actual but in a hyperrealist logic of the deterrence of the real by the virtual'.[14] Amid the deluge of images, the reality of the conflict is lost. In addition, the media coverage of the war was so heavily edited that it bore practically no relation to the reality of the conflict. However, this is to neglect the fact that the Gulf War was nevertheless a scene of violence. Dorian's attitude is indicative of the postmodern waning of the affect, which results in inhuman responses to suffering.

Early in the novel, Wotton and Dorian attend a charity reception for the homeless organized by Wotton's mother, the aristocratic Phyllis Hawtree: "'My mother,'" Wotton whispered, "is an intelligent woman who views the distressing of the social fabric with the very real emotion she withholds from all those around her'" (30). Hawtree is concerned with man in the abstract rather than the men and women around her, deploying an ethics predicated upon the notion of man as an essential category that transcends differences. Human rights appear to be 'natural' and inalienable because the category of man has been raised to the level of a transcendental absolute. By contrast, anti-humanists such as Michel Foucault, Louis Althusser and Jacques Lacan have consistently worked to debunk the notion of an abstract human essence. Foucault posits that man is a constructed historical concept that is incapable of founding a universal ethics of human rights. Althusser argues that the humanism of human rights is an abstract ideology particular to the capitalist sociocultural order. As explored throughout this book, Jacques Lacan disrupts the centrality of the ego by naming it as an imaginary concept of unity. Man contains no eternal substance or 'nature'. Alain Badiou develops these positions to argue that the liberal humanist belief in the essential category of man has resulted in an ethical ideology that preserves the status quo. Consequently, the indeterminate blurring of ethics and aesthetics characteristic of the postmodern era effectively conceals the structures that reinforce the ideologies of late capitalism.

Badiou argues that traditionally, ethics are predicated upon the prior existence of evil and subsequently on the conception of man as a victim. It is far easier to establish consensus on the nature of what is evil than what is good. Human rights are fundamentally negative insofar as they are ultimately the right not to suffer, not to feel pain, not to starve and so on. As Badiou states: 'ethics subordinates the identification of the subject to the universal recognition of the evil that is done to him. Ethics thus defines man *as a victim*. [. . .] man is *the being who is capable of recognizing himself as a victim*.'[15] Badiou argues that such a conception of man reduces him to his animality, evades political thought and stigmatizes any ethical consensus that advocates the Good. At the charity event, Wotton and Dorian encounter a minor character known as Jane who apologizes by way of introduction:

The apology was not just for the interruption – it was for *everything*. For colonialism and racism and sexism; for the massacres of Amritsar and Sharpeville and Londonderry; for introducing syphilis to Europe and opium to China and alcoholism to the Aboriginals; for the little Princes in the Tower *and the Tower itself.* (32)

Jane is a Duchess who engages in philanthropic efforts without self-reflection; her affected asceticism is undermined by her excessive wealth. Indeed, Wotton is quick to point out the irony of the owner of a house, 'which would offer a great deal of shelter for a great many youths', attending a reception for Homeless Youths (33). As Self himself states: 'It's always those who have most to lose by a genuine levelling of the economic playing field who take the keenest interest in persuading other people to give away their money.'[16] Jane thinks of herself as a conscientious benefactor and subjects others to the moral imperative to intervene. However, this ethical ideology sustains the global system of economic injustice by insisting on a division between the victim and the benefactor. As Badiou states in *Ethics*:

> Since the barbarity of the situation is considered only in terms of 'human rights' – whereas in fact we are always dealing with a political situation, one that calls for a political thought-practice, one that is peopled by its own authentic actors – it is perceived, from the heights of our apparently civil peace, as the uncivilized that demands of the civilized a civilizing intervention. (13)

Philanthropic events such as the Homeless Youth reception and the dinner table discussion of the Balkans conflict consider these situations in terms of a strict binary opposition between victim and benefactor. Badiou would understand this to be a contemporary form of colonization through moral superiority. He argues that every humanitarian expedition and intervention carries with it an unacknowledged Western discourse of power that carries the implicit judgement that other nations are inferior or uncivilized. Against the philanthropic discourse of benefactor and victim promoted by Jane and his mother, Wotton states: 'I'm trying to warn Dorian off this man-of-the-people act. Hypocrisy won't suit his nature' (31). Consequently, despite displaying a postmodern aesthetic, *Dorian* can be understood to be a criticism of both postmodern ethics and the discourse of human rights.

Badiou's conception of ethical ideology is derived in part from Lacan's understanding of the philanthropic drive. This is related to the mirror stage as discussed in the Introduction. The mirror stage inaugurates a series of alienating identifications that constitute the illusion of an autonomous stable ego. These external images function as projections of the ideal ego that generates both narcissism and aggression in the subject: 'aggressivity is the correlative tendency of a mode of identification that we call narcissistic, and which determines the formal structure of man's ego and of the register of entities characteristic of his world'.[17] The subject narcissistically desires his ideal image and aggressively wants to take its place. This leads Lacan to describe philanthropy in terms of an ethical ideology that perceives an ideal world and aggressively attempts to make that ideal a reality. Lacan states: 'we can find no promise in altruistic feeling, we who lay bare the aggressiveness that underlies the activities of the philanthropist, the idealist, the pedagogue, and even the reformer' (80–1). Lacan's reading of philanthropy links it with aggressivity and the pursuit of an idealized image. In this respect, Lacan's critique of grand philanthropic projects can be linked to Lyotard's criticism of grand totalizing narratives. Both emphasize the fantasy-structure of the One to be illusory. The following section discusses the ways in which Self's text draws on the central magical realist trope of Wilde's novel in order to reinvigorate discussion of ethics and aesthetics in the wake of postmodernism.

Cathode Narcissus

The central image of the novel is Baz Hallward's video installation named Cathode Narcissus that consists of nine monitors, all displaying Dorian's naked form. This is a re-visioning of the painting from Wilde's text with which the eponymous character exchanges his soul for eternal youth: 'He never caught cold, he never had a headache, he never experienced the slightest physical discomfort save that caused by obvious abrasions of the physical world' (207). Dorian's initial encounter with the Cathode Narcissus is reminiscent of Lacan's mirror stage. However, whereas the infant greets his or her image with jubilant activity, Dorian experiences aggressivity and jealousy. The Cathode Narcissus is an ideal image of Dorian that will not decay and die. Indeed, M. Hunter Hayes sees in the Cathode Narcissus a rich metaphor: 'Gray inhabits a pixilated society, one in which the illusion of youth can be preserved onscreen through television and film media' (155). This has particular resonance with the emergence of the mythology of the 'new man' in the 1980s, which reflected a new politics of masculinity. The new man supposedly defied traditional models of masculinity to become 'a potent symbol for men and women searching for new images and visions of masculinity in the wake of feminism and the men's movement'.[18] The new man was an ideal figure who embraced female roles and qualities while retaining his masculinity. As Rowena Chapman states, he had 'a wholehearted acceptance of himself as a sexual object, embracing narcissism with open arms' (228). However, it was the narcissistic image that came to dominate perceptions of the new man. Dorian exemplifies such a model because he is initially objectified by the idealized art work before entering into a self-conscious narcissism. The unearthly power of the installation is such that, 'all who looked upon it became involuntary voyeurs' (42). This is reflective of the bombardment of images of the ideal man, 'in the million brilliant mirrors of magazines, newspapers, advertising hoardings, TV, cinema and video'.[19] Contemporary man is constructed as a narcissistic voyeur who seeks his ideal image through consumption and technological intervention. As Baudrillard argues:

> All representation implies malefience, from the event of being seduced by one's own image in the water, like Narcissus [. . .] to the mortal reversal of the vast array of technical equipment that today man disguises in his own image.[20]

Both Self and Baudrillard highlight the construction of men as an image for consumption and suggest that there exists only a thin line between narcissism and aggression.

Dorian's narcissism is combined with a postmodern aesthetic in which he adopts a series of styles and fashions at the moment they appear: 'Dorian was the mother of all mothers, showing us how to give birth to our own images' (129). The maternal imagery signifies his adoption of feminine attributes. Whereas shopping and consuming were traditionally feminine activities, Dorian fully embraces consumer capitalism by adopting the changing fashions and fulfilling both the economic and sexual market's imperatives to preserve his youthful appearance. This leads him to conceive of himself as a commodity-form: 'the product has changed, Baz, believe me; it's only the packaging that remains the same' (141). Slavoj Žižek argues that following Foucault, the subject is empowered to construct their self without reference to any transcendental absolute:

> we have a turn against that universalist ethics which results in a kind of aestheticization of ethics: each subject must, without any support from universal rules, build his own mode of self-mastery [. . .] produce himself as a subject, find his own particular art of living.[21]

This social constructivist argument positions the subject as self-affirming through the deliberate construction of his or her particular mode of subjectivity. Dorian's reinventions throughout the 1980s and 1990s epitomize the self-construction of the subject. As Wotton comments: 'Dorian can be whatever you want him to be – a punk or a parvenu, a dodgy geezer or a doting courtier, a witty fop or a City yuppy [. . .] he revelled in every opportunity that London offered him to assume an imposture' (108). Dorian's ability to make every social role his own demonstrates that status and morality in the wake of postmodernism is predicated upon performance and the image.

Dorian's conspicuous consumption is mirrored by his overt sexuality. As Hallward states: 'He's unashamed . . . he belongs to a totally new generation, the first gay generation to come out of the shadows' (12). Indeed, David Alderson argues that 'gay men have assumed greater public visibility, becoming symbols [. . .] of the economic and ideological liberalization of late modernity'.[22] Dorian's confrontation with his ideal image in the form of the Cathode Narcissus mirrors the proliferation of media depicting the idealized image of the new man and the construction of narcissistic desire within men. This is indicative of the intersection between the rapidly burgeoning gay culture of the 1980s and the construction of the image of the new man. Both were constructed as symbols of economic and ideological liberation by the marketplace. Indeed, the image of the new man was the perfect ideological accompaniment to consumer capitalism. As Mark Simpson argues, 'the imperfection of image and body next to ideal ensures that desire is never satisfied and that the consumer never loses his appetite' (96). This suggests that homosexuality has become naturalized at the cost of the assimilation and commodification of its counter-culture. This demonstrates how previously marginalized groups are subsumed into newly normative positions by capital.

The most significant difference between the painting in Wilde's original text and Self's Cathode Narcissus is the replacement of a singular representation with a multiplicity of shifting images. This is symptomatic of the endless sliding semblances emblematic of the postmodern condition. However, rather than a numbing repetition of the same, the nine monitors generate the effect of a single aesthetic moment. In order to understand the significance of aesthetics for both Wilde and Self, it is useful to turn to the work of Walter Pater. Writing in the nineteenth century, Pater was a formative influence on the Aesthetic Movement. In the conclusion to his seminal text *The Renaissance*, Pater contrasts the inconstant fashions of the period with the singular aesthetic moment:

> Each moment some form grows perfect in hand or face; some tone on
> the hills or the sea is choicer than the rest; some mood of passion or

insight or intellectual excitement is irresistibly real and attractive to us, – for that moment only. Not the fruit of experience, but experience itself, is the end.[23]

This nineteenth-century description of the aesthetic moment stands in stark contrast with Baudrillard's desert analogy. Against the series of interchangeable semblances characteristic of postmodern culture, Pater's aesthetic moment stands as an interval reminiscent of Wordsworth's 'spots of time' that unites the senses. The artists and writers of the Aesthetic movement held that the primary purpose of Art is to convey pleasure and should be esteemed over moral, social and didactic practices. As Pater states: 'To burn always with this hard, gem-like flame, to maintain this ecstasy, is success in life' (152). Despite the ostensibly amoral character of Aestheticism, there is an ethical position to be found within Pater's discourse. For Pater, the Good, as in the 'good life', is to be found in the appreciation of beauty. Consequently the ethical imperative of the Aesthetic movement is that the subject must stay true to the aesthetic moment. This formulation has resonance with Alain Badiou's philosophy of the event and subsequent ethics of fidelity. Against the indeterminacy of the postmodern aesthetic, Badiou reinstates the philosophical notions of Being and truth and this enables the possibility of an ethics that rejects the ideologies of late capitalism.

Ethics of the Event

Alain Badiou is a contemporary French philosopher who argues against the Levinasian ethics of the Other as well as the discourse of human rights. Instead, he posits a subjective fidelity that renders the subject a militant of the truth. As Lisa Downing states, 'it is the modern obsession with protecting the other and the self from victimhood that gets in the way for Badiou' (153). Badiou's argument against the adoption of victimhood as an ethical principle is related to Friedrich Nietzsche's discussion of master and slave morality. Master morality is rooted in a principle of spontaneous growth and self-assertion: 'all noble [master] morality grows out of a triumphant saying "yes" to itself'.[24] By contrast, slave morality is a set of values born out of *creative ressentiment* by the underclasses. These underclasses were defined by their repression and could give value to their existence only by saying '"no" on principle to everything that is "outside", "other", "non-self": and *this* "no" is its [slave morality's] creative deed' (21). The active principle of the master's 'good' was constructed through the imposition of a 'natural' order that posited a direct correlation between power and moral superiority. By contrast, those who failed to achieve social legitimacy were therefore deemed to be 'bad'. Nietzsche argues that the development of Christianity was instrumental in the emergence of a slave morality that valorized the poor, the weak and the oppressed by positing the existence of a spiritual hierarchy, independent of material constraints. It is from this *creative ressentiment* that the concept of 'evil' first emerged. Slave morality perceives life as primarily oppressive and positions those with power, those that master morality perceives as 'good' as in fact, 'evil'. Nietzsche exposes morality as a discourse that changes over time; constraining and directing human actions and therefore the very nature of consensual reality. This view resonates with Badiou, for whom ethics is a totalizing grand narrative that effaces the need for individual thought when confronted with a situation in its particularity. Contemporary ethics can be seen as fundamentally conservative and working to either justify the acts of those in power, or promote an abstract, idealistic egalitarian politics. This is a contemporary version of the conflict between master and slave moralities. Indeed, Nietzsche argues that all higher and mixed cultures attempt 'a mediation between the two [. . .] the discrimination of values has originated either amongst the powerful, the rulers, or amongst the ruled' (xiv). As Badiou states in *Ethics*, this constitutes a conception of ethics as 'the spiritual supplement of the consensus' (32), thereby promoting conformity to the status quo and obfuscating genuine emancipatory thought.

For Badiou, there is a division between the ordinary realm of knowledge and an exceptional state that stands outside of the status quo. The realm of knowledge is dominated and structured by the ruling class. Following Althusser, this is reality as structured by naming, classification and ideology. Subjects are interpellated through and by the identity categories they inhabit. In contrast with this, Badiou posits the existence of an exceptional realm of singular truths that persist through the militant proclamation of individuals who position themselves as subjects of a truth. For Badiou, truth is not a phenomenological or scientifically verifiable category. Instead, truth should be understood as a form of fidelity. Raymond Geuss states:

> The basic sense of 'true' is that in which Jesus says of himself that he is the truth. To say that Jesus is the truth is to say that his life is the true life, i.e. the good life, the exemplary life, the life that is a model for humans, the life to which we all should aspire to be faithful.[25]

As such, fidelity to a truth stands against the status quo and the dominant ideology of the hegemonic sociocultural order. Access to this realm of truth is achieved through a break with the ordinary situation in which it takes place, namely, an encounter with an event. In Badiou's seminal text *Being and Event*, the event is understood as that which cannot be discerned in ontology, 'in the double sense that it can only be *thought* by anticipating its abstract form, and it can only be *revealed* in the retroaction of an interventional practice which is itself entirely thought through'.[26] This formulation indicates that the event and the subject are mutually constitutive as the subject comes into being by naming and subsequently displaying fidelity to the truth-process of the event. Consequently, the event cannot be proved, only affirmed.

Badiou's philosophy of the event offers a radical alternative to postmodern ethics. He rejects both the notion of a single, organizing principle to the world as well as an ethics concerned with the Other. For Badiou, there is no all-embracing One. Consequently, multiplicity is all that there is: 'The multiple from which ontology makes up its situation is composed solely of multiplicities. There is no one. In other words, every multiple is a multiple of multiples' (29). There is no defined concept of the multiple because this would be to reduce it to one. Instead, there are only pure inconsistent multiples. It is for this reason that Badiou equates ontology with mathematics. He is unconcerned with differences because infinite alterity is simply what there is. As he states in *Ethics*, 'the whole ethical predication based upon recognition of the other should be purely and simply abandoned' (25). Identity groupings are insignificant because there are infinite multiplicities contained within these groups. Instead, these groupings deny ethical judgement of a concrete political situation in its particularity. Badiou's ethics relates instead to a militant fidelity to a truth born out of the event. The imperceptible switch between Dorian and the Cathode Narcissus stands as an exemplary example of such an event:

> Inside the dark studio the nine monitors were sharply outlined. Across their faces, hissing with static, the fluid images of Dorian presented a cascade of motion. There was a soundtrack as well, an insistent thrumming beat entwined with a breathy fluting. Dorian was transfixed for a few moments, but then he moved closer and began to sway in time with his own televisual images. Nine naked Dorians and one clothed. In synchrony, youth and the images of youth waltzed to the heavenly and eternal music of self-consciousness. (22)

This moment of synchrony is both an aesthetic moment as understood by Pater and an event as theorized by Badiou. This is the moment at which

Dorian's soul is imperceptibly switched with that of the Cathode Narcissus. It is a point of minimal difference between representation and reality that is not empirically demonstrable and consequently takes place within an exceptional state beyond the ordinary realm of knowledge. Subsequently, Dorian becomes a self-conscious subject rather than simply an object of desire for Wotton and Hallward. He is formed as a subject who revels in multiplicity, fluidity and masquerade, and challenges the stasis of social hierarchies and hetero-normative relations.

According to Badiou, truth is not a transcendental absolute but is painstakingly constructed through fidelity to the event. As demonstrated by the Cathode Narcissus, the event is unpredictable and seizes the subject. Indeed, Badiou argues in *Being and Event* that the subject is a subject only in relation to the movement of the process of truth generated by the event: 'the subject is solely the finitude of the generic procedure, the local effects of an evental fidelity' (406).[27] By displaying fidelity to the event, the subject creates and sustains a truth-process that embodies the void of the preceding situation. For example, Marx can be understood to be an event for political thought because he names the proletariat who previously functioned as the hidden structural support, or void, of early bourgeois societies. The event Marx inscribes is the situated void of the earlier situation. Just as the event erupts as an immanent break with the status quo, fidelity is measured through the process of sustaining the event's continuing rupture. Consequently, truth is a process that is constructed by fidelity to the event. As this schema indicates, fidelity is never certain. Indeed, the potential revolutionaries in *Fight Club and Millennium People* demonstrate that there can never be proof that the subject is displaying fidelity to the cause if it is situated beyond the realms of normative social experience. The truth-process is sustained as a continuing break that disrupts and violates established knowledge systems and ideologies. For Dorian, this takes the form of the disruption and violation of all fixed identity categories and normative sexual relations. Dorian inscribes the event as the void at the heart of conceptions of identity and forces a rearrangement of previous knowledge. Instead of identity being a fixed category, Dorian emphasizes its fluidity.

Badiou's affirmative truth-process shares a structural homology with Nietzsche's master morality. Evil only has an existence through the subversion of this system. In *Ethics*, Badiou identifies three ways in which this subversion can take place, which correspond to the three stages of the truth-process; terror, betrayal and disaster:

to believe that an event convokes not the void of the earlier situation, but its plenitude, is Evil in the sense of *simulacrum*, or, *terror*; to fail to live

up to a fidelity is Evil in the sense of *betrayal,* betrayal in oneself of the
Immortal that you are; to identify a truth with total power is Evil in the
sense of *disaster.* (71)

As the narrative follows Dorian in the wake of the event, it becomes clear
that he embodies each aspect of evil as defined by Badiou's schema. As he
states in *Being and Event,* an evental site is 'the *minimal* effect of structure
which can be conceived; it is such that it belongs to the situation, whilst
what belongs to it in turn does not' (171). The event is a border effect that
touches upon the void or the Real, insofar as all access to the Real is of the
order of an encounter. As Lacan states: 'the moral law, the moral command,
the presence of the moral agency in our activity, insofar as it is structured by
the symbolic, is that through which the real is actualised'.[28] Consequently,
Badiou's ethic of truths bears a structural homology with Lacan's ethics of
the Real. Lacan's imperative to 'Stay true to your desire' is the precursor to
Badiou's insistence on the subject's continuing fidelity to the event.

The first form of evil identified by Badiou is terror that arises out of
fidelity to a simulacrum of the event. As Pater cautions with respect to the
aesthetic event, 'be sure that it is passion – that it does yield you this fruit
of a quickened, multiplied consciousness' (153). Dorian's progress through
the novel is a simulacrum of a truth-process that bears the formal traits of
fidelity to an event. However, rather than connoting the void of an earlier
situation he represents the appearance of plenitude and energy as surfaces
become substance. Dorian's truth-process conveys the fluidity of identity
but rather than naming the void of the former situation, this knowledge
becomes a fetish that he uses to disrupt both normative and minoritarian identity groupings. The void of the situation depicted in *Dorian* should
be understood as the oppressed homosexual community, which Dorian
should have inscribed in the same way as Marx inscribes the proletariat.
Indeed, the Cathode Narcissus was conceived as a truth. As Hallward states:
'I did try to say a true thing in all this . . .', although the exact nature of
this truth remains resolutely ambiguous for the artist: '. . . 'bout you, me,
'bout bein' gay, 'bout . . . stuff' (51). Dorian was supposed to represent an
evental break that names the former void, consequently displacing normative socio-sexual discourse: 'He's unashamed – not like us. He belongs to a
totally new generation, the first gay generation to come out of the shadows'
(12). However, rather than adhering to the universalized truth of the void,
Dorian demonstrates fidelity only to the self-sustaining hedonism of an
absolutely fluid identity. He is able to manufacture (in)appropriate selves
for a variety of social scenarios by manipulating the social discourses that

order reality. By swapping his soul with the video installation, Dorian exists as a simulacrum with no 'real' bodily referent. Without the risk of physical consequence, Dorian feels no ethical demand. Instead he is compelled to perform murderous acts and it is frequently inferred that 'Dorian was the AIDS Mary, the malevolent and intentional transmitter of the virus' (112). Acquired Immunodeficiency Syndrome (AIDS) is the result of debilitating damage to the immune system caused by the Human Immunodeficiency Virus (HIV). This is the antithesis of Dorian's invulnerable status. Instead the virus reflects his omnivorous sexual predations that strip away social defences: 'usually he'd have a titbit on his arm, a beautiful straight boy he was in the process of subtly warping, or a respectable wee wifey whom he'd encouraged to slip the noose' (98). This constitutes a rearranging of previously established knowledge but brings with it terror and violence. As he confronts a group of recently bereaved homosexuals: 'You're all delicate little flowers, aren't you, boys. The whole death thing shakes you up so, and that *nasty* moral majority saying it was all your minority fault' (111). Rather than naming the fluidity of identity as a universal truth, Dorian manipulates this knowledge into a simulacrum of truth. As such it constitutes in Badiou's phrase, 'terror directed at everyone' (*Ethics* 77).

Badiou classifies the second form of evil as betrayal of a truth-process: 'a crisis of fidelity is always what puts to the test, following the collapse of an image, the sole maxim of consistency (and thus of ethics): "Keep going!"' (78–9). Dorian himself destroys the Cathode Narcissus out of fear of its discovery and public exposure. Perceived threats arrive from numerous sources in quick succession. Dorian takes in and cares for Helen, a destitute past girlfriend and her baby, which gives him the opportunity to, 'be vile in new and exciting ways' (246). This includes infecting her with HIV and swinging the baby from the top of the staircase: 'You've got plenty of time . . . Dorian was spitting as the baby screamed. You're so fucking young and healthy, *you've* got plenty of time . . . while I'm old and sick' (251). The baby comes to undermine his ideal self-image and eventually Helen directly challenges Dorian: 'At first [. . .] I found your silky hair and smooth skin a turn-on, but to be frank, Dorian, they give the creeps now' (246). In contrast to every other character, Helen is repulsed rather than attracted to him and this undermines his narcissistic truth-process. At the same time, the police start to question Dorian about a murder he has previously committed and ask to see the Cathode Narcissus. Further to this, Dorian's former accomplice, Alan Campbell, attempts to blackmail him by either damaging or exposing the Cathode Narcissus. These threats unnerve Dorian and spur him to betray his fidelity to the truth-process. Rather than the immortality of a truth-process, the Cathode Narcissus begins to signify his limitation as a subject constructed through and by the event.

Dorian is confronted with a conflict between the immortal truth-process and his human animality. Unable to simply renounce the immortality granted by the Cathode Narcissus, Dorian has to convince himself that its power is illusory: 'He didn't need *all* the tapes – why would he? He probably never had' (249). Dorian tapes over all the tapes save one, therefore concealing his concealer. This method relies upon the assumption of a meta level beyond the Cathode Narcissus that enables Dorian to re-present the representation. As explored above, the ego is ultimately a fantasy construct that presents the illusion of a unified, stable subjectivity, beneath which lies the multiplicity and flux of the unconscious. By taping over eight of the nine tapes, Dorian subtracts his multiplicity to one, signifying the ego as a unified whole. Of course, for Badiou this is an unsustainable illusion because multiplicity is all that exists. The multiple lies at the very base of being, as the not yet symbolically structured multitude of experience. Crucially, this multitude is not a multitude of Ones, since they have not been symbolically integrated. The Cathode Narcissus embodies the ethical demand placed upon Dorian. As nine images bound into a structured sequence and named as a singular art form, the Cathode Narcissus represents a structured multiple. By taping over eight of the nine tapes, Dorian reduces the multiplicity of the situation to a pure One. However, there can be no pure One in the same way as the subject's perception of himself as an autonomous stable ego is illusory. By turning against the Cathode Narcissus and attempting to reduce himself to a stable One rather than a fluid multiple, Dorian betrays the truth-process.

Dorian becomes increasingly psychotic, eventually killing his pitiful digital counterpart with a switchblade and therefore himself. After Wotton finally succumbs to the AIDS virus, the novel cuts to a short coda in which the 'real' Dorian reflects upon the preceding text – supposedly written by the 'real' Henry Wotton. Here Dorian is a respected pillar of the community, a successful businessman, philanthropist and supporter of the Labour government. Baz's artwork is no longer repressed. Instead it embodies gay pride and is disseminated across the democratic space of the internet. It is from this position of 'reality' that Dorian is able to assert that the author had 'taken colossal liberties with the truth!' (259). However, the 'real' Dorian redoubles the mistake the 'textual' Dorian made by conceiving of the phenomenological world as a meta level separate from representations. Indeed, the gradual intrusion of the previous text into Dorian's reality asserts that there is no metalanguage. As Lacan states, there is no metalanguage insofar as 'all language implies a metalanguage, it's already a metalanguage of its own register'.[29] Dorian makes the same mistake that he made in the preceding text; he believes himself to be operating on a meta level, removed from representative discourse. Ultimately Ginger (his nemesis in the novel) appears and kills him in 'reality'. The post-structuralist critic would understand this to signify that truth is merely an effect of discursive articulation. However, in *The Philosophical Discourse of Modernity*, Habermas critiques Foucault's discursive universe by deconstructing his genealogy of the human sciences as a discourse in itself, which operates on an unsupportable meta level. Foucault's analysis of power criticizes the discourse of truth that supports it, but this paradoxically presumes Foucault himself to be speaking from a position of truth. This is the fallacy of post-structuralist criticism. When deconstructing positions of authority and power, the post-structuralist conveniently excludes him or herself from such a deconstruction. Foucault's discursive universe privileges the endless sliding of metonymy over the metaphoric cut. There is an analogy between metaphor and Badiou's concept of the event. Metaphor acts as a cut in the symbolic fabric through the substitution of one word for another. In the absence of the word, it falls upon the structure of the surrounding sentence to convoke meaning. This is reflected in the closing sentence in which Ginger finally kills Dorian: 'But by now he was also coming to terms with the fact that the beautiful new tie Ginger had just given him with his knife was a warm, sticky, fluid thing, and hardly likely to remain fashionable for very long at all' (278). This final sentence introduces a literal cut into Dorian as well as a metaphor that cuts through Dorian's discursive universe. Lacan is clear that the return of the repressed functions as a metaphoric substitution and it is through this linguistic device that Self stages a final traumatic encounter with the Real, beyond aesthetic relativism. It is here, beyond the structure of the Symbolic order, that Dorian encounters the moral law.

Dorian also embodies evil in the form of disaster. This is the identification of a truth-process with total power, to the extent that it overrides other truths. Since the multiple of a situation is named from the perspective of a truth, the absolutization of a truth names *all* the elements of a situation, including the unnameable. According to Badiou, the unnameable is the, 'one multiple existing in the situation, which remains inaccessible to truthful nominations, and is exclusively reserved to opinion, to the language of the situation' (*Ethics* 85). Dorian embodies an aesthetic absolute; he is 'absolutely divine, he's a true original, he's *gorgeous*' (11), which is mirrored by his belief in the totalizing power of his truth-process to the extent that it engulfs the Real of a situation. This is a passion for the Real that eliminates opinion by forcing one 'absolute' truth; in Dorian's case, that identity is absolutely fluid. Due to the plurality of truths in Badiou's schema, no truth can ever be absolute. Consequently it is from the perspective of the unnameable that totalizing structures that dictate the 'truth' of a situation can be undermined. Badiou cites some examples of the unnameable in four key areas. These include disciplines such as mathematics, which consist of non-contradictory thought, and love, which is rooted in the nameless passion between two individuals. For mathematics, Badiou states that non-contradiction is the element that cannot be named or indeed proven from within that system. Similarly, *jouissance*, sexual pleasure or the complete unification of the self with the Other, remains as the unnameable within love, which is a truth about the Two, or a non-dialectical antagonism. Dorian's reality is composed of endlessly sliding metonymy and self-conscious narratives. It is a world in which truth is reduced to a discursive effect, and accordingly truth is precisely what cannot be named. Dorian's passion for the Real and belief in the absolute power of his 'truth' is a disaster for Badiou's 'ethic of truths' because it denies the universality of the truth process.

Will Self's *Dorian* depicts a postmodern universe in which semblances frictionlessly slide over one another. The only thing that is fixed is the absence of a stable identity. Ethical consistency appears to be impossible in the face of the fluidity and retroactivity of the Symbolic. However, Badiou's schema allows ethics to be approached as a subjective process rather than through pure abstractions. For Badiou, the subject is formed in relation to the event, through fidelity to the truth-process, produced in relation to a concrete situation. Rather than relativism, this ethical system lays emphasis upon situated universalism. Will Self's *Dorian: An Imitation* is simultaneously demonstrative and critical of the motivational deficit in contemporary ethics, caused by the ideologically invested hyperreal. The dominance of the image has constructed an entirely relativistic system of values: 'Evil is to morality as magnolia is to paint [. . .] it's an unpleasant shade of meaning, far too liberally applied, purely on the basis that it isn't white' (201). It is the text's non-coincidence with itself, as evinced by Dorian's initial narcissistic split, the coda, and the final, structurally signifying tie/cut that renders the gaps and inconsistencies in the discursive universe discernable. It is through gaps such as these that Badiou's event can be glimpsed, producing a perspective from which Dorian's hedonistic and immoral exploits can be conceived as positions of radical evil.

Concluding Remarks

Dorian: An Imitation employs a postmodern aesthetic in order to question the ethics of this mode of thought. There are two main approaches to postmodernism encapsulated by the split between postmodernism's ability to construct new forms out of a variety of artistic traditions, and the loss of normative stability in which genres and forms are indistinguishably mixed. Theorists such as Jean-François Lyotard and Zygmunt Bauman argue that postmodernism offers a powerful mode of critique of authority, hierarchy and fixed normative positions. By contrast, writers such as Jean Baudrillard and Paul Virilio perceive postmodernism to be a flattening of forms into a homogeneous mass that produces apathy and a waning of the affect. In order to move beyond this aporia between playful critique and an affectless lack of conviction, it has proven useful to turn to the work of Alain Badiou who offers an ethics rooted in fidelity to the event. Following the anti-humanist tradition, he offers a critique of human rights as an ideological system of thought predicated upon an essentialist conception of man. The subordination of ethics to an ideology that preserves the status quo sustains the global system of economic injustice while obfuscating the need for political thought when confronted with a situation in its particularity. This reveals philanthropy to be bound up in the fantasy structure of the One because it presupposes an idealized world and aggressively attempts to realize it.

Against the radical indeterminacy of postmodernism, Alain Badiou reinstates the philosophical notions of being and truth. He renders the human animal as a subject only insofar as he or she displays fidelity to the event. The event is understood as part of the exceptional realm that stands unnamed and outside of the status quo. As such, fidelity to the event always takes the form of a militant radicalism. Truth is understood not as a transcendental absolute or as a verifiable category but as a form of fidelity. The event stands as a break with the existing situation, which offers an ethics based on affirmative principles. However, fidelity can never be certain or proved and it is from this basis that Badiou is able to name evil, not as a pre-existing quantity but solely in relation to the Good. The ethics of the event is predicated upon the subject's rearrangement of previously established knowledge in pursuance of fidelity to the truth-process. However, it is easy to slip back into established categories and discourses. This can be read in relation to the Copernican revolution as a decentering that ineluctably returns to the One. The importance of Badiou's work lies in his positioning of ethics as a subjective process rather than as a pure abstraction. As such, it provides a way through the multiplicities favoured by the logic of postmodernism.

Chapter 5

Sex Tourism and the Politics of Enjoyment in Michel Houellebecq's *Platform*

Michel Houellebecq's *Platform* is a meditation on the question of enjoyment within human society. Through the protagonist Michel, the author explores three interrelated themes. The first concerns the polyvalent ways in which enjoyment is signified. Should enjoyment be treated as a substance or a signification? What is happiness and how do we know what we desire? This is a theme Houellebecq has pursued since the publication of his collection of poems *The Pursuit of Happiness* in 1992. Secondly, *Platform* constitutes a satirical critique of neoliberal capitalism and the globalized marketplace. For Houellebecq, globalization is a contemporary form of colonization that produces conditions of inequality, oppression and alienation on a vast scale. His critique focuses upon the travel and tourism industry that 'might stand as a symbol of the new face of modern capitalism. In the year 2000, for the first time, the tourist industry became – in terms of turnover – the biggest economic activity in the world.'[1] In particular, he draws out the obscene underside of tourism by bringing sex to the fore. His depiction of the increasing commodification of both sex and the exotic Other takes the contemporary discourse of consumer culture to its logical extreme. His narrator contrasts the Western sociocultural order, which is rich in financial capital but has a population that is increasingly atomized, with Eastern countries such as India and Thailand, which are poverty-stricken but rich in bodies and the provision of sensual experience. In this way, Houellebecq's narrator exposes global capitalism to be a system predicated upon the colonization of the Other and the usurpation of natural resources. However, rather than minerals, ore or territory, the resources depicted in the text are the bodies of young girls. Finally, Houellebecq's novel focuses on the politics of enjoyment. As one reviewer states: 'he reduces the world's ills – racism, political extremism, economic inequalities – to an intrinsic conflict over young women's vaginas'.[2] It is my contention that what initially appears reductive in Houellebecq's oeuvre actually opens up questions about group formation and the structure of desire. Drawing on psychoanalytic discourse, this chapter explores these three aspects of enjoyment – its signification, commodification and politicization – in relation to the construction of the desiring subject within neoliberal capitalism. As *Platform* demonstrates, enjoyment functions as a constitutive element of global capitalism in the twenty-first century.

Houellebecq employs a satiric technique reminiscent of Jonathan Swift's parodic political pamphlet 'A Modest Proposal'. Here, Swift examines the conditions of oppression in Ireland and proposes what appears to be the next logical step, namely that the conditions of overpopulation and famine would be solved if the Irish would consent to eat their children whilst selling their surplus to the English for consumption. In a similar way, Houellebecq examines the global inequalities that have developed in tandem with the rise of neoliberal capitalism and posits a simple albeit unpalatable solution by standard Western norms. In the text, Western civilization is depicted as increasingly decadent and marked by stratified class divisions. Indeed, the Western subject is presented as increasingly removed from sensual contact. By contrast, the East is depicted as poor in financial capital but rich in natural resources, that is, in bodies. The characters in *Platform* make a simple equation between the wealthy yet sexually unfulfilled Western man, and the poor yet sensual Eastern body and propose a basic trade in the form of regulated sex tourism.

Michel Houellebecq self-consciously blurs the division between the author and narrator by naming the main protagonist Michel. As Katherine Gantz states: 'with notable overlap between his own life story and those of his characters, it is admittedly often difficult to distinguish where Houellebecq's fiction leaves off and his personal commentary begins'.[3] However, to immediately conflate the two would be disingenuous and tantamount to stating that Joseph K in *The Trial* and K in *The Castle* are synonymous with Franz Kafka. By naming his narrator after himself, Houellebecq questions the traditional distance held between the author and his or her fictional work. The dividing line between fiction and essay signals the question of distance between the narrator and the world he observes. Gantz positions Houellebecq's narrators and their prolific social commentary as contemporary versions of the turn-of-the century *flâneur*: 'a worldly urban stroller, the *flâneur* moves among the crowds, watching, participating, but never entirely assimilating' (150). This is exemplified by the first part of *Platform* when Michel goes on a package tour to Thailand. Whilst remaining part of the group, Michel also feels isolated and is able to dispassionately comment on the social dynamics around him: 'the establishment of micro-groups can only be detected after the first excursion, sometimes after the first communal meal' (36). Like the nineteenth-century *flâneur*, Michel is positioned within the crowd but is also an articulate spectator able to comment on its dynamics. This simultaneously implies closeness and distance, echoing the relationship between Houellebecq and his narrator. This is further reflected by the title of the novel. A platform implies a space elevated above the quotidian, upon which the speaker can broadcast their polemical views. This indicates that Michel functions as a voyeuristic spectator from within who functions as a platform for Houellebecq's controversial views. This has wider repercussions for the novel form in general as a fictional space that provides a 'safe' platform from which the author can experiment in radical thought. Towards the end of the novel, Michel reflects on a memory of climbing up to a platform:

> I had climbed to the top of an electricity pylon high in the mountains. As I was going up, I didn't once look at my feet. When I reached the platform at the top, the descent seemed complicated and dangerous. The mountain ranges stretched as far as the eye could see, crowned with eternal snows. It would have been much simpler to stay there, or to jump. I was stopped, *in extremis*, by the thought of being crushed; but otherwise, I think I could have rejoiced endlessly in my flight. (322)

This literal platform exists above the concerns of the everyday. The view of mountains and 'eternal snows' heralds a Romantic sense of the sublime and signifies that the platform for Michel and by extension for Houellebecq is a transcendental space for contemplation. This passage supports Gantz's argument that as a *flâneur* who treads the fine line between observation and participation, Michel is paradoxically a part of and held apart from the crowd.

The final sense of the word 'platform' is derived from economics. A platform functions as an intermediary between two sides of a market with two distinct user groups that provide each other with network benefits. As the economists Jean-Charles Rochet and Jean Tirole state:

> many if not most markets with network externalities are characterized by the presence of two distinct sides whose ultimate benefit stems from interacting through a common platform. Platform owners or sponsors in these industries must address the celebrated 'chicken-and-the-egg problem' and be careful to 'get both sides on board'.[4]

A network externality is the effect that one user of a service has on the value of that product to other people. A good example of this is that the more people who own telephones, the more valuable the telephone is to each user. For the purposes of the novel, the platform stands as a bridge that orchestrates supply and demand between two networks. In the second part of the novel, Michel works with his partner Valérie to rejuvenate the ailing tourist industry by offering travel packages based on sex tourism in the Third World. From an economic perspective, this plan makes perfect sense and stands in line with globalized trade practices. In this way, Houellebecq is satirically replicating the thought of global economy. It is left to the reader to contemplate and impose moral judgement.

Platform charts three distinct phases in Michel's life. In the first part, following the death of his father Michel travels on a package tour to Thailand where he has sex with local women. This section subjects to critique the Western colonization of the Orient through the travel and tourism industry. Michel's ostensibly immoral actions unveil the hypocrisy of his fellow travellers whose search for an 'authentic' Other is packaged, marketed and reduced to the level of the commodity-form. The second part of the novel details Michel's and Valérie's plan to legitimize and regulate Third World sex tourism. This satirizes the ideologies of global capitalism by presenting a plan that acknowledges and utilizes global inequalities rather than attempting to obfuscate or reduce them. This empowers the reader to make their own critique. In the final part of the novel, a terrorist attack on the first sex tourism endorsing 'Aphrodite' resort results in Valérie's death. This part examines the ways in which racial, sexual and nationalistic violence is predicated upon group modes of enjoyment. By examining the signification, commodification and politicization of enjoyment in each section of the novel, this chapter offers a critique of one of the most naturalized ideologies of the contemporary sociocultural order.

The Signification of Enjoyment

Enjoyment has become a naturalized discourse within Western civilization. Subjects are commonly told that an act is morally good 'so long as you enjoy it'. Advertising campaigns increasing exhort individuals to take enjoyment from the commodity-form. As Slavoj Žižek argues, contemporary civilization is determined by the superego imperative to 'Enjoy!' This formulation draws together the capitalist dynamics of surplus-value and the libidinal dynamics of surplus-enjoyment. Enjoyment typically signifies as a surplus over standard satisfactions such as food, warmth or shelter. However, for Lacan, enjoyment is related to the signifier and therefore directly linked to castration, primarily understood as the experience of lack. Steering away from Freud's literal reading of castration, Lacan understands it as a linguistic term through which the subject enters into the Symbolic order while renouncing the *jouissance* (plenitude or satisfaction) experienced in the Imaginary. Entry into the Symbolic is the inaugural moment of alienation that entails the subject's replacement of the thing with the signifier. At this moment *jouissance* is lost and the subject becomes a barred or lacking subject. However, as Bruce Fink argues, 'what happens to the jouissance that is sacrificed? Where does it go? Is it simply annihilated? Does it simply vanish? Or does it shift to a different level or locus? The answer seems clear: it shifts to the Other.'[5] This means that the *jouissance* that is lost in the transition from the Imaginary to the Symbolic is refound in speech. Through entry into the Other as language, the subject takes a portion of the *jouissance* circulating in the Other.

The relationship between castration and *jouissance* indicates that enjoyment is extracted from and circulates outside the subject and as such can be added to or modified by others. As such, it bears a structural homology with Marx's surplus value. The capitalist system is predicated upon the extraction from the worker of a surplus value. The capitalist takes from the worker interest or profit rather than returning it to his employees. The worker never takes enjoyment from the surplus product and instead loses it. This renders the worker a subject alienated from his or her labour. The capitalist functions as the Other who enjoys while the worker sacrifices him or herself for the Other's *jouissance*. Just as capitalism extracts surplus-labour from the worker in order to ensure profitability and growth, so entry into the Symbolic order demands surplus-enjoyment from the speaking subject and this ensures the continued proliferation of civilization and culture. The capitalist system is unique insofar as other modes of production have previously found accordance with the social relation. However, capitalism is marked by a contradiction between the social mode of production and the individual, private mode of appropriation. This contradiction at the heart of the capitalist system causes it to continuously revolutionize itself and incessantly develop its own conditions of production. As Michel states, 'capitalism, by its very nature, is a permanent state of war, a constant struggle which can never end' (284). The 'normal' state of capitalism is one of incessant development, revolution and imbalance in a constant attempt to resolve its internal contradiction. Slavoj Žižek argues that this paradox defines Lacan's concept of surplus enjoyment:

> It is not a surplus which simply attaches itself to some 'normal', funda-
> mental enjoyment, because *enjoyment as such emerges only in this surplus*,
> because it is constitutively an 'excess'. If we subtract the surplus we lose
> enjoyment itself, just as capitalism, which can survive only by incessantly
> revolutionizing its own material conditions, ceases to exist if it 'stays
> the same', if it achieves an internal balance. This, then, is the homol-
> ogy between surplus-value – the 'cause' which sets in motion the capital-
> ist process of production – and surplus-enjoyment, the object-cause of
> desire.[6]

Surplus value and surplus enjoyment mark the paradoxical coincidence of limit and excess. Both capital and desire are linked because they form the bridge that draws the subject into the circuits of exchange of the Other.

Surplus enjoyment is homologous to capital and the rule of general equivalence. This is the value against which all other values are measured. For the subject, enjoyment signifies as a value against which activities and relations are measured. It is useful at this point to draw on Freud's notion of the unary trait that operates within group dynamics as the minimal point of signification of the subject's enjoyment. This is expounded in 'Group Psychology and the Analysis of the Ego' when Freud begins to link psycho-analytic thought to the social and the political. He draws on a number of examples of identification that stand as the earliest and most basic form of emotional bond between individuals. For instance, one of his patients, Dora inherited a cough in imitation of her beloved father. This cough is an exam-ple of one subject imitating just one aspect of another and is the only ele-ment required for identification to take place. Freud also uses the example of a group of girls in a boarding school in which identification is established devoid of any other objective relation to the person who is being imitated:

> Supposing, for instance, that one of the girls in a boarding school has
> had a letter from someone with whom she is secretly in love which arouses
> her jealousy, and that she reacts to it with a fit of hysterics; then some of
> her friends who know about it will catch the fit, as we say, by mental infec-
> tion. The mechanism is that of identification based upon the possibility
> or desire of putting oneself in the same situation. The other girls would
> like to have a secret love affair too, and under the influence of a sense of
> guilt they also accept the suffering involved in it.[7]

Freud is clear that these symptoms are not exhibited by the other girls out of sympathy but through identification with the trait that emerged at a moment of crisis. This identification marks the point of minimal coincidence between two egos. It is clear from these examples that the unary trait is completely arbitrary but nonetheless bears significance for the subjects concerned. It is significant that the inaugural moment of identification in the boarding school example is centred on a moment of loss. It is at the point when one of the girls loses her object of desire that the trait is repeated amongst the group as a whole. As such, this identification becomes a source of a supplementary satisfaction or enjoyment.

For Jacques Lacan, the unary trait is, 'the simplest form of mark, which properly speaking is the origin of the signifier'.[8] This shifts the concept of enjoyment away from the notion of an original loss upon entry into the Symbolic to, 'a notion of loss which is closer to the notion of *waste*, of a useless surplus or remainder, which is inherent in and essential to *jouissance* as such'.[9] Enjoyment should be read as a form of waste. As such, the inaugural loss is not simply a lack or an absence but has a substance. It exists yet serves no purpose. Significantly, for Lacan, enjoyment is not indelibly associated with transgression. Instead, as he states in *Seminar XVII*:

> [it] only comes into play by chance, an initial contingency, an accident. The living being that ticks over normally purrs along with pleasure. If *jouissance* is unusual, and if it is ratified by having the sanction of the unary trait and repetition, which henceforth institutes it as a mark – if this happens, it can only originate in a very minor variation in the sense of *jouissance*. These variations, after all, will never be extreme, not even in the practices I raised before. (50)

By practices, Lacan is referring specifically to masochism and sadism. His point is that enjoyment is not a transgression of the sociocultural order. Instead, it is an intrinsic aspect of capitalism. The subject encounters a surplus enjoyment that represents a deviation from normative acts of pleasure. However, this deviation is never extreme and is instituted into the Symbolic, becoming a signification in the process. Through his famous phrase 'a signifier is what represents the subject for another signifier', Lacan is declaring that the subject can only take enjoyment and therefore enter into identification with other subjects through the structure of language in the form of the signifier. Consequently, enjoyment can be understood as the central point of identification that forms the unspoken bond around which communities are formed. The unary trait is the point of minimal difference or the simplest form of inscription that draws together groups and communities. As such, it can be argued that enjoyment stands at the heart of conflict between identity groups and social minorities.

Lacan is clear that enjoyment is not transgressive but an intrinsic component in the smooth functioning of the socio-symbolic order. This formulation is reflected in Houellebecq's critique of Western society. In *Platform*, Michel meets with the artist Bertrand Bredane, a purveyor of the grotesque. He takes Michel and Valérie to Bar Bar, a sadomasochistic club in which perverse and extreme forms of sexual practice take place: 'Some nights, customers had needles pushed through their balls or the heads of their cocks; once he'd even seen a guy whose dominator had torn out a fingernail with a pair of pliers' (187). The name 'Bar Bar' is a repetition of the same signifier that denotes the point of minimal difference. Like the fight club, it functions as a minimal inscription that invisibly draws together a group into mutual identification through a shared enjoyment. Valérie expresses revulsion at sadomasochistic practice and is answered by an associate of Bredane's: 'I don't see the problem. It's a contract that's all' (187). This response indicates that sadomasochistic practice, as depicted in the novel, is subservient to symbolic laws and mercantile discourse in particular. Valérie states: 'I don't believe you can *freely consent* to humiliation and suffering' (187). Sadomasochistic practice enacts an overt return to a master and slave dialectic as represented by the spectacle of a woman gagged and handcuffed in a cage: 'She was, as was the custom of the place, a slave whose master was going to auction her off for the evening' (186). Again a codified set of precise rules guide the extent of the suffering inflicted upon the individual. Valérie criticizes the lack of sensual, physical contact in favour of multitudinous, fetishized objects, such as whips, chains and so on: 'they need to be re-educated, to be loved, to be taught what pleasure is' (190). Michel perceives the enjoyment taken from sadomasochism as, 'the apotheosis of sexuality, its ultimate form. Each person remains trapped in his skin, completely given over to his feelings of individuality' (191). In this scene, sex is regarded as a parody of itself, provided through a contractual agreement: 'we have become cold, rational, acutely conscious of our individual existence and our rights' (244). This detached position of neutral self-observation establishes a direct link between the subject's enjoyment and the Symbolic order: 'organised S&M with its rules could only exist among cultured, cerebral people for whom sex has lost all attraction' (245). In this instance, sadomasochism can be regarded as the overdetermination of sex. The signifier dominates to the detriment of bodily experience. What has the potential to be a transgressive and potentially subversive act is brought back within a set of heavily codified norms mediated through and by the signifier.

In interview, Michel Houellebecq has stated that:, 'my typical narrator is often in the position of zigzagging between holes of nothingness. And strangely enough he doesn't fall in.'[10] In *Platform*, Michel moves between a series of emotional holes starting with the death of his father and ending with his traumatized response to Valérie's death. Each hole is significant for occasioning a significant shift in the coordinates of Michel's desire. The death of his father causes him to seek enjoyment on package holidays whilst Valérie's death causes him to withdraw from the circuits of desire altogether. These opposing responses can be understood in relation to Jacques-Alain Miller's definitions of a hole and a lack: 'lack is spatial, designating a void within a space, while the hole is more radical – it designates the point at which this spatial order itself breaks down'.[11] This difference signifies the difference between drive and desire. Whereas desire is grounded in a constitutive lack, or the void that structures reality; drive circulates about a hole, a gap in the order of being. Although *Platform* is ostensibly about desire, it becomes apparent that this cyclical system is underpinned by drive. Although desire is fluid, it is drive that sets it in motion. This psychoanalytic structure is embodied by the structure of capitalism. Valérie states: 'I think you're the love of my life, and I don't ask for anything more than that. But that's not possible: I have to ask for more. I'm trapped in a system from which I get so little, which I know is futile; but I don't know how to get out' (163). Valérie acknowledges the fluidity of desire but simultaneously recognizes that she is bound to the demands of drive as instigated by the impersonal capitalist machine. Michel comments on 'the curse of the tourist, caught up in the frenetic search for places that are "not touristy", which his very presence undermines, forever forced to move on, following a plan whose very fulfilment, little by little, renders it futile' (311). Desire is an impossible demand to fill a lack that is constantly shifting. Capitalism and in particular the tourist industry stimulates desire for ever new objects, experiences and modes of enjoyment. However, drive operates within the libidinal dynamics of capitalism in a more fundamental way. As Žižek states in '*Objet a* in Social Links': 'it is the impersonal compulsion to engage in the endless circular movement of expanded self-reproduction' (118). The death of his father is for Michel an experience of lack that draws him into the capitalist circuits of exchange. By contrast, following Valérie's death, Michel experiences real trauma in the form of a hole that marks the point at which the bond between the subject and the Symbolic order breaks down.

Platform demonstrates that enjoyment is indissolubly linked to the structure of signification. By opening with the line, 'Father died last year' (3), the novel self-consciously mimics the opening to Albert Camus' *The Outsider*, which evokes a similar sense of affectless alienation. However, in *Platform* it is the father rather than the mother who dies. Indeed, the mother is conspicuously absent. As discussed in the chapter on *Lunar Park*, the father has particular significance within psychoanalytic discourse as the figure who prohibits enjoyment. Indeed, the father is positioned within the Oedipus complex as the agent of castration. Michel's apparent dislike for his father suggests that he is still coming to terms with this prohibitive function: 'I quickly visualised a moron in shorts – his face wrinkled, but otherwise very like mine – building up his pectorals with hopeless vigour. Father, I said to myself, Father, you have built your house upon sand' (4). The father's athletic and sexually promiscuous character contrasts with Michel's slight frame and awkward attitude towards sex. By insulting his father and emphasizing the futility of his life, Michel is attempting to elide the fantasy that it is the father who is the castrator. For Michel, the death of the father reveals the gap between the real father and his symbolic function. Indeed, his death reveals that prohibition resides not in the body but in the Name-of-the-Father, which, as a signifier, holds universal value. As Lacan states in *Seminar XVII*, 'the dead father is what guards *jouissance*, is where the prohibition of *jouissance* started, where it stemmed from' (123). For Lacan, the dead father is the site of an impossibility because he fulfils a symbolic function as the bearer of knowledge and authority but logically cannot know that he is dead. As such, the figure of the dead father touches upon the Real, which is radically distinguished from the rules and logic of the Symbolic order. Consequently, the death of Michel's father generates resentment as Michel comes to realize that his father was not the cause of his inability to seek enjoyment. Instead, it is the signifier or the Name-of-the-Father, internalized as an agent of castration, that is the marker of prohibition that has restricted Michel's enjoyment. As Lacan argues, 'Castration is an essentially symbolic function, that is, is conceivable from nowhere else than the articulation of signifiers' (124). This indicates that enjoyment and lack are bound up with the logic of signification. This link between enjoyment and signification is evoked when Michel spends his compassionate leave searching through holiday brochures: 'I was particularly fond of the star-ratings system, which indicated the intensity of the pleasure one was entitled to hope for. I wasn't happy, but I valued happiness and continued to aspire to it' (14). The figure of the dead father functions as a spur to Michel to pursue his desire, conceived of as a quantifiable category, down codified and well-trammelled pathways. Indeed, this chapter will now trace the ways in which enjoyment is harnessed and commodified by the system of globalized capitalism.

The Ethics of Enjoyment

Having explored the ways in which enjoyment functions as an unspoken signification that draws together otherwise disparate groups, I will now discuss the ways in which it is harnessed by the machinery of global capitalism. This is a key theme of Houellebecq's satiric text. Rather than engaging with the ethical issues at play in global inequalities, the narrator of *Platform* perceives economic imbalance as a business opportunity:

> You have several hundred million Westerners who have everything they could want but no longer manage to obtain sexual satisfaction: they spend their lives looking, but they don't find it and they are completely miserable. On the other hand, you have several billion people who have nothing, who are starving, who die young, who live in conditions unfit for human habitation and who have nothing left to sell except their bodies and their unspoiled sexuality. It's simple, it's really simple to understand: it's an ideal trading opportunity. (242)

This passage demonstrates the ways in which the obscene underside of the late capitalist system is disavowed by its citizens. Michel knows well that global capitalism generates severe inequalities but rather than deploring these conditions, treats them as part of the inevitable outcome of the dominant sociocultural order. This in turn naturalizes the obscene underside of global capitalism in a way that disrupts the reader's expectations. By explicitly rendering young girls' bodies as a commodity-form ripe for consumption by the affluent West, Houellebecq establishes the coordinates for a radical critique of the circuits of global exchange. This critique operates through the juxtaposition of the French social milieu with the experience of Thailand from the perspective of the tourist.

Against the cultural stereotype that France is a place of freedom, artistry and hedonism, Michel argues that it is, 'a sinister country, utterly sinister and bureaucratic' (64). The sadomasochistic club exemplifies the image of a sociocultural order in which sex is dominated by signification and codified by rigorous social norms. Michel notes that Parisian girls 'weren't remotely interested in sex, only in seduction – and even then it was a kind of elitist, trashy, bizarre seduction that was not in the least bit erotic' (206).

Michel despairs of a world in which signification and fantasy-structures stand between and remove direct sensual contact. For Lacan there is no sexual relation unmediated by a fantasy-structure. Michel's enjoyment of Thai girls is no less of a signification than sadomasochistic practice. However, the sadomasochism depicted in the novel remains contactless and is held fully under the sway of the signifier. It is useful to contrast this world of affectless relations with Michel's experience in Thailand.

Michel's holiday juxtaposes explicit sexual scenes with uncomfortable social interactions. This exemplifies the gap between the two sociocultural orders: 'on package tours people talk to each other a lot, but it's a forced camaraderie; they know perfectly well they'll never see each other again. It's very rare for them to have a sexual relationship' (159). Michel finds himself alienated within the unwritten rules of the social group: 'no one came to sit beside me. I had clearly missed my first opportunity to integrate into the group' (34). It is clear that Michel's enjoyment does not coincide with the others. He fails to identify with the unary trait that sustains the group dynamic, be it their nationality, gender or the very fact of being a tourist. In particular, Michel does not experience the Oriental Other in the same way. He fails to derive enjoyment from tourism's sanitized system of staging encounters with the Other. For instance, the experience of traditional Thai dance is described as, 'Not bad, really, but a bit expensive and terrifyingly cultural; everyone involved had at least a masters degree' (43). The Oriental Other is contained with a codified system of Western norms. In contrast to the rest of the group, Michel seeks enjoyment in Thai massage parlours, self-consciously conforming to the model of the consumer as 'a rational individual seeking to maximize his satisfaction while taking price into consideration' (14). Both Michel and the group take enjoyment in relation to money and the signifier. However, Michel is unambiguous about his libidinal impulses that for the group are stimulated but not satisfied by the experience of being a tourist.

There is a widely perceived disjuncture between travel and tourism. Travel is seen as an authentic experience whereas tourists are guided to non-threatening experiences of the Oriental Other. This is highlighted by the tour guide's reflections on two Thai tribes: 'Karen tribe good, deemed Sôn, brave, children good study in school, no problem.' By contrast, the Akha tribe are 'incapable of giving up growing opium poppies, their traditional activity. Akhas bad, [. . .] they are completely useless' (65). This contrast between the two tribes is indicative of the imposition of Western values on native cultures. Tourism ultimately reflects the tourist's preconceived values. Michel and the others are only permitted to see the Karen tribe because they adhere to the Western fantasy of the harmless, inclusive Other who responds positively to ideological apparatus. This is in contrast to the Akhas who retain their traditions. The Karens are decreed 'good' because they coincide with an acceptable image of the tribal Other because they have renounced their cultural identity. They are, 'more or less indifferent to the cause of Karen independence', and have constructed an, 'ecological paradise, which an international clientele could now enjoy' (66). The construction of Western enjoyment in the wilderness stands at odds with enunciated Western expectations: "'If you go abroad," Josiane barked, "It is in order to eat the *local* food and to observe *local* customs"' (70). The marked disparity between the tourists' manifest desire to encounter Otherness and their latent desire to explore the familiar implies a degree of fetishistic disavowal. Their experience with the hostile jungle and an indigenous Other is mediated by a codified system of Western values that frame the Other for Western consumption. They are not 'authentic' travellers, but disavow this knowledge in order to take enjoyment from the performance of Otherness and ethnicity.

The Other is valued so long as he or she is not really Other. The tourist industry is predicated upon the experience of the new and the exotic but must commodify this experience, thereby bringing it back into a codified system of norms. The French philosopher Alain Badiou comments on multiculturalism and the Western experience of the Other:

> Our suspicions are first aroused when we see that the self-declared apostles of ethics and of the 'right to difference' are clearly *horrified by any sustained difference.* For them, African customs are barbaric, Muslims are dreadful, the Chinese are totalitarian, and so on. As a matter of fact, this celebrated 'other' is acceptable only if he is a *good* other – which is to say what exactly, if not *the same as us?*[13]

Michel displays aversion towards his fellow travellers because they clamour for the experience of the Other but are horrified by the idea of going to a Thai massage parlour. They are ostensibly accepting of difference but the prostitution network returns the exploitative practice of Western imperialism to them in an inverted form. Sustained contact with the obscene underside of Western ideology is traumatic and shocking. By contrast, at the conclusion of the holiday, Michel wanders through the airport's shopping arcade: 'Even though the departures hall was completed roofed-over, the shops were built in the form of huts, with teak uprights and roofs thatched with palm leaves' (131). This scene stands as a microcosm of the tourist experience. The Western tourist consumes the experience of the Other within the frame and shelter of Western ideals. The shops sell a combination of international standards and local products. However, they are all bound together by the rule of general equivalence: 'every item had a barcode' (131). The experience of Otherness is systematically commodified, codified and thereby brought within the Western signifying chain in a sanitized and unthreatening manner.

Midway through the novel, Houellebecq delivers a brief history of Thailand and its entry on to the global stage. This description delivers three distinct stages. The first is a long-running conflict with Burma. The causes of this conflict are lost in history but resulted in Burma's conquest of Thailand in the eighteenth century. However, Thai culture continued to prevail in the form of Buddhism: 'The image of the Buddha, on the other hand, was very much in evidence and had retained all of its significance' (80). Even under military conquest, Thailand retained its cultural identity. Following this, Thailand entered into a period of stability: 'For two centuries (actually, up to the present day) the kingdom knew no serious foreign wars, nor any civil or religious wars for that matter; it also succeeded in avoiding any form of colonisation' (81). This description deliberately presents a utopian picture of a land free from oppression or strife. Houellebecq contrasts this image with Thailand's entry on to the global stage:

> Thailand had become part of the free world, meaning the market economy; for five years it had been suffering a terrible economic crisis which had reduced the currency to less than half its previous value and brought the most successful businesses to the brink of ruin. (81)

The Burmese conquest of Thailand parallels Western financial colonization. However, whereas the Burmese looted and pillaged Thailand's material treasures whilst making relatively little impact on its culture or traditions, the global economy presents itself under the banner of freedom. This is the freedom to trade and masks the concomitant colonization and destruction of Thai culture.

Houellebecq demonstrates that the sole beneficiary of Thailand's entry into the free market economy is the already affluent West. The city of Surat Thani had been an important site for the metallurgical industries and more recently plays a significant role in machine assembly; an industry necessary for the sustenance and development of Western travel agencies. Michel encounters two Western tourists who are event organizers working for a public relations company. Their travel and lifestyle is dependent on the Thai machine assembly industry but their salary is approximately 25 times that of a metal worker in Surat Thani. This striking economic inequality gives some indication of the reasons for the availability of prostitutes in the Third World. Michel delivers a breakdown of Thai prostitution rates: 'For a whole night, I think the price was about four or five thousand baht – about a month's salary for an unskilled Thai worker' (107). In a country trading on and thereby exposed to the free market economy, Thai workers receive a minimal wage. The tourist industry offers an opportunity to earn far more from relatively rich travellers. As such, Thai culture has undergone significant changes in its attempt to satisfy the desire of the Western tourist. Without offering a direct moral judgement on prostitution, Houellebecq portrays free-market capitalism as a systemic and naturalized form of colonization that exploits Thailand's natural assets, be they rich iron ore or young girls' bodies. The labour of the East is utilized to sustain the leisure of the West.

Later in the novel, Michel and Valérie go on holiday to Cuba. Here, Michel detects a similar system to that in Thailand. Cuba is portrayed as a country that cannot sustain itself in the industrial age. Wages are insufficient and workers must supplement their labour in a tourist-related capacity. The situation is comparable to that in Thailand insofar as the official systems of work are relatively insufficient in comparison to the opportunities afford by the tourist industry: 'The bronzed men and women weaving between the tourists thought of us purely as wallets on legs, there was no point in deluding oneself; but it was just the same in every third-world country' (224). Here the social relation is completely subsumed by the economic imperative. Furthermore, when confronted with the absence of industrial output in Cuba, Michel is made aware of his and his companion's own lack of knowledge with regard to production methods:

> We had not the least idea about casting metal, manufacturing parts, thermoforming plastics. Not to mention more complex objects like fibre optics or microprocessors. We lived in a world made up of objects whose manufacture, possible uses and functions were completely alien to us. (225)

Michel is suddenly defamiliarized and alienated from the objects around him. This is indicative of the archetypal Western consumer's removal from the modes of production. Michael Hardt and Antonio Negri discuss the blurring of the division between labour and leisure in the post-Fordist industries of the West. As discussed in the chapter on *Millennium People*, they define immaterial labour as 'labour that produces immaterial products, such as information, knowledges, ideas, images, relationships, and affects'.[14] The Western subject manages information and capital rather than directly producing goods. Immaterial labour deconstructs the division between labour and leisure to capitalize on the productivity of the social relation in the form of non-remunerated life. The Italian social theorist Paolo Virno states: 'Labour and non-labour develop an identical form of productivity, based on the exercise of generic human facilities: language, memory, sociability, ethical and aesthetic inclinations, the capacity for abstraction and learning.'[15] Rather than freeing the subject from the demands of labour, immaterial labour marks the infiltration of capitalist ideology into every aspect of the subject's life. The division between leisure and labour is lost amidst the imperative for ever increasing productivity.

Michel's sex tourism strategy employs an unapologetically rational discourse that overtly displays the ideology of the global marketplace and thereby exposes it to critique: 'If sex was really to come into the category of tradable commodities, the best solution was probably to involve money, that universal mediator which already made it possible to assure an exact equivalence between intelligence, talent and technical competence' (298). The abstract rule of number presents a neutral exterior which conceals the systemic violence that sustains the system. Empirical analysis indicates that prostitution often develops alongside conventional tourism: 'tourist development has been associated with the emergence of an informal prostitution sector *as well as* the reproduction of an existing, formally organised sector'.[16] The official face of tourism is supported by its obscene accompaniment in the form of either formally organized or unregulated prostitution. Michel's plan to create sex tourist resorts is unashamedly exploitative, using economic advantage to secure sex:

As a wealthy European I could obtain food and the services of women more cheaply in other countries; as a decadent European, conscious of my approaching death, and given over entirely to selfishness, I could see no reason to deprive myself of these things. (299)

Houellebecq fails to convincingly critique child prostitution, gender inequalities or indeed, the issue of venereal disease in his text. Michel's institutionalization of prostitution makes no attempt to end unequal and exploitative sexual encounters. However, Houellebecq's narrator is refreshingly devoid of hypocrisy and by clearly articulating the logic and exploitative practices of globalization, the reader is able to subject it to critique.

Indeed, Houllebecq makes his narrator's position as a *flâneur* clear from the start: 'I observe the world as it unfurls, I thought; proceeding empirically, in good faith, I observe it; I can do no more than observe' (286). Houellebecq's text does not produce an overt criticism of sex tourism but does unveil the hypocrisy of the West. As such, the text supports Julia Davidson's argument that 'many of the countries which are exploited by multinational tourism conglomerates are simultaneously being exploited as a source of cheap labour by other transnational corporations' (87). Prostitution helps enable a low-wage economy which is of benefit to these transnational corporations. Women and children in countries such as Thailand often live in poverty and have several dependents. The potential income from prostitution is far higher than the limited alternatives, which are also dependent upon the tourist trade, such as begging or flower-selling. Rather than seeking to morally condemn the political economy or even the participants of sex tourism, Houellebecq is seeking to demonstrate the inconsistencies involved in Western civilization's ethical value system.

The Politics of Enjoyment

The novel concludes with a terrorist attack on one of the newly opened resorts, during which Valérie is shot and killed. This violent conclusion draws out the political effects of enjoyment and offers insight into communities and civilizations. The violence of the terrorist attack appears seemingly out of nowhere. As discussed in the chapter on *Millennium People*, Slavoj Žižek offers a theorization of the gap between systemic and subjective violence. Žižek draws on the example of Nikolai Lossky, an anti-communist bourgeois intellectual who was expelled from Russia by the Soviet government in 1922. From the comfortable space of bourgeois norms and values, the eruption of Leninism appeared as a violent incursion: 'What they didn't understand was that in the guise of this irrational subjective violence, they were getting back the message they had sent out themselves in its true inverted form.'[17] Lossky had lived a comfortable, privileged life that coincided perfectly with the dominant bourgeois ideology. However, this sociocultural order was predicated upon a systemic form of violence that operated invisibly against marginalized groups such as the oppressed proletariat. The subjective violence of the Leninist revolt granted visibility to these oppressed groups and appeared seemingly out of nowhere. Subjective violence is a particularized form of violence that is made visible through conflict with the dominant sociocultural order. Systemic violence is far more coercive because it exists as violence in its universal form and consequently is much harder to perceive as such. Houellebecq's novel portrays the tourist industry as a systemic form of violence that subjects the Oriental Other. The discourse of leisure and enjoyment is increasingly naturalized and its smooth operation conceals the antagonisms and gross inequalities in the global free markets. The terrorist attack that concludes *Platform* is this violence returned in its inverted form. Ultimately, the subjective violence of the terrorist attack is a powerful indictment of the tourist industry that reveals the inconsistencies and inequalities of Western capitalism.

The media response to the attack is universal condemnation of both the Muslim terrorists and the holiday club: 'The journalist accused the Aurore group in no uncertain terms of promoting sex tourism in third-world countries, and added that, in the circumstances, the reaction of the Muslims was understandable' (340). However, rather than being interpreted as simply a clash of religious beliefs, the terrorist attack should be read as the point at which two communities' forms of enjoyment clash. Following Lacan, Jacques-Alain Miller debates what grounds the alterity of the Other. Lacan asks 'what is the Other of the Other?' The answer cannot be the subject because this would indicate the existence of a unified, autonomous ego. Instead, he is forced to conclude that there is no Other of the Other as such, but various categories of alterity and plurality. Miller focuses on the figure of the Neighbour in Christian discourse or *le prochain* meaning 'the one who is close'. The Neighbour is not someone in physical proximity but someone who is always 'too close'. This should be linked to the discourse of enjoyment. The Neighbour is someone who takes enjoyment in a different way to the subject. It makes them simultaneously alien and too close. Indeed, Miller argues that '*Jouissance* is precisely what grounds the alterity of the Other when there is no Other of the Other'.[18] It is difference in terms of enjoyment that renders the Other as Other. Accordingly, discourses predicated upon identity such as race, gender, nationality and sexuality can be understood to be the outcome of perceptions of how the Other enjoys. As Miller states:

Racism is founded on what one imagines about the Other's *jouissance*; it is hatred of the particular way, of the Other's own way, of experiencing *jouissance*. We may well think that racism exists because our Islamic neighbour is too noisy when he has parties. However, what is really at stake is that he takes his *jouissance* in a way different from ours. Thus the Other's proximity exacerbates racism: as soon as there is closeness, there is a confrontation of incompatible modes of *jouissance*. (79–80)

The Other is Other because of the ways in which he or she takes enjoyment. Close proximity with the Neighbour or Other leads to conflict. This is demonstrated by the Muslim terrorist attack on the Western leisure resort. The first section of this chapter examined the significance of the unary trait for Freud's theory of group psychology. The unary trait is the minimal point of inscription that draws together a community around a common mark. The community is formed around a mode of enjoyment with which every member can identify. Consequently, conflict with other communities can be seen to originate over a conflict between two incompatible unary traits. As such, although race and religious belief exist, they exist only insofar as they are discourses or traditions of subjective positions grounded in relation to the unary trait.

There is always an aspect of the Neighbour that is unknown to the subject. Lacan identifies this unknown element as the Thing or *das Ding*: 'The *Ding* is the element that is initially isolated by the subject in his experience of the *Nebenmensch* as being by its very nature alien, *Fremde*.'[19] The subject for Lacan is not a given but is presumed. No matter how well one subject is known by another, there is still a minimal requirement of belief required to perceive the Other as another subject rather than as a biological machine devoid of depth. This point at which another subject is perceived to be a semblance devoid of substance is the place of the Thing. It is the point of absolute alerity that locates the Neighbour despite his proximity. In *Platform*, the Thing is located in the space of the Other's enjoyment. What one subject desires may be perceived as 'evil' or perverse to another. Houellebecq demonstrates that enjoyment is the space that marks the Other as Other. Michel points out that many Muslims transgress Islamic law to participate in Western ideals of enjoyment: 'I had been surprised by the presence of people from Arab countries, in fact, they came for exactly the same reasons as Westerners, with one slight difference: they threw themselves into debauchery with much more enthusiasm' (309). It is by seeing the Muslim Other as the same as Westerners that the figure of the Thingly Neighbour appears. As Žižek states in *Violence*:

> Since a Neighbour is, as Freud suspected long ago, primarily a thing, a traumatic intruder, someone whose different way of life (or, rather, way of *jouissance* materialized in its social practices and rituals) disturbs us, throws the balance of our way of life off the rails, when it comes too close, this can lead to an aggressive reaction aimed at getting rid of this disturbing intruder. (50)

Whereas the Muslim community is perceived to obey its own codified system of norms, coincidence around the same point of enjoyment as Westerners leads to conflict. The tourist industry marks the point at which modes of enjoyment are thrown into relief as each identity is homogenized under the banner of the tourist. The point at which the Other appears as the Same causes conflict because paradoxically, it emphasizes their Otherness.

Platform's closing scene is foreshadowed by a separate outbreak of violence. Two weeks before the opening of the Aphrodite club in Thailand, a German tourist and a Thai girl are kidnapped by an Islamic terrorist sect. Whilst the German is castrated and has his throat cut, 'the young girl had been stoned to death, she had been beaten with extraordinary violence; everywhere her skin was ripped open, her body was little more than a swelling, barely recognisable' (308). It is clear that the cause of the attack was not simply hatred of the Western Other but hatred of the Other's enjoyment. For this reason, it is significant that the German tourist was castrated, thereby depriving him of the means of enjoyment. However, the most excessive acts of violence were directed at the girl. She signifies as the privileged object-cause of desire, and it is as if by ripping open her skin, the terrorists were trying to locate the indefinable *objet a*. The media suggest that the reason for the attack is because the girl and the tourist were in contravention of Islamic law. However, this is indicative of the impotence of interpretation in the face of violence. This justification resorts to a belief in the fundamental difference of the Other that obfuscates the true resentment brought about by the German's conspicuous enjoyment of the Other's privileged object. Ultimately, it conceals the idiotic and self-reflexive enjoyment taken from violently removing the possibility of taking enjoyment from the girl, now literally reduced to an object.

The link between violence and enjoyment is reinforced by the opening of the novel and the death of Michel's father at the hands of the brother of the Muslim girl he was having an affair with. Again, the girl's Muslim identity or ethnic origin is relatively unimportant. Instead, violence is caused by resentment of the Other's enjoyment. Writing in response to Levinas in *Seminar VII*, Lacan disparages the hypocrisy of an ethics that valorizes the Other: 'what I want is the good of others in the image of my own. That doesn't cost so much. What I want is the good of others provided that it remain in the image of my own' (187). Lacan is satirizing Western multicultural ethics that consider the Other to be 'good' so long as he or she is deprived of his or her Otherness. Paradoxically, it is when the Other appears as the Same that his or her alterity is emphasized and the Thingliness of the Neighbour appears. When Michel returns to Bangkok, he discovers that many of the bars ban

Muslims with the justification: '*We respect your Muslim faith: we don't want you to drink whisky and enjoy Thai girls*' (309). This prohibition effectively keeps the Muslim Other at a distance by clearly differentiating between modes of enjoyment. Without the experience of direct contact with the Other, their Otherness can be preserved. Paradoxically, close proximity to the Other would demonstrate their difference.

Concluding Remarks

The increasing spread of the Western sociocultural order under the guise of globalization conflicts with Islamic value-systems and beliefs. Within the context of an aggressive economic and cultural expansionism alongside the globalization (and implicit homogenization) of social values, tolerance of the Other can be perceived to be a form of antagonism that implicitly affirms the Western position of dominance and superiority whilst disavowing the systemic violence inherent to universalized sociocultural orders. Edward Said comments on the difficulties involved in writing about the Arab world in a passage worth quoting at length:

> If Orientalist scholarship traditionally taught that Muslims were no more than fatalistic children tyrannized by their mindset, their *ulama*, and their wild-eyed political leaders into resisting the West and progress, was it not the case that every political scientist, anthropologist, and sociologist worthy of trust could show that, given a reasonable chance, something resembling the American way of life might be introduced into the Islamic world via consumer goods, anti-Communist propaganda, and 'good' leaders? The one main difficulty with the Islamic world, however, was that, unlike India and China, it had never really been pacified or defeated. For reasons which seemed always to defy the understanding of scholars, Islam continued to sway over its adherents, who, it came regularly to be argued, were unwilling to accept reality or at least that part of reality in which Western superiority was demonstrable.[20]

Orientalism portrays Muslims as resistant to progress and modernization. At the same time, the Islamic world stands apart and asserts its own version of reality, thereby resisting the encroachments of Western hegemony. As such, Orientalism functions as a 'rational' ideological support for the capitalist colonization of the East. However, Islam directly conflicts with the globalized development of the marketplace precisely because it is not bound by ethnicity or territory. Islamic law is directly opposed to development, the dominant cultural ideology of the West. Instead of the capitalist drive towards ever more excessive enjoyments, Islam produces its own reality, imposing its own order on the world. It can be said that Muslims take enjoyment from their renunciation of Western enjoyment in a similar way to ascetics who take another form of enjoyment from their denial of enjoyment. Said argues that Western perception of the Islamic world is one of a population who are brutally oppressed by their mythologizing religious and political leaders who irrationally reject the development and prosperity of the West. This view constructs the population as repressed consumers rather than an Other who takes enjoyment in a different way. Orientalist discourse naturalizes the 'American way of life' by portraying consumer culture as something 'normal' that Muslims would embrace if freed from their 'oppressive' Muslim law. Michel takes the same position throughout the text. The Other is not really Other but socially and ideologically repressed. The importation of cultural images of enjoyment indicates the ways in which the Other is rendered in an acceptable light, that is, deprived of their Otherness. This is brought into relief by the advertising campaign for the Aphrodite clubs that indicate the ways in which Orientalist discourse constructs the exotic Other: 'In every photo the local girls were topless, wearing miniscule G-strings or see-through skirts; photographed on the beach or right in the hotel rooms, they smiled teasingly, ran their tongues over their lips: it was almost impossible to misunderstand' (296). However, it should be argued that these adverts are misunderstood. These are 'presented' or 'induced' images that actively construct the place by guiding expectation. It is true that, 'marketing has long made use of idealized sexual images and information to sell products'.[21] However, instead of the journey or the location, it is the fetishized body of the Other that is sold. As Graham Dann notes, in the language of tourism:

> travel may be readily compared to the phenomenon of love in terms of its varieties, approaches, games and conquests; travel is a disorienting process in which one abandons the familiarity of home for exciting new amorous experiences elsewhere where the destination becomes a woman.[22]

In light of Houellebecq's satiric critique, it is clear that the destination is not a woman but the promise of enjoyment delivered from the gendered, racialized and oppressed Other.

Michel Houellebecq's *Platform* is about loss, desire and enjoyment and their relation to the ideologies of late capitalism. Enjoyment embodies

an integral part of global consumer culture but also has political consequences in relation to issues of violence and group dynamics. Enjoyment
is a naturalized discourse within the capitalist sociocultural order, which
sustains the fantasy that satisfaction is achievable. Following Lacan, when
the subject enters into language and the Symbolic order he is linguisti-
cally castrated and renunciates the plenitude found within the Imaginary.
Enjoyment is ineluctably linked to the signifier because lost *jouissance* or
plenitude is refound through speech. This formulation establishes a clear
link between circuits of desire, signification and the social relation. The
dominant expression of the circulation of enjoyment is money, which operates as the law of general equivalence. This renders all named substances
equivocal and thereby binds and flattens them into a fantasy of wholeness.
This correlation is further supported by Lacan's link between surplus-enjoyment and Marx's surplus-value. As this chapter has demonstrated, desire
and enjoyment are integral aspects of the machinery of capitalism. Just as
money functions as a unit of exchange between commodity-forms, enjoyment signifies as a value against which social relations are measured.

Freud's unary trait forms the basis for the psychoanalysis of group
dynamics. The unary trait is the minimal form of mark or inscription
that binds a community through identification. This identification is a
supplementary satisfaction for the subject's experience of alienation and
loss following castration and their entry into the Symbolic order. Indeed,
this provides a formulation of enjoyment as a supplement that attempts to
fill in but ultimately sustains the lack at the heart of the subject. As such,
enjoyment sustains the fantasy-structure of the One that supports the illusion of the autonomous stable ego held within a coherent structure of
codified norms and traditions. This supplementation can take a number
of forms including the enjoyment taken from the renunciation or denial
of enjoyment as demonstrated by the example of the Christian tradition
of asceticism and denial. Enjoyment should be regarded as a substance or
waste material that highlights points of conflict or antagonism between
two competing groups, often demarcated through an identity politics of
race, gender or sexuality. In particular, enjoyment as marketed and sold by
the tourist industry marks a contemporary form of colonization through
the commodification of the Other. This commodification produces an
Other who is not really Other, that is, one who has been brought to reflect
Western norms, values and traditions. In the final chapter of this book,
I will explore the ways in which the fiction of Tama Janowitz challenges
many of these norms and reinvigorates the need for feminist critique.

Chapter 6

Feminism, Satire and Critique in the Work of Tama Janowitz

Tama Janowitz is a contemporary satirist who was named as a member of the Brat Pack alongside Bret Easton Ellis and Jay McInerney for her often grotesque depictions of life in New York. Her best known work is *Slaves of New York* (1986), which was later adapted into a film in 1989 by Merchant-Ivory Productions. This initially strange pairing found creative synergy when the lavish costumes and set design for which Merchant-Ivory are renowned were transferred from their traditional Edwardian milieu to a vivid depiction of the decadent New York elite in the 1980s. Further to this, Merchant-Ivory films typically focus on the theme of individual disillusionment with the freedoms promised by society and this finds contemporary resonance in Janowitz's focus on the role of women in the twenty-first century. In this chapter, I will discuss the significance of a series of Janowitz's increasingly acerbic satires including *The Male Cross-Dresser Support Group* (1992), *A Certain Age* (1999) and *Peyton Amberg* (2003). Each novel parodies and inverts the conventions of mainstream culture in order to eloquently portray the glamour of New York in close juxtaposition with its obscene underside. Janowitz employs a series of female narrators from a variety of ages and class backgrounds. By depicting consumer culture's increased focus on women as a key target market and demographic as displayed by numerous popular shows such as *Sex and the City* and *Gilmore Girls* alongside their obscene counterpart in the form of scenes of drug-taking, violence and sexual abuse, inspired in part by Bret Easton Ellis' *American Psycho*, Janowitz's wide-ranging and complex oeuvre is unified around the attempt to rejuvenate questions of female emancipation within a culture that has seemingly replaced fundamental rights with the illusions of consumer society. In line with previous chapters in this book, I argue that despite appearing fragmented and diffuse, patriarchal ideology generates conditions of indeterminacy in order to evade critique.

In Janowitz's collection of non-fiction entitled *Area Code 212* she comments on the publication of her first novel, *American Dad* (1981). She initially found that the chapters she sent to publishers were unanimously rejected until she sent them out, unaltered, under a man's name. Following this shift in gender, she was immediately approached by *Esquire* and *The Paris Review*. She states:

> I wanted to publish that book under the name Tom A. Janowitz because I felt I would be making a point, that things hadn't changed all that much since the Brontë's wrote under men's names, and George Eliot and George Sand and so forth.[1]

As this quotation indicates, Tama Janowitz is concerned with questions of female identity and feminist politics in a period in which feminism is widely regarded to have reached its end. Recent scholarship, spearheaded by Susan Faludi's *Backlash* published in 1992, has argued that since the 1990s the traditional concerns of feminist politics have been either deemed irrelevant to the concerns of contemporary women or to have achieved its aims of women's enfranchisement and freedom. Indeed, as work by Yvonne Tasker and Diane Negra has indicated, popular culture is increasingly characterized by a heightened focus on women as consumers who are seemingly liberated from the traditional concerns of feminist politics. Against this shift in mainstream culture, Janowitz seeks to contest the claim that the need for a feminist politics is either irrelevant or anachronistic. Indeed, her fiction locates women's ongoing oppression throughout almost every sector of society, thereby highlighting the continuing need for a collective women's movement. This chapter is divided into three parts that each examine Janowitz's satirical stance on a key theme for feminist critics in the wake of postmodernism. First, through a reading of *The Male Cross-Dresser Support Group* I question whether feminism functions as an effective politics for working-class women and explore the ways in which Janowitz employs what is widely regarded as a predominantly masculine form in order to form her critique. Next, in a discussion of the themes deployed in *A Certain Age*, I explore the significance of marriage and ageing for women in Western society. Finally, through a reading of *Peyton Amberg*, I discuss the themes of adultery and domesticity in order to suggest that even women who appear to be economically liberated and socially mobile continue to be bound by patriarchal ideology. As such, Janowitz's work explores a series of wildly different perspectives and voices that are collectively linked through a common concern with the role of women in postfeminist society. However, before moving on to an exploration of the specificities of Janowitz's oeuvre, it is necessary to engage in a brief discussion of significant feminist debates at the turn of the twenty-first century.

The continuing importance of feminism in the twenty-first century is implicitly linked to the transition from solid modernism to liquid modernity identified by Zygmunt Bauman. This sociocultural shift has resulted in the obfuscation of the 'women question' amidst the celebration of choice, political ambivalence and self-conscious materialism endemic to consumer culture. As Misha Kavka argues in *Feminist Consequences*, in the wake of postmodernism, feminism, an already fractured movement, has become increasingly diffuse: 'the problem is not the death or the end of feminism, but, rather, coming to terms with the fact that political, strategic and interpretative power has been so great as to produce innumerable modes of doing'.[2] Consequently, it has become increasingly difficult to attribute a single unity of purpose to the feminist movement and this ambivalence has functioned as both a strength and a weakness. Contemporary feminist critics such as Sarah Gamble, Stacy Gillis, Elaine Showalter and Luce Irigaray characterize the woman's movement in the form of waves. In an interview conducted by Gillian Howie, Irigaray states: 'if the stages in feminist movement correspond to waves, this could suggest a moving ceaselessly [. . .] thus, the matter would be of a permanent but instable and not autonomous movement which could never assume a definitive meaning or form'.[3] This conception of the women's movement would suggest that the metaphor of fluidity has been of benefit to feminist politics. First wave feminism was founded in the nineteenth-century women's movement as a political programme for the inclusion of women in response to 'a common exclusion from political, social, public and economic life'.[4] Second wave feminism, developed in the 1960s and 1970s, was concerned with broader social relations and focused on specific issues such as the family, the workplace and reproductive rights. Finally, third wave feminism was influenced by the anti-essentialist arguments developed out of post-structuralist thought. As Alison Stone argues, 'the central target of anti-essentialist critique was the belief – arguably widely held amongst second wave feminists – that there are shared characteristics common to all women, which unify them as a group'.[5] The third wave constituted a critique of the relations of power and exclusion that underpinned general claims about women. Indeed, the unifying essence common to second wave feminists was overwhelmingly defined by the concerns of white, middle-class, Western women of a certain age. As we shall see, Janowitz's satiric fiction works to undo the notion of a unified feminine self by displaying contemporary culture from a variety of perspectives. However, the third wave emphasis on anti-essentialism also implied that women did not exist as a distinct social group and consequently undermined the possibility of solidarity and collective social or political action. As such, the transition from the political aims of the first wave, followed by the second wave's critique of the patriarchal structure of society, to the anti-essentialist critique of third wave feminism finds resonance with the broader cultural trends identified within this book. Indeed, the transition from a collective politics to diffuse critique can be understood as the demise of a feminist grand narrative in the face of the postmodern celebration of indeterminacy and fragmentation as well as the concomitant rise of consumer culture. However, as Janowitz's work demonstrates, despite the apparent conditions of indeterminacy that characterize the postmodern era, patriarchal authority still continues to have real effects on women's lived experience.

Tama Janowitz's satiric engagement with the role of women in contemporary society exposes the ways in which the traditional concerns of feminist politics have been submerged beneath the fluid desires of consumer culture. Indeed, it can be argued that consumer culture mimics and repackages feminist desire in an easily consumable form, divested of its radical potential. Within popular culture, depictions of feminism range from ironic dismissal to placing it in the role of the scapegoat for the anxieties faced by women in the twenty-first century. As Negra and Tasker state, 'postfeminist culture is evidently postmodern in character, its self-reflexivity mobilizing the terms of its own critique'.[6] They are part of a growing body of contemporary feminist scholarship that has identified an urgent need to critically engage with the tropes of postfeminist culture and the ways in which it frequently neutralizes feminist critique. Key examples of these seemingly liberated postfeminist texts include *Bridget Jones's Diary*, *Sex and the City*, *Ally McBeal* and *What Not to Wear*. These are examples of a female-centred popular culture that celebrates the hegemony of consumer society under which women are seemingly free to construct their identities in any way they choose. As such, they assume that women have achieved equality at the turn of the twenty-first century while simultaneously placing the blame for the fears and anxieties faced by women who desire a career, children, marriage, as well as to appear younger, slimmer, more intelligent and more desirable at the hands of the women's movement. In its self-conscious mimicry and subversion of popular conceptions of women's role in contemporary society, Tama Janowitz's work can be read as a response to the emerging postfeminist culture. The three novels under discussion combine a distinctive blend of comedy and horror that draws on the tropes of both transgressive literature and sensationalist 'chick lit'. As such, Janowitz exposes many of the blind spots of postfeminist culture including its limited depiction of working-class and ageing women. In addition, it is important to note that Janowitz is writing within a traditionally male-dominated genre. Consequently, this chapter will explore the ways in which satire is conventionally associated with masculinity and questions why female satirists such as Fay Weldon, Muriel Spark and Doris Lessing are not granted the same degree of visibility as their male counterparts. After all, surely after centuries of oppression, women have a greater need to write satire than men?

Women Writing Satire

So far this book has been concerned with the work of a series of male satirists. Each in turn has been linked to themes of violence, revolution and transgression. However, as Janowitz's fiction demonstrates, satire is not a solely masculine domain. Indeed, recent scholarship by Lisa Wilson has revealed that in the eighteenth century, women writers wrote narrative satire in numbers nearly equal to their male counterparts. Wilson notes that female satirists in the Romantic period, 'self-consciously manipulated gendered conventions regarding authorship, they adopted explicitly satirical personae, and their narrators appealed directly to their (usually female) readers in order to achieve their satiric aims'.[7] This paints a picture not of a genre dominated by male authors and agendas but of a literary space in which women writers could connect to their audience while challenging and shaping genre conventions. However, despite the evidence presented in Wilson's thesis, the unfortunate common conception is that women do not and should not write satire. As Gary Dyer states, 'both men and women traditionally have seen satire, more than other genres, as distinctly masculine'.[8] Despite the existence of female satirists, the prevailing cultural truism remains that women are not capable of writing satire. This can be linked to the theory of the male gaze expounded by Laura Mulvey in her seminal essay titled 'Visual Pleasure and Narrative Cinema' originally published in *Screen* in 1975. Mulvey argues that within patriarchal society, men are regarded as active subjects and bearers of the look while women are rendered as passive objects who connote 'to-be-looked-at-ness'. She states:

woman then stands in patriarchal culture as a signifier for the male other, bound by a symbolic order in which man can live out his fantasies and obsessions through linguistic command by imposing them on the silent image of woman still tied to her place as bearer, not maker, of meaning.[9]

Indeed, writing satire can be understood to be akin to employing the male gaze in order to render otherwise autonomous subjects as objects for scrutiny and correction. As such, women writing satire can be understood as analogous to women adopting the male gaze with the attendant possibility of inverting its form in order to function as a critical tool against patriarchy. Indeed, it is significant that for centuries ridiculing others has been commonly understood to render women unattractive. Consequently, the cultural blindness concerning women satirists continues to operate as an ideological support for patriarchal society. For this reason, Janowitz's adoption of a masculine form constitutes a radical subversion of the patriarchal hegemony of not only reason, law and order but of critique and the comic spirit.

The male dominance of the satiric genre can be located in the etymology of the word 'satyr', which is the root of the word 'satyriasis', meaning excessively great venereal desire in the male. This etymological link is one that has been submerged but indicates why the form has traditionally been seen as predominantly masculine. In addition to this, the feminist critic Ethel Sloane notes: 'everyone knows that a nymphomaniac is a woman with an excessive sex drive. Why is it that hardly anyone knows the same conditions in males is satyriasis?'[10] Sloane's question indicates again that women have traditionally been understood to be passive material in relation to the active male subject. Indeed, the application of medical labels to excessive sexuality in women contrasts with the cultural valorization of virility in men. In addition, this etymological link supplements the discussion of the 'satyr' as a half man-half beast in the Introduction. The figure of the barbaric and savage satyr is representative of both sexuality and blackness inviting parallels with Western civilization's reception of black identity. Blackness has traditionally functioned as the Other to white civilization by signifying inferiority, sexuality and an almost metaphysical stasis. However, Western civilization's determination to produce clear hierarchical boundaries between different categories of race was overtly challenged by the threat of miscegenation. In light of this, the figure of the satyr as a half man-half beast constitutes a radical challenge to civilized hierarchies and normative sexuality. As the film theorist Richard Dyer notes, 'inter-racial (non-white on white) rape is represented as bestiality storming the citadel of civilization – but this often implies that sexuality itself is bestial and antithetical to civilization'.[11] This creates the paradoxical situation whereby white civilization attempts to repress sex but in order to ensure the survival of the race, they have to have sex: 'the means of reproducing whiteness are not themselves pure white' (26). Black identity is crucial for the formation of white identity but simultaneously exposes the gaps and inconsistencies in an otherwise monolithic sense of self. This parallels satire's position within the Western sociocultural order insofar as its display of obscenity functions as the Other to civilized values. As such, satire can be understood to be the perfect form for Janowitz's depiction of women's oppression within the seemingly liberal, self-empowering postfeminist age. In what follows, I will discuss the significance of three novels for ongoing feminist debates as Janowitz confronts issues of class, ageing and adultery.

Class and Cross-Dressing

In *The Male Cross-Dresser Support Group*, Janowitz explores the social milieu of New York from both male and female perspectives. Not only does Pamela, the narrator, engage in transvestism but Janowitz herself can be said to be engaged in an act of literary cross-dressing as she adopts a predominantly masculine form. Cross-dressing has a rich place in the comic tradition as evidenced by texts as diverse as Shakespeare's *As You Like It* and the 1959 film *Some Like It Hot* in which Tony Curtis and Jack Lemmon disguise themselves as women in order to avoid the attention of the mob. More recently,the films of Pedro Almodóvar have stimulated discussion of drag and debates on gender inequalities. Indeed, Janowitz's satire on gendered norms displays a notable influence from Jonathan Swift's scatological poems such as 'The Lady's Dressing Room' that parodies the assumptions of the assumed male reader in order to produce a potentially ambivalent critique. As the young suitor Strephon explores Celia's private rooms, he discovers a series of grotesque objects that are normally concealed from the sight of young men. Concluding with the discovery of Celia's chamber pot, he delivers the immortal line: 'Oh! Celia, Celia, Celia shits!'[12] To the naive male eye, this poem could be understood to identify and condemn an individual case of deviancy. On a more serious note, it could be understood to project a broader seam of misogyny against women who construct themselves as objects of desire while failing to conceal their bodily functions. In this light, the absent Celia appears to be representative of stereotypes about women as manipulative, devious and corrupt. However, the majority of readers would agree that the poem functions as a critique of the earnest narrator who indulges in masculine fantasies of idealized images of femininity that the real Celia cannot attain. In a similar way, in the *Male Cross-Dresser Support Group*, Janowitz refuses to depict her female narrator as anything but uncouth, badly dressed and impoverished in order to challenge male-dominated aesthetic conventions that dictate that women depicted in art and literature must be beautiful. Indeed, Pamela is an engaging narrator precisely because her combination of naivety, cynicism and paranoia paints the world around her in a bizarre mixture of comedy and horror.

Near the start of the novel, Pamela unwillingly adopts a young boy named Abdhul who has started to sleep on the street outside her basement flat. Following a series of unfortunate events at the magazine where she works, she is threatened with police action and decides to leave the city. Taking Abdhul with her, she embarks on a road trip filled with blackly comic scenes including the burning down of her father's house, shooting toads with a hallucinating shopkeeper and various misadventures with a decapitated head found on the highway. Suddenly, while staying at a hotel, Abdhul goes missing and Pamela resolves to return to New York disguised as a man in order to find him. Throughout the novel, a maternal bond slowly develops between Pamela and Abdhul. Indeed, as an adoptive mother herself, Janowitz is careful to debunk essentialist notions of a biological link between mother and child. In a similar fashion to the fictional representation of Bret Easton Ellis in *Lunar Park*, it is clear that father or motherhood is not a natural or instinctual state but one that is learned. As Pamela notes early on in the novel, 'something was wrong with my behaviour; I was like a mockery, a parody, of what I dimly remembered as being a mother'.[13] This statement denaturalizes conventional images of maternal sufficiency and suggests that Pamela is constantly searching for contentment. By embarking on the road trip with Abdhul, Pamela undergoes a transition from her mundane existence in New York to a life of ceaseless movement. At the novel's conclusion it is revealed that Abdhul has not been lost but has found sanctuary with Pamela's mother, enabling him to go to school, work as a golf caddy and go on dates. However, rather than ending with a scene of blissful reunion and a return to normative domestic life, Abdhul reveals that he is saving money to buy a car in order to reinitiate the road trip: '"Oh, come on, Pamela," he said. "What's happened to you? That's not like us. You don't want to get too conventional do you?"' (314). The private domestic sphere is depicted as a temporary refuge before a return to the public encounters on the road. In this way, the novel gestures towards the standard trope of narrative closure in the form of a family reunion while simultaneously highlighting its artificiality. Consequently, the novel indicates that the maternal bond between mother and child is an ineluctable fantasy-structure of the One. In line with the conventions of the satiric genre, narrative closure is portrayed as insufficient and contingent upon societal expectations.

Throughout the novel, Janowitz highlights the fixed roles that men and women occupy in relation to the structures of fantasy and desire. Two scenes in particular depict moments when Pamela experiences sexual fantasies from either male or female subject positions. Her ability to experience both perspectives indicates that desire is fluid. At the same time, the particular circumstances that generate each fantasy suggest that there are two distinct symbolic structures in which desire is inscribed. The first instance follows an extended comic sequence in which Pamela's employer Amber finds herself trapped beneath a wash basin in a public toilet. Pamela states:

> I saw myself grabbing this woman, who was absolutely undesirable, at least from my point of view, with great chunky big legs, big animal legs, like an elephant, with a huge ass, and I saw myself grabbing her and fucking the hell out of her, right there on the floor, yes, I could see myself, ramming a penis into her, a big fat dick into her huge pussy. (107)

The crudity and violence of this image indicates that Pamela is engaged in a hyperbolic masculine fantasy prompted by a reversal in the power relation between Amber and herself. Rather than seeing her boss as her superior, Pamela now sees Amber as a passive object and herself as an active subject. This disrupts the notion of sexual difference as biological and immutable. At the same time, it suggests that there is an unconscious structure that determines masculine desire. As Pamela notes, 'for a second it was as if some male mind had occupied mine' (107). The second incident occurs when Pamela stops at a shop located in a rural backwater. Here she knocks over a stack of cans, which fall on her. As she lies prone beneath them, the grotesque shopkeeper approaches and she finds herself engaging in an extended rape fantasy:

> There was nothing wrong with a rape-fantasy, it still didn't mean the person actually *wanted* to be raped. All it meant was that one portion of my brain wanted to lie around passively while some man came along and held my arms down, overcome with animal desire for me that he was unable to control. (205)

It should be noted that Janowitz does not adequately engage with the problematic issue of rape and her narrator rather hastily asserts a clear division
between fantasy and reality. Indeed, the scene's status as comic satire does
not neutralize its potentially pernicious effects. However, as Pamela notes,
this is a fantasy that emerges unbidden from her unconscious. Like the
first scene, this fantasy is catalyzed by a sudden reversal in which an individual is suddenly rendered passive. In order to explore this further, it will
prove useful to draw on Jacques Lacan's symbolic logic of sexuation that
indicates that sexual difference is a psychic structure unconsciously chosen
by the subject.

Pamela's exaggerated fantasies of alternately masculine empowerment
and feminine passivity suggest that patriarchal norms are embedded at the
level of language and the unconscious. For Lacan, sexual difference is not
rooted in biological essence but neither is it a purely discursive construct.
Instead, it is located within the unconscious, which cannot be reduced to
either society or the body. As such, sexual difference is determined through
an unconscious choice in terms of either absence or presence, which establishes a place for the subject within the social fabric. As discussed throughout this book, for Lacan, the transition from the Imaginary stage into the
Symbolic order marks the subject's entry into language and concomitant
loss of satisfaction and illusory unity. Without elaborating the intricacies of
the Aristotelian logic that Lacan draws upon, suffice it to say that Lacan's
formulaic treatment of sexual difference outlines a structure in which all
male and female speaking beings inscribe themselves within the socio-
symbolic in distinct ways. Whereas male-identified subjects enter into language under the threat of castration, female-identified subjects are always
already castrated. Both male and female sexes experience lack insofar as
they are split between the body and their symbolic identity but approach
this lack in different ways. As Elizabeth Wright states: 'each speaking being
can choose to inscribe itself on either side, although this will be a "forced"
choice, imposed by the parameters of the history of the subject's unconscious'.[14] Against claims that Freud and Lacan were engaged in a misogynist
discourse, it should be noted that their understanding of sexual difference
is descriptive rather than prescriptive and consequently offers insight into
the ways in which unconscious structures of desire have been co-opted
as a structural support for patriarchal society. Although Lacan's formulae of sexuation indicate that the subject must choose between one of two
identificatory positions, it does suggest that object-choice and desire can
cut across biological constraints. As such, Lacan's sexuation theory offers
a powerful critique of fixed gender roles without removing all structures

and values. It offers a critique of conceptions of fixed, autonomous subjects without deconstructing identity categories altogether. Consequently, sexuation can offer feminism the opportunity to reengage with the structures of patriarchal oppression without slipping into endless indeterminacy and fluidity.

The Male Cross-Dresser Support Group offers a view of women's role in society from the perspective of a working-class woman. Against the image of the young, independent and emancipated woman disseminated by postfeminist mass media, Pamela is depicted as untidy, disorganized and unintelligent by conventional standards. Her particular worldview offers a naive look at standards and conventions of everyday life, thereby opening them up to critique. In particular, she displays a dismissive and condemnatory attitude towards the gains of the women's movement:

> Stuck at the end of the twentieth century, when everyone went around saying women were equal to men and no one admitted to the silent subtext – that the only real status for women was to align themselves with a rich and famous man. Even women who had made it on their own – famous blond rock stars, or TV journalists, or supreme court judges – were frankly viewed with contempt, albeit fascination. (54)

This perspective constitutes a deviation from the image of women presented within mainstream media at the close of the twentieth century. Indeed, it signals a degree of class blindness within the feminist movement while highlighting the overriding significance of the economy over concerns about gender equality. In line with this, postfeminist media signifies alternately as a depoliticized and anti-feminist backlash or as an opportunity for women to freely construct their identity. Stéphanie Genz and Benjamin A. Brabon make a case for a positive reading of postfeminism. They argue that 'postfeminism is doubly coded in political terms and is part of a neo-liberal political economy that relies on the image of an "enterprising self" characterised by initiative, ambition and personal responsibility'.[15] As such, it can be seen to be a necessary response to changes in relationships, freedom of choice and the increasing deployment of traditionally feminist ideas in mainstream culture at the turn of the twenty-first century. However, it also functions as an ideological support for consumer culture and operates as the antithesis of public and collective campaigns for female emancipation and equality. Despite the social and political changes that have taken place in the twentieth century, Janowitz's text demonstrates that in many ways, women continue to inhabit a position subordinate to men: 'it was one thing to pretend things had changed for women; but in fact they hadn't' (54). This perspective suggests that although select individuals have been successful in different areas of endeavour and commerce, for the majority of working-class women, the new opportunities promised by neoliberal enterprise culture remain inaccessible. Indeed, advances towards equality in the workplace are torturously slow and subject to frequent reversals. Although more women than ever are emerging from university and entering into professional careers, they frequently find themselves failing to reach senior management levels. With this in mind, it is more urgent than ever to consider the possibility of collective political action. In addition, the opportunity to engage in the range of diverse lifestyle choices celebrated by postfeminist media almost entirely occludes questions of race and class. Suzanne Leonard argues that 'as a feminist icon, the modern woman worker is, predictably, white and upper or middle class, as were the women whose discourse fomented the working woman as a feminist model in the 1960s and 1970s'.[16] From this perspective, celebrating the gains of privileged and well-educated women can be seen to be premature since it presupposes a new idealized image of women as vital, youthful, playful and enterprising. For this reason, Janowitz's confused, struggling and difficult narrator offers fresh insight into women's place in society.

The differences in the treatment of men and women are demonstrated at the start and the conclusion of the novel. In the beginning, Pamela is treated with either derision by her female line manager or as a sexual object by her male boss. However, at the novel's conclusion, she returns to New York disguised as Paul and the same people who had treated her with disdain now flatter her. As Amber states: '"I've always gone wild over men in glasses. I bet all the women are just crazy about you." "Just lately," I said' (284). This sycophantic display indicates that aspirational values at the turn of the twenty-first century are to be economically successful and socially ambitious. In an analysis of the postfeminist drama, *Gilmore Girls*, Diane Negra argues that the show, 'suggests that those who don't have the cultural or economic capital to stylize their lives are merely ridiculous whilst those whose lives lie beyond white hometown affluence are held in contempt'.[17] This show is indicative of more pernicious and widespread attitudes that judge those who are unable or unwilling to participate in the lifestyle choices constitutive of prescribed standards of wellbeing in the wake of postmodernism. Because of her wild hair, unkempt appearance and lack of enterprising spirit, Pamela is treated with disdain by the denizens of New York. This is reflected in Janowitz's own experience of living in New York as recounted in *Area Code 212*. Indeed, in one particularly memorable tale, recounted to an audience of graduate students, the author once went for a job interview dressed as Morticia Addams. By cross-dressing, Pamela reveals that the structural inequalities of society continue to be demarcated along both class and gender lines. Her dual experience as alternately male and female indicates that gender categories are fluid. However, the formulae of sexuation identified by Lacan indicate that a structural difference between men and women continues to exist. Like the transition from Pamela to Paul, Janowitz's adoption of the satiric form is a mode of literary cross-dressing. Indeed, as Janowitz states in *Area Code 212*, she had always attempted to, 'write about men as objects in the way men had always written about women' (93). This is a reversal of gendered binaries that challenges inequalities predicated upon biological difference and indicates the ways in which the socio-symbolic fabric continues to maintain patriarchal norms in a period in which feminism is depicted within mainstream culture on a spectrum ranging from irrelevant to pernicious. The theme of women's ongoing oppression is continued in *A Certain Age* in which Janowitz casts her satiric gaze squarely on the issue of conspicuous consumption and ageing for women at the turn of the twenty-first century.

The Postfeminist Lifecycle

As discussed throughout this book, the postmodern subject has been conceived in terms that problematize the concept of the autonomous stable ego in order to stress its discursive construction. This approach emphasizes fluidity rather than stability and valorizes multiplicity over singularity. On the one hand, this approach has benefitted the feminist cause. As Stephen Best and Douglas Kellner state: 'the postmodern emphasis on plurality, difference and heterogeneity has had immense appeal to those who have found themselves marginalised and excluded from the voice of Reason, Truth and Objectivity'.[18] In this respect, the postmodern understanding of the subject has enabled new forms of critique to emerge that call to account the structures of power that have bound 'woman' as a fixed, essential category for centuries. However, although postmodernism can be seen to have benefitted the feminist movement by providing the critical tools necessary in order to deconstruct and undermine otherwise fixed categories, there is an underlying tension between the two movements. In *The*

Politics of Postmodernism, Linda Hutcheon defines the relationship between postmodern aesthetics and feminist politics as a complicitous critique:

> The difference between the postmodern and the feminist can be seen in the potential quietism of the political ambiguities or paradoxes of postmodernism. The many feminist social agendas demand a theory of agency, but such a theory is visibly lacking in postmodernism, caught as it is in a certain negativity that may be inherent in any critique of cultural dominants.[19]

This quotation marks the central aporia between postmodernism as a self-reflexive form that deconstructs all forms of positive agency and feminism as a collective movement with specific political aims. Deconstruction is primarily a form of critique rather than an act in itself although it certainly can catalyse effective political action. This uneasy relationship between indeterminate critique and concrete social issue is encapsulated in the title of Janowitz's fifth novel, *A Certain Age.* On the one hand, the title ironically refers to the age of postmodernism in which all known values have become *un*certain. On the other hand, it refers to one of the key social concerns facing women in the twenty-first century, namely ageing and the cultural perceptions regarding the ticking of the biological clock. In this novel, Janowitz highlights the fluidity of all values by depicting the constant shifts in fashion and endless circulation of commodities within the passively nihilistic consumer society of premillennial New York. The narrative follows the plight of Florence, a single woman in search of a wealthy husband against the background of glamour and conspicuous consumption of the Manhattan elite. However, the scenes of decadence, dinner parties and dates are contrasted with the final third of the novel in which Florence descends into a nightmarish world of violence, drug-taking and transgression that challenges the illusion that New York in the twenty-first century is a space of possibility, freedom and class mobility for women.

Florence's search for her ideal husband provides the narrative impetus that leads her through stages of obsession, desperation and disillusionment. The plot begins as a feminized version of the quest narrative, introduced in the opening pages when Florence reminisces about her mother: 'she had always encouraged Florence to go back East, to marry rich, to return to spawn like a reintroduced salmon'.[20] As this unflattering image suggests, the quest for marriage is directly linked to the twin ideological imperatives of economic enterprise and reproductive futurity. Through this ambivalent persona, Janowitz is quick to interrogate the ways in which these constructed imperatives – to marry, grow wealthy and reproduce – are presented as natural. Florence's mother 'had managed somehow, to imprint this on Florence – or perhaps it went deeper, imprinted on her strands of DNA like a celestial map carved on an ancient Aztec necklace' (6). This particular simile conveys an image of ancient civilizations in which rules and laws were constructed and became sedimented over time. Indeed, as the work of Michel Foucault demonstrates, a law that was originally contingent appears natural and eternal with the passing of time. At the same time, within the decadent milieu of Manhattan's social elite, Janowitz is interposing the less salubrious image of imitation jewellery sold to naive tourists as 'original' or 'authentic'. Indeed, the opening of the novel places naturalized images of twenty-first century woman's quest for the ideal husband alongside scenes of vacuous decadence within a social milieu devoid of affect:

> The lives of these people seemed so unreal; nothing here was any more serious than the action unfolding in a film. It was only a matter of time before she, too, joined their ranks, abandoning feelings – anguish, despair, hope, caring, understanding – thoughts, wishes, dreams, ideals. (36)

This is a world devoid of affect in which values are fluid and the experience of suffering appears only as a distant memory. Violent or political action is undifferentiated from the distant events occurring on a television screen. Indeed, echoing Fredric Jameson's diagnosis of the postmodern era, Florence finds herself, 'overcome with nostalgia for something she had never experienced' (77). However, within this world of conspicuous consumption, as a single woman in her mid-thirties, Florence is acutely aware of her precarious placement within the social hierarchy. Consequently, within a world characterized by indeterminate and constantly shifting sociocultural signifiers in terms of fashions, styles, banal conversation topics, bars and restaurants, Florence is constantly labouring to maintain her own status. Indeed, as she reminds herself during an unexpected trip to a noisy club in Queens, 'associate too long with the wrong types and she would join their ranks' (65). This fear of social exclusion is indicative of the individualist consumer ethic that forecloses the possibility of collective feminist politics.

In order to maintain her precarious social position within an ever-changing social landscape, Florence discusses her body in terms of property and exchange: 'most of her income went on maintenance for herself. Her nails and toenails were manicured and polished in the palest silver-pink, her legs waxed, as were eyebrows and facial hair' (43). This recital develops into an extensive and detailed inventory that echoes Patrick Bateman's equally extended monologues in Bret Easton Ellis' *American Psycho*. However, Florence's expensive upkeep remains for the most part inconspicuous to her male suitors. A key example of this occurs when Florence spends 5 hours and 300 dollars every month on, 'slivers of honey and amber in her hair, so subtle as to appear natural' (43). However, when the narrative is focalized through a male character, her hair is unflatteringly regarded: 'Her blond hair, the colour of dirty honey, hung down in messy chunks' (51–2). Instead, these expensive and time-consuming rituals signify in a combative manner towards other women since, in the novel, they are the only people who can differentiate between different lifestyle choices. In turn, this indicates that consumer culture's valorization of the individual and celebration of a myriad of lifestyle choices concomitantly occludes the possibility of collective female solidarity against the patriarchal hegemony. This is keenly expressed halfway through the novel when the narrative voice, focalized through Florence, compares women to dogs competitively seeking to establish themselves in a pack based upon a host of different signifiers of social status: 'she couldn't see the importance of friendships with women. It didn't occur to her to confide in someone [. . .] Women were objects with which to compete' (141). Although blackly humorous, the attitude displayed by Florence indicates that she has internalized the imperatives of patriarchal consumer society, thereby relegating the gains made by the women's movement to a distant memory. Indeed, Florence's comparison of women with dogs is reminiscent of the patriarchal myth of the Great Chain of Being that is composed of a series of hierarchical relationships in which women are placed between man and beast. Janowitz's satirical eye suggests that, devoid of a common language and unable to confide in one another within a competitive and economically driven society, women will internalize seemingly anachronistic and pernicious patriarchal ideologies thereby foreclosing the possibility of liberating feminist politics.

The internalization of pernicious patriarchal attitudes is also witnessed in Florence's attitude to sexual relations and her cynical denial of agency. Indeed, following a one-night-stand with a married man, she justifies her actions not in terms of female sexual empowerment or as a transgression of oppressive and codified norms but because, 'her body meant so little to her, except as a commodity that nobody seemed to want to buy or own; she might as well hand it over to him for a few hours at a reduced rate' (129). In a similar manner to Stewart Home's treatment of prostitution, discussed in the Introduction, Janowitz directly links the conditions of economic oppression to gender subordination. Consequently, Florence treats her body as passive material to be traded on the libidinal economy. Indeed, her speech is frequently interspersed with mercantile discourse. This stands in direct contrast to Hélène Cixous' call for women to emancipate themselves by 'writing the body', that is, reinscribing female subjectivity in ways that generate new potentialities within the socio-symbolic fabric. Indeed, Florence's capitulation signals a refusal of her own agency and reinscribes her subordinate position. This self-conscious reduction of the self is symptomatic of the postmodern condition and concomitant deconstruction of the subject. Within the dominant cultural paradigm that celebrates individualism and freedom of choice, Florence finds herself confronted with indeterminacy and is constantly searching for the latest fashion or trend. Consequently, the innumerable lifestyle choices Florence must negotiate on a daily basis obfuscate the ideologies of patriarchal society. By voicing the obscene accompaniment to Florence's conspicuous consumption, Janowitz is able to bring the ideologies of patriarchal consumer society to light, thereby exposing them to critique.

This section has demonstrated that the question of agency is of central importance for Janowitz's depiction of the plight of the single woman in New York. On the one hand, consumer culture seemingly privileges the individual and offers freedom and scope to self-consciously sculpt an identity. On the other hand, the novel suggests that women continue to be bound by naturalized patriarchal ideologies and are impelled to seek a wealthy husband. Diane Negra in *What a Girl Wants?* characterizes this paradigm as an aspect of 'time crisis'. She argues that postfeminist culture has:

> accelerated the consumerist maturity of girls, carving out new demographic categories such as that of the 'tween'; it has forcefully renewed conservative social ideologies centering on the necessity of marriage for young women and the glorification of pregnancy; and it has heightened the visibility of midlife women often cast as desperate to retain or recover their value as postfeminist subjects. (47)

As Tama Janowitz's satiric fiction demonstrates, women are increasingly aware of their age and position within a myriad of overlapping consumer demographics. Within the increased speed of everyday life, women are increasingly confronted with the patriarchal imperative to marry and reproduce, couched in an essentialist rhetoric. In order to retain value within consumer culture, women must appear youthful, healthy and fertile. In *Area Code 212*, Janowitz states:

> as a woman one is immediately categorised by the outside world, based on one's age. No longer, perhaps, is one a spinster at an unmarried twenty-two, but at thirty a woman is 'desperate' and by simply announcing 'forty' as a woman one is truly past the point of sexual desirability. (46)

As Janowitz notes, women are impelled to conform to aspirational lifestyles appropriate to their age group. Consequently, the increased speed of everyday life, remarked upon by theorists such as Paul Virilio, has significant ramifications for women's role in society. Women are increasingly regarded as overworked, rushed and subject to the mythology of the 'biological clock'. Indeed, Tasker and Negra argue that within postfeminist culture, 'female adulthood is defined as a state of chronic temporal crisis' (10). The cultural mythology of the 'biological clock', developed from scientific measurements of fertility from menarche to menopause, has had a range of effects on women's health, diet, grooming, education, career and the institution of marriage. The increased cultural emphasis on fertility and ageing has led women to experience time-pressured conflict between their education, career and personal goals and the desire to reproduce.

The onset of 'time crisis' in the wake of postmodernism simultaneously generates indeterminacy as women are bombarded with conflicting cultural and 'biological' imperatives while reinforcing patriarchal ideologies that ascribe value to the female subject primarily in relation to her reproductive capacity. As Diana Negra argues, 'in postfeminist culture the single woman stands as the most conspicuously time-beset example of contemporary femininity, her singlehood encoded as a particularly temporal failure and a drifting off course from the normative stages of the female lifestyle' (61). Janowitz dramatizes this perspective in a typically hyperbolic manner in order to expose it to ridicule. Accordingly, Florence not only 'drifts off course' but in the final third of the novel engages in drug abuse, theft and sexual encounters that border on prostitution. The categorization of women on the basis of their age and thereby on their fertility reduces female subjectivity to the level of a (reproductive) object. Janowitz's critique of masculine fantasies about women on this subject returns us again to Laura Mulvey's criticism of the 'male gaze' that reaffirms the binary opposition between the active male and the passive female. Following Lacan, Mulvey argues that desire is embedded in the gaze and accordingly feminist writers in the 1970s and 1980s focused their critique on images of women presented as a consumable object. However, as Angela McRobbie argues, this form of feminist politics has become increasingly portrayed within postfeminist culture as irrelevant to the fully enfranchised female consumer of the twenty-first century. Echoing Janowitz's ongoing concerns, she asks: 'is this then, the New Deal for New Labour's "modern" young women: female individualization and the new meritocracy at the expense of feminist politics?'[21] In particular, McRobbie points to the overtly sexist Wonderbra advertisements from the mid-1990s in which images of the model Eva Herzigova gratuitously invited the male gaze. Indeed, the lack of a sustained feminist backlash against the provocative nature of this image indicated that a distanced, ironic attitude had become the cultural norm. As such, sexism and patriarchal ideologies have re-emerged (if they ever went away) in a new and arguably more pernicious form. Rather than presenting itself as a monolithic structure that inscribes a natural order of being, patriarchal ideology at the turn of the twenty-first century presents itself as a diffuse, fragmented and vitiated discourse. However, despite mainstream culture's depictions of women as emancipated, they continue to be bound to the imperatives of the patriarchal market economy. As Florence states: 'no one wanted to admit it, but even now the highest status for women in New York was to be married to a rich man' (178). Beneath the layers of conspicuous consumption and lifestyle choices, the coordinates of 'success' continue to be determined by patriarchal authority and the economy. Later in the novel, in an uncharacteristic act of kindness, Florence gives a homeless woman 50 cents, observing that 'there was a hole in the woman, a hole that could never be filled, no different from her own empty space' (273). This moment is indicative of the often ambivalent tone of the novel as a whole. On the one hand, it offers a brief glimpse of the possibility of female solidarity irrespective of class difference. On the other hand, it demonstrates the extent to which Florence has internalized patriarchal ideologies insofar as she conceives of herself and other women as castrated beings or rather subjects of lack who are constantly denied wholeness. In a continuation of the theme of women and economics, in the following section, I will discuss Tama Janowitz's *Peyton Amberg* and the ways in which this novel questions women's freedom of choice within a world dominated by global systems of exchange.

Adultery and Domesticity

In *Peyton Amberg*, Tama Janowitz depicts a woman who possesses the financial security and nuclear family that Pamela lacks and has achieved

Florence's fantasy of gaining a wealthy husband. However, as the novel progresses, it becomes apparent that this is an idealized image that is soon disrupted by the banality of domestic life and the temptations of adultery. Indeed, this novel highlights the conflict between quotidian experience and the limitlessness of desire. Even when Peyton engages in extramarital relations, she is bound by guilt and unable to escape the limitations of patriarchal society. Rather than being possessed as legal property, she becomes a plaything of a succession of wealthy men. Consequently, the novel uncompromisingly portrays women as trapped in the double bind of constantly seeking self-sufficiency within patriarchal society yet failing to achieve satisfaction.

Unlike Pamela who has no fixed income and Florence who remains single and alone, Peyton Amberg is married to a relatively wealthy and successful dentist. However, Peyton feels increasingly suffocated within her life of banal domesticity and engages in a series of affairs with different men around the world. This text speaks to the concerns of Janowitz's earlier novels by confirming that the normative lifestyles that Pamela and Florence are expected to desire are illusory ideals. Even within her relatively privileged position, Peyton is subject to the twin ideologies of patriarchal society and the machinations of globalized capitalism. Following her marriage to Barry, Peyton continues to work as a travel agent but has little interest in her marital obligations of domesticity or motherhood. Indeed, she feels little affection for her son, thereby reaffirming Janowitz's critique of the 'naturalness' of the maternal bond begun in *The Male Cross-Dresser Support Group*. Peyton's working life signals a shift in the coordinates of women's oppression and indicates a degree of success for the feminist politics of the twentieth century. Indeed, Charlotte Perkins Gilman argued in 'Women and Economics' at the turn of the twentieth century that women must ensure independent financial security in order to separate the 'economic relation' from the 'sex relation'. This position was later taken up by Virginia Woolf in her seminal essay, 'A Room of One's Own'. However, despite this signifier of relative freedom, Peyton is ineluctably bound to her husband as a dependent due to her increasingly affluent lifestyle. This is supported by her fear of poverty. Espying a disruptive and obese family on a plane she imagines the horror of inhabiting a class lower than her own in a hyperbolic light:

> she imagined them returning to some poor hovel in a slum, creatures bred for eons to serve as peasant-workers, inhabiting the banks of petrochemical wastelands, fed on the rotting carcasses of chickens who in

turn had been fed on too many hormones. If she hadn't married Barry, that would definitely have been the route she was on.[22]

Despite the ostensible success of Gilman's call for women to ensure financial security through employment, Peyton's experience demonstrates that the economic imperative continues to dominate her life choices and indicates the lack of class mobility granted to single women. As discussed in the first chapter, fear has been elevated to the role of a cultural dominant that generates conditions of uncertainty and indecision leading to the reinscription of the status quo. Within these conditions, the only release Peyton finds is in a series of adulterous liaisons that ultimately leave her unfulfilled. Once again, Janowitz's satirical depiction of women's place in society exposes the ways in which women at the turn of the twenty-first century continue to be bound between the public sphere of waged labour and the private institution of marriage.

Following Gilman, labour and marriage would appear to stand in conflict with one another since the opportunity to work seemingly relieves women from financial dependency on men. However, as Suzanne Leonard argues, 'despite the record number of female workers now employed in contemporary American culture, the popular conception of marriage as the most vaunted and desirable institution in women's lives has changed little' (102). Leonard suggests that the popular conception of marriage is that it stands as a choice rather than a compromise for women. However, Janowitz is quick to subject this prevailing attitude to critique. Although Peyton is ostensibly given the choice to enter into marriage, her impoverished background and the promise of class mobility conspire to render this a false choice. This indicates that economic imperatives (even if not instigated at the level of dependency) continue to play a dominant role in women's lives. Indeed, as soon as Peyton agrees to marry Barry she is swiftly deprived of agency and treated as an object of exchange by his extended family. It swiftly becomes apparent that Grace, Barry's mother, will be planning the entire event: 'the whole concept, the wedding, seemed to be a public offering to a deranged, controlling, obsessive-compulsive god, who, in her case, was Grace' (157). Following the event that takes place in a blur of champagne, dancing and cake, Peyton realizes that 'what had taken place had happened to someone else, all that fuss, she might just as well not have been there at all; in fact, she didn't really feel she had been' (159). For centuries, the institution of marriage has been a site of conflict between economic allegiances and love. The significance of Janowitz's contribution is that this is a critique of marriage in an era when none should be necessary.

The institution of marriage within Western society has traditionally been one of economic and legal convenience that establishes normative sexual relations between individuals. As Peter Goodrich notes, 'at the beginning of our era of amorous laws [. . .] marriage was a property relation, a servitude of the feminine, an arrangement between fathers and not necessarily based upon any kind of affective relationship between the couple'.[23] However, in the twentieth century, marriage has increasingly been seen as expression of love, while the social and legal aspects are concealed. Although Peyton is initially attracted to Barry and is keen to find financial security by securing a wealthy husband, as the realization that she is dependent upon him becomes clear, her desire turns to disgust. However, despite escaping the boundaries of domestic servitude by engaging in a series of adulterous liaisons, Peyton soon discovers that devoid of her social status, she is adopted and discarded as an object by a series of men. When she reminisces about her sexual encounters, she realizes that the men she slept with had no interest in her subjectivity or wellbeing beyond the satisfaction of their own sexual appetites. At this point Peyton realizes how exposed and vulnerable she is and the bonds of marriage signify as shelter from a hostile world: 'her life had been a field of landmines that she had accidentally managed to avoid stepping on. She had not even known the landmines were out there [. . .] one misstep and walls would crumble around her' (295). However, rather than moralizing about extramarital affairs, Janowitz demonstrates that despite the status of adultery as a structural transgression of marriage, which offers the possibility of sexual liberation, it frequently functions as a system of patriarchal control. Peyton's seemingly transgressive acts generate guilt and fail to provide satisfaction, thereby reaffirming patriarchal rule and presenting marital relations as desirable and normative in the process.

Janowitz's text highlights the seemingly impossible double bind faced by women at the turn of the twenty-first century. On the one hand, within an alienating and increasingly fragmented, globalized world, the desire for companionship and economic security is more important than ever. On the other hand, seemingly liberating avenues of escape, including illicit affairs and adulterous relations, expose women to unrestrained currents of masculine desire and public condemnation. This is a theme that is increasingly acknowledged, not least by postfeminist shows such as *Sex and the City* that, for the most part, provide a sympathetic portrayal of single women who seek career success and celebrate their emancipated lifestyles. However, Janowitz's satiric fiction continues to present feminism as a key area for ongoing debate in the twenty-first century.

Concluding Remarks

Within the supposedly liberal Western society at the dawn of the twenty-first century, it is still relatively unusual to find women writing in either the satiric or comic tradition. As discussed above, women were traditionally supposed to appear amenable to the male gaze, rather than subjecting patriarchal norms to ridicule or critique. Against this cultural trend, Tama Janowitz has constructed an oeuvre that self-consciously adopts a masculine form in order to expose the continued subordination of women to critique. Despite appearing to be an increasingly vitiated discourse, patriarchal ideology has been submerged beneath postfeminist culture's celebration of fluidity, multiplicity and consumer lifestyles. Indeed, patriarchal ideology functions as a fantasy-structure of the One, which ineluctably works to preserve the status quo. Against this cultural dominant, Janowitz posits an urgent need to re-engage in collective feminist debate in order to confront the ongoing issues of class, ageing and marriage in the twenty-first century. Janowitz's satiric fiction indicates that there is far broader scope for criticism of postfeminist culture. Indeed, the cultural truism that women do not engage in satiric critique is a pernicious ideological construct that obfuscates a range of critical tools from usage by the feminist movement. Consequently, feminism remains an issue of paramount concern in the wake of postmodernism.

This ongoing concern with a cultural dominant that is seemingly rendered diffuse is reflected by all of the authors discussed in this book. Each writer works to reveal and undo the pernicious ideologies that continue to produce systems predicated on injustice and inequality within contemporary society. By looking back to the past, these writers challenge the conventions of the present and indicate new directions for literary critique. Although suspicious of the impact of postmodern culture on our lives, these writers refuse to engage in nostalgic returns to the monolithic ideologies of the past. As such these writers reconfigure satiric critique in order to make clear social and political interventions within an era clouded by mystifications, reflexivity, indeterminacy and the concomitant motivational deficit to be found in contemporary ethics and politics. Consequently, the arguments presented in *Ethics and Desire in the Wake of Postmodernism* connect the methods of literary practice employed by satirists writing in an era of indeterminacy and uncertainty to ongoing debates on the issues of fear, nihilism, revolution, ethics, enjoyment and feminism. Placing these issues at the forefront of literary debate provides insight into the ways in which authors at the turn of the twenty-first century make visible the naturalized ideologies of our time.

Notes

Introduction

1. Thomas Docherty, *After Theory* (Edinburgh: Edinburgh University Press, 1996), 1.
2. Alain Badiou, *The Century* (Cambridge: Polity, 2007), 6.
3. Jürgen Habermas, 'Modernity – An Incomplete Project' in *Postmodern Debates*, Hal Foster (ed.) (London: Pluto, 1985), 9.
4. Stephen Ross (ed.), *Modernism and Theory: A Critical Debate* (London: Routledge, 2008), 1–2.
5. Jacques Derrida, *Writing and Difference*, Alan Bass (trans.) (London: Routledge, 1978), 352.
6. Antonio Calcagno, *Badiou and Derrida: Politics, Events and Their Time* (London: Continuum, 2007), 50.
7. Josh Toth, *The Passing of Postmodernism: A Spectroanalysis of the Contemporary* (New York: SUNY Press, 2010), 38.
8. Jean-Francois Lyotard, *The Postmodern Condition: A Report on Knowledge*, G. Bennington and B. Massumi (trans.) (Minneapolis: University of Minneapolis Press, 1984), xxiv.
9. Jean-Luc Nancy, *The Birth to Presence*, Brian Holmes (trans.) (Stanford: Standford University Press, 1993), 144–5.
10. Jean Baudrillard, *The Gulf War Did Not Take Place*, Paul Patton (trans.) (Sydney: Power Institute of Fine Arts, 1995).
11. Harvie Ferguson, 'Glamour and the End of Irony' *The Hedgehog Review*, Fall 1999, 10–16.
12. Jacques Rancière, *The Emancipated Spectator*, Gregory Elliot (trans.) (London: Verso, 2009), 25.
13. Zygmunt Bauman, *Liquid Modernity* (Cambridge: Polity, 2000), 14.
14. Dustin Griffin, *Satire: A Critical Reintroduction* (Lexington: University Press of Kentucky, 1994), 6.
15. Horace and Persius, *The Satires of Horace and Persius*, Niall Rudd (trans.) (London: Penguin, 2005), 76.
16. John Dryden, *Works*, 4:79; hereafter cited in text by volume and page number.
17. Jacques Lacan, *Seminar XX: Encore: On Feminine Sexuality, The Limits of Love and Knowledge*, Bruce Fink (trans.) (London: Norton, 1998), 42.
18. Mladen Dolar, 'Hegel as the Other Side of Psychoanalysis' in *Jacques Lacan and the Other Side of Psychoanalysis: Reflections on Seminar XVII*, Justin Clemens and Russell Grigg (eds) (London: Duke University Press, 2006), 132.

19 Bruce Fink, 'Knowledge and Jouissance' in *Reading Seminar XX: Lacan's Major Work on Love, Knowledge, and Feminine Sexuality*, Susanne Barnard and Bruce Fink (eds) (New York: SUNY Press, 2002), 29.
20 Scott Wilson, *The Order of Joy* (New York: SUNY Press, 2008), xv.
21 Henri Bergson, *Laughter: An Essay on the Meaning of the Comic* (London: Macmillan, 1921), 9.
22 Alenka Zupančič, *The Odd One In* (London: Verso, 2008), 55–6.
23 Stewart Home, *Down & Out in Shoreditch and Hoxton* (London: Do-Not Press, 2004), 112.
24 See pages 105, 123, 126.
25 Northrop Frye, 'The Nature of Satire' *University of Toronto Quarterly*, 14 (1944), 78.
26 Sigmund Freud, 'Jokes and their Relation to the Unconscious' in *The Standard Edition of the Complete Psychological Works of Sigmund Freud*, Vol. 8, James Strachey (trans.) (London: Vintage, 1905), 119.
27 Sigmund Freud, 'Humour' in *The Standard Edition of the Complete Psychological Works of Sigmund Freud*, Vol. 21, James Strachey (trans.) (London: Vintage, 1927), 166.
28 Sigmund Freud, 'Civilisation and Its Discontents' in *The Standard Edition of the Complete Psychological Works of Sigmund Freud*, Vol. 21, James Strachey (trans.) (London: Vintage, 1930), 66.
29 Jacques Lacan, *Écrits*, Bruce Fink (trans.) (London: Norton, 2006), 324.
30 Slavoj Žižek, *The Sublime Object of Ideology* (London: Verso, 1989), 45.
31 Jacques Lacan, *Seminar XI: The Four Fundamental Concepts of Psychoanalysis*, Alan Sheridan (trans.) (London: Norton, 1981), 60.
32 Jacques Lacan, *My Teaching* (London: Verso, 2008), 65.
33 Michel Houellebecq, *The Possibility of an Island*, Gavin Bowd (trans.) (London: Phoenix, 2006), 323.
34 Gabriella van den Hoven, 'A Child Through the Mirror' in *The Later Lacan: An Introduction*, Veronique Voruz and Bogdan Wolf (eds) (New York: SUNY Press, 2007), 129.
35 Roland Barthes, *Mythologies*, Annette Lavers (trans.) (London: Vintage, 2000), 40.
36 Jacques Lacan, *Seminar VII: The Ethics of Psychoanalysis*, Dennis Porter (trans.) (London: Norton, 1992), 144.
37 Chuck Palahniuk, *Invisible Monsters* (London: Vintage, 2000), 54.
38 Slavoj Žižek, 'A Plea for Leninist Intolerance' *Critical Inquiry*, 28: 2 (2000), 545.
39 Slavoj Žižek, *The Parallax View* (Cambridge, MA: MIT Press, 2006), 347.
40 Sigmund Freud, 'Fetishism' in *The Standard Edition of the Complete Psychological Works of Sigmund Freud*, Vol. 21, James Strachey (trans.) (London: Vintage, 1927), 154.
41 F. R. Leavis, *The Great Tradition* (London: Chatto and Windus, 1948), 15.
42 Charles Dickens, *Bleak House* (London: Penguin, 1971), 13.
43 Alain-Philippe Durand and Naomi Mandel, *Novels of the Contemporary Extreme* (London: Continuum, 2006), 1.
44 Georges Bataille, *Eroticism*, Mary Dalwood (trans.) (London: Marion Boyars, 1987), 63.

Chapter 1

[1] Frank Furedi, *Culture of Fear Revisited: Risk-taking and the Morality of Low Expectation* (London: Continuum, 2006), 1.

[2] Brett Easton Ellis, *Lunar Park* (London: Picador, 2005), 30.

[3] Sigmund Freud, 'The Uncanny' in *The Standard Edition of the Complete Psychological Works of Sigmund Freud*, Vol. 17, James Strachey (trans.) (London: Vintage, 1919), 220.

[4] C. D. Broad, *Kant: An Introduction* (Cambridge: Cambridge University Press, 1978), 211.

[5] Sigmund Freud, 'The Antithetical Meaning of Primal Words' in *The Standard Edition of the Complete Psychological Works of Sigmund Freud*, Vol. 11, James Strachey (trans.) (London: Vintage, 1910), 161.

[6] For further examples and discussion of the family narrative see Slavoj Žižek, *In Defense of Lost Causes* (London: Verso, 2008), 52–94.

[7] See Sigmund Freud, 'On Narcissism: An Introduction.' *The Standard Edition of the Complete Psychological Works of Sigmund Freud*, Vol. 1, James Strachey (trans.) (London: 1953–1966), 67–104.

[8] Eva-Maria Simms, 'Uncanny Dolls: Images of Death in Rilke and Freud' in *New Literary History*, 27: 4, Autumn 1996, 671.

[9] Anthony Vidler, *The Architectural Uncanny: Essays in the Modern Unhomely* (Cambridge, MA: MIT Press, 1992), 17.

[10] Nicholas Royle, *The Uncanny* (Manchester: Manchester University Press, 2003), vii.

[11] For Freud's two versions of the myth of the primal horde and its leader see 'Totem and Taboo' and 'Moses and Monotheism' 13: 1–161 and 23: 3–140 respectively.

[12] Jacques Lacan, *Seminar XVII: The Other Side of Psychoanalysis*, Russell Grigg (trans.) (London: Norton, 2007), 127.

[13] Paul Verhaeghe, 'The Collapse of the Function of the Father and its Effect on Gender Roles' in *Sexuation*, Renata Salecl (ed.) (London: Duke University Press, 2000), 135.

[14] See Alain Badiou, *Logics of Worlds*, Alberto Toscano (trans.) (London: Continuum, 2009).

[15] Lorenzo Chiesa, *Subjectivity and Otherness* (Cambridge, MA: MIT Press, 2007), 35.

[16] Jacques-Alain Miller, 'Extimité' in *Lacanian Theory of Discourse: Subject, Structure and Society*, Mark Bracher, Marshall W. Alcorn, Jr., Ronald J. Corthell, and Françoise Massardier-Kenney (eds) (New York: New York University Press, 1994), 76.

[17] Jerry Flieger, *Is Oedipus Online? Siting Freud After Freud* (Cambridge, MA: MIT Press, 2005), 238.

[18] The small other is 'the other who is not really other, but a reflection and projection of the ego.' See Dylan Evans, *An Introductory Dictionary of Lacanian Psychoanalysis* (London: Routledge, 2006), 132–3.

[19] Albert Camus, *Camus at Combat: Writing 1944–1947*, Arthur Goldhammer (trans.) (Princeton: Princeton University Press, 2007), 257.

Chapter 2

1 Bülent Diken and Carsten Bagge Laustsen, *Enjoy Your Fight!* – *'Fight Club' as a Symptom of the Network Society* (Lancaster: Department of Sociology, Lancaster University, 2002).

2 Mark Bracher, 'Introduction' in *Lacanian Theory of Discourse: Subject, Structure and Society* Mark Bracher, Marshall W. Alcorn, Jr., Ronald J. Corthell, and Françoise Massardier-Kenney (eds) (New York: New York University Press, 1994), 1.

3 Chuck Palahniuk, *Fight Club* (London: Vintage, 2006), 41.

4 Fredric Jameson, *Postmodernism: Or, the Cultural Logic of Late Capitalism* (London: Verso, 1992), 202.

5 Jacques Lacan, *Seminar I: Freud's Papers on Technique,* John Forrester (trans.) (New York: Norton, 1991), 193.

6 Friedrich Nietzsche, *The Anti-Christ, Ecce Homo, Twilight of the Idols and Other Writings*, Judith Norman (trans.) (Cambridge: Cambridge University Press, 2005), 169.

7 Mladen Dolar, '"I Shall Be with You on Your Wedding-Night": Lacan and the Uncanny' in *October* Vol. 58, Rendering the Real (Autumn, 1991), 12.

8 Bice Benvenuto and Roger Kennedy, *The Works of Jacques Lacan: An Introduction* (London: Free Association Books, 1986), 62.

9 Philip Shaw, *The Sublime* (London: Routledge, 2006), 133.

10 Alenka Zupančič, *The Shortest Shadow: Nietzsche's Philosophy of the Two* (Cambridge, MA: MIT Press, 2003), 8.

11 Friedrich Nietzsche, *Thus Spoke Zarathustra*, R. J. Hollingdale (trans.) (Harmondsworth: Penguin, 2003), 336.

12 Theodore Adorno, *The Culture Industry: Selected Essays on Mass Culture* (London: Routledge, 2001), 99.

13 Slavoj Žižek, *For They Know Not What They Do: Enjoyment as a Political Factor* (London: Verso, 2002), lxxvii.

14 David Fontana, *Psychology, Religion, and Spirituality* (Oxford: Blackwell, 2003), 162.

Chapter 3

1 Fredric Jameson, *Postmodernism, or, The Cultural Logic of Late Capitalism* (London: Verso, 1991), 178.

2 J. G. Ballard, *Millennium People* (London: Harper Perennial, 2003), 5.

3 David Hawkes, *Ideology* (London: Routledge, 2003), 1.

4 Jean Baudrillard, *Simulacra and Simulation*, Sheila Faria Glaser (trans.) (Michigan: University of Michigan Press, 1994), 155.

5 Antonio Negri, *The Porcelain Workshop: For a New Grammar of Politics*, Noura Wedell (trans.) (Los Angeles: Semiotext(e), 2008), 21.

6 This is graphically demonstrated in Werner Herzog's documentary, *Grizzly Man*, in which Timothy Treadwell, a man who lives with bears in the wild, is inexplicably fascinated with the bear's excrement and openly perceives it to be a gift from the bears to him.

[7] Slavoj Žižek, *The Puppet and the Dwarf: The Perverse Core of Christianity* (Cambridge, MA: MIT Press, 2003), 130.

[8] Jean Baudrillard, *The Consumer Society* (London: SAGE, 1998), 75.

[9] Slavoj Žižek, *Violence: Six Sideways Reflections* (London: Profile, 2008), 1.

[10] David Cunningham, 'Obituary: J.G. Ballard, 1930–2009' in *Radical Philosophy* 156, July/August 2009, 66.

[11] This is supported by the recurrent promise of gap-year tours to aid the subject in the discovery of a 'new you' and orchestrate an 'escape to the real world'. See especially the literature provided by www.gapyear.com and www.i-to-i. com. Gap-year companies promise to free the subject from the constraints and boundaries of 'everyday' life. However, this apparent emancipation is a device that ultimately better integrates the individual into society, as demonstrated by the increased importance of extra-curricular travel ascribed by potential graduate employers.

[12] On 14th March 2007 the National Film Theatre was relaunched as the BFI Southbank, merging with the Museum of the Moving Image (MOMI). Interestingly, following MOMI's temporary closure in 1999, a letter to the *London Evening Standard* on 31st August 1999 claimed that this was cultural vandalism by the BFI. This was no doubt a significant influence on Ballard's rather more literal depiction of cultural vandalism.

[13] See Philip Tew, 'Situating the Violence of J.G. Ballard's Postmillennial Fiction: The Possibilities of Sacrifice, the Certainties of Trauma' in *J.G. Ballard: Contemporary Critical Perspectives*, Jeanette Baxter (ed.) (London: Continuum, 2008).

[14] Andrzej Gasiorek, *J.G. Ballard* (Manchester: Manchester University Press, 2005), 173.

[15] Jacques Lacan, *Seminar III: The Psychoses*, Russell Grigg (trans.) (London: Norton, 1993), 198.

[16] Slavoj Žižek, *The Plague of Fantasies* (London: Verso, 2008), ix.

Chapter 4

[1] Lewis Caroll, *Alice's Adventures in Wonderland and Through the Looking Glass* (London: Bloomsbury, 2003), xii–xiii.

[2] M. Hunter Hayes, *Understanding Will Self* (Columbia: University of South Carolina Press, 2007), 148.

[3] Will Self, *Dorian: An Imitation* (London: Penguin, 2002), 3.

[4] Peter Widdowson, '"Writing Back": Contemporary Re-visionary Fiction' in *Textual Practice* 20: 3 (2006), 304.

[5] Fredric Jameson, *The Cultural Turn* (London: Verso, 2009), 7.

[6] Stephen Connor, 'Rewriting Wrong: On the Ethics of Literary Reversion' in *Postmodern Literary Theory: An Anthology*, Niall Lucy (ed.) (Oxford: Blackwell, 2000), 124.

[7] Jean-François Lyotard, *The Postmodern Condition*, Geoff Bennington and Brian Massumi (trans.) (Minneapolis: University of Minnesota Press, 1984), xxiv.

8 Zygmunt Bauman, *Postmodern Ethics* (Oxford: Blackwell, 1993), 3.

9 Jean Baudrillard, *Simulacra and Simulation*, Sheila Faria Glaser (trans.) (Michigan: University of Michigan Press, 1994), 6.

10 Jean Baudrillard, *America*, Chris Turner (trans.) (London: Verso, 2010), 121.

11 Walter Benjamin, *Illuminations*, Harry Zorn (trans.) (London: Pimlico, 1999), 215.

12 Lisa Downing and Libby Saxton, *Film and Ethics: Foreclosed Encounters* (London: Routledge, 2010), 148.

13 Fredric Jameson, *Postmodernism, or the Cultural Logic of Late Capitalism* (London: Verso, 1991), 76.

14 Jean Baudrillard, *The Gulf War Did Not Take Place*, Paul Patto (trans.) (Sydney: Power Institute of Fine Arts, 1995), 27.

15 Alain Badiou, *Ethics: An Essay on the Understanding of Evil*, Peter Hallward (trans.) (London: Verso, 2001), 10.

16 Will Self, *Feeding Frenzy* (London: Viking, 2001), 317.

17 Jacques Lacan, *Écrits*, Bruce Fink (trans.) (London: Norton, 2006), 89.

18 Rowena Chapman, 'The Great Pretender: Variations on the New Man Theme' in *Male Order: Unwrapping Masculinity*, Rowena Chapman and Jonathan Rutherford (eds) (London: Lawrence & Wishart, 1988), 226.

19 Mark Simpson, *Male Impersonators* (London: Cassell, 1994), 95.

20 Jean Baudrillard, *Symbolic Exchange and Death*, Iain Hamilton Grant (trans.) (London: SAGE, 1993), 84.

21 Slavoj Žižek, *The Sublime Object of Ideology* (London: Verso, 2008), xxiv.

22 David Alderson, '"Not Everyone Knows Fuck All About Foucault": Will Self's *Dorian* and Post-Gay Culture' in *Textual Practice* 19: 3 (2005), 319.

23 Walter Pater, *The Renaissance: Studies in Art and Poetry* (Oxford: Oxford University Press, 1986), 152.

24 Friedrich Nietzsche, *On the Genealogy of Morality*, Carol Diethe (trans.) (Cambridge: Cambridge University, 1994), 21.

25 Raymond Geuss, 'Review of Alain Badiou's *Ethics*' in *The European Journal of Philosophy* 9: 3 (2001), 389.

26 Alain Badiou, *Being and Event*, Oliver Feltham (trans.) (London: Continuum, 2005), 179.

27 Note 'evental' (événementiel) is a translator's neologism to signify 'of the event'.

28 Jacques Lacan, *Seminar VII: The Ethics of Psychoanalysis*, Dennis Potter (trans.) (London: Norton, 1992), 20.

29 Jacques Lacan, *Seminar III: The Psychoses*, Russell Grigg (trans.) (London: Norton, 1993), 226.

Chapter 5

1 Michel Houellebecq, *Platform*, Frank Wynne (trans.) (London: Vintage, 2003), 29.

2 Gretchen Rous Besser, '*Platforme* by Michel Houellebecq' in *The Paris Review* 76: 3 (2003), 641.

³ Katherine Gantz, 'Strolling with Houellebecq: The Textual Terrain of Postmodern *Flânerie*' in *Journal of Modern Literature* 28: 3 (2005), 149.

⁴ Jean-Charles Rochet and Jean Tirole, 'Platform Competition in Two-Sided Markets' in *Journal of the European Economic Association* 1: 4 (2001), 990.

⁵ Bruce Fink, *The Lacanian Subject: Between Language and Jouissance* (Princeton: Princeton University Press, 1995), 99.

⁶ Slavoj Žižek, *The Sublime Object of Ideology* (London: Verso, 1989), 54.

⁷ Sigmund Freud, 'Group Psychology and the Analysis of the Ego' in *The Standard Edition of the Complete Psychological Works of Sigmund Freud*, Vol. 18, James Strachey (trans.) (London: Vintage, 1921), 107.

⁸ Jacques Lacan, *Seminar XVII: The Other Side of Psychoanalysis*, Russell Grigg (trans.) (London: Norton, 2007), 46.

⁹ Alenka Zupančič, 'When Surplus Enjoyment Meets Surplus Value' in *Reflections on Seminar XVII: Jacques Lacan and the Other Side of Psychoanalysis*, Justin Clemens and Russell Grigg (eds) (London: Duke University Press, 2006), 157.

¹⁰ Michel Houellebecq quoted in *The Guardian* (17th September 2005).

¹¹ Slavoj Žižek, '*Objet a* in Social Links' *Reflections on Seminar XVII: Jacques Lacan and the Other Side of Psychoanalysis*, Justin Clemens and Russell Grigg (eds) (London: Duke University Press, 2006), 117.

¹² Sigmund Freud, 'Totem and Taboo' in *The Standard Edition of the Complete Psychological Works of Sigmund Freud*, Vol. 13, James Strachey (trans.) (London: Vintage, 1921), 143.

¹³ Alain Badiou, *Ethics: An Essay on the Understanding of Evil*, Peter Hallward (trans.) (London: Verso, 2001), 24.

¹⁴ Michael Hardt and Antonio Negri, *Multitude: War and Democracy in the Age of Empire* (London: Penguin, 2006), 66.

¹⁵ Paolo Virno, *A Grammar of the Multitude: For an Analysis of Contemporary Forms of Life*, Isabella Bertoletti (trans.) (Los Angeles: Semiotext(e), 2004), 103.

¹⁶ Julia O'Connell Davidson, *Prostitution, Power and Freedom* (Cambridge: Polity, 1998), 76.

¹⁷ Slavoj Žižek, *Violence: Six Sideways Reflections* (London: Profile, 2008), 9.

¹⁸ Jacques-Alain Miller, 'Extimité' in *Lacanian Theory of Discourse: Subject, Structure and Society*, Mark Bracher, Marshall W. Alcorn, Jr., Ronald J. Corthell, and Françoise Massardier-Kenney (eds) (New York: New York University Press, 1994), 79.

¹⁹ Jacques Lacan, *Seminar VII: The Ethics of Psychoanalysis*, Dennis Porter (trans.) (New York: Norton, 1992), 52.

²⁰ Edward Said, *The Politics of Dispossession: The Struggle for Palestinian Self-Determination 1969–1994* (London: Vintage, 1995), 61.

²¹ Martin Oppermann, *Sex Tourism and Prostitution: Aspects of Leisure, Recreation and Work* (New York: Cognizant Communication, 1998), 20.

²² Graham Dann, *The Language of Tourism* (London: CAB International, 1996), 127.

Chapter 6

¹ Tama Janowitz, *Area Code 212: New York Days, New York Nights* (London: Bloomsbury, 2002), 109.

2   Misha Kavka, 'Introduction' in *Feminist Consequences: Theory for the New Century*, Elisabeth Bronfen and Misha Kavka (eds) (New York: Columbia University Press, 2001), xi.

3   Interview with Luce Irigaray in Gillian Howie, *Third Wave Feminism: A Critical Exploration*, Stacy Gillis, Gillian Howie and Rebecca Munford (eds) (Basingstoke: Palgrave Macmillan, 2007), 283.

4   Stacy Gillis, Gillian Howie and Rebecca Munford (eds), *Third Wave Feminism: A Critical Exploration* (Basingstoke: Palgrave Macmillan, 2007), xxi.

5   Alison Stone, 'On the Genealogy of Women: A Defence of Anti-Essentialism' in *Third Wave Feminism: A Critical Exploration*. Stacy Gillis, Gillian Howie and Rebecca Munford (eds) (Basingstoke: Palgrave Macmillan, 2007), 16.

6   Diane Negra and Yvonne Tasker, 'Feminist Politics and Postfeminist Culture' in *Interrogating Postfeminism: Gender and the Politics of Popular Culture*, Yvonne Tasker and Diane Negra (eds) (London: Duke University Press, 2007), 22.

7   Lisa Wilson, 'British Women Writing Satirical Novels in the Romantic Period: Gendering Authorship and Narrative Voice', *Romantic Textualities: Literature and Print Culture, 1780–1840* 17, Summer 2007, 25.

8   Gary Dyer, *British Satire and the Politics of Style, 1789–1832* (Cambridge: Cambridge University Press, 1997), 151.

9   Laura Mulvey, *Visual and Other Pleasures* (Basingstoke: Palgrave Macmillan, 2009), 15.

10 Ethel Sloane, *Biology of Women* (London: Virago, 1999), 50.

11 Richard Dyer, *White: Essays on Race and Culture* (London: Routledge, 1997), 26.

12 Jonathan Swift, *Poems* (London: Everyman, 1998), 86.

13 Tama Janowitz, *The Male Cross-Dresser Support Group* (Basingstoke: Picador, 1992), 74.

14 Elizabeth Wright, *Lacan and Postfeminism* (Cambridge: Icon, 2000), 31–2.

15 Stéphanie Genz and Benjamin A. Brabon, *Postfeminism: Cultural Texts and Theories* (Edinburgh: Edinburgh University Press, 2009), 166.

16 Suzanne Leonard, '"I Hate My Job, I Hate Everybody Here" Adultery, Boredom, and the Working Girl in Twenty-First Century American Cinema', *Interrogating Postfeminism: Gender and the Politics of Popular Culture*, Yvonne Tasker and Diane Negra (eds) (London: Duke University Press, 2007), 101.

17 Diane Negra, *What a Girl Wants? Fantasizing the Reclamation of Self in Postfeminism* (London: Routledge, 2009), 30.

18 Steven Best and Douglas Kellner, *Postmodern Theory: Critical Interrogations* (London: Macmillan, 1991), 207.

19 Linda Hutcheon, *The Politics of Postmodernism* (London: Routledge, 2002), 22.

20 Tama Janowitz, *A Certain Age* (London: Bloomsbury, 1999), 6.

21 Angela McRobbie, 'Postfeminism and Popular Culture: Bridget Jones and the New Gender Regime', *Interrogating Postfeminism: Gender and the Politics of Popular Culture*, Yvonne Tasker and Diane Negra (eds) (London: Duke University Press, 2007), 32.

22 Tama Janowitz, *Peyton Amberg* (London: Bloomsbury, 2003), 11.

23 Peter Goodrich, *The Laws of Love: A Brief Historical and Practical Manual* (Basingstoke: Palgrave Macmillan, 2006), 143.

Bibliography

Adorno, Theodor, *The Culture Industry: Selected Essays on Mass Culture* (London: Routledge, 2001).

Alderson, David, '"Not Everyone Knows Fuck All About Foucault": Will Self's *Dorian* and Post-Gay Culture', *Textual Practice* (2005) 19 (3), 309–30.

Azari, Ehsan, *Lacan and the Destiny of Literature: Desire Jouissance and the Sinthome, Donne, Joyce and Ashbery* (London: Continuum, 2008).

Badiou, Alain, *Ethics: An Essay on the Understanding of Evil*, Peter Hallward (trans.) (London: Verso, 2001).

— *Saint Paul: The Foundation of Universalism*, Ray Brassier (trans.) (Stanford: Stanford University Press, 2003).

— *Being and Event*, Oliver Feltham (trans.) (London: Continuum, 2005).

— *The Century*, Alberto Toscano (trans.) (Cambridge: Polity, 2007).

— *Logics of Worlds*, Alberto Toscano (trans.) (London: Continuum, 2008).

Ballard, J. G., *Running Wild* (New York: Farrar, Straus and Giroux, 1988).

— *Cocaine Nights* (London: Harper Perennial, 1996).

— *Super-Cannes* (London: Harper Perennial, 2000).

— *Millennium People* (London: Harper Perennial, 2003).

— *Kingdom Come* (London: Harper Perennial, 2006).

Barthes, Roland, *Mythologies*, Annette Lavers (trans.) (London: Vintage, 1972).

Bataille, Georges, *Eroticism*, Mary Dalwood (trans.) (London: Marion Boyars, 1987).

Baudrillard, Jean, *Symbolic Exchange and Death*, Iain Hamilton Grant (trans.) (London: SAGE, 1993).

— *Simulacra and Simulation*, Sheila Faria Glaser (trans.) (Michigan: University of Michigan Press, 1994).

— *The Gulf War Did Not Take Place*, Paul Patton (trans.) (Sydney: Power Institute of Fine Arts, 1995).

— *The Consumer Society: Myths and Structures*, George Ritzer (trans.) (London: SAGE, 1998).

— *America*, Chris Turner (trans.) (London: Verso, 2010).

Bauman, Zygmunt, *Postmodern Ethics* (Oxford: Blackwell, 1993).

— *Liquid Modernity* (Cambridge: Polity, 2000).

— *Liquid Times: Living in an Age of Uncertainty* (Cambridge: Polity, 2007).

Benjamin, Walter, *Illuminations*, Harry Zorn (trans.) (London: Pimlico, 1999).

Benvenuto, Bice and Roger Kennedy, *The Works of Jacques Lacan: An Introduction* (London: Free Association Books, 1986).

Bergson, Henri, *Laughter: An Essay on the Meaning of the Comic* (London: Macmillan, 1921).

Besser, Gretchen Rous, '*Platforme* by Michel Houellebecq', *The French Review* (2003) 76 (3), 640–1.

Best, Steven and Douglas Kellner, *Postmodern Theory: Critical Interrogations* (London: Macmillan, 1991).

Bosteels, Bruno, 'The Jargon of Finitude: Or, Materialism Today', *Radical Philosophy* (2009) 155, 41–7.

Bracher, Mark, 'Introduction' in *Lacanian Theory of Discourse: Subject, Structure and Society* Mark Bracher, Marshall W. Alcorn, Jr., Ronald J. Corthell and Françoise Massardier-Kenney (eds) (New York: New York University Press, 1994).

Broad, C. D., *Kant: An Introduction* (Cambridge: Cambridge University Press, 1978).

Bürger, Peter, *Theory of the Avant-Garde*, Michael Shaw (trans.) (Minneapolis: University of Minnesota Press, 1984).

Butler, Judith, *Gender Trouble: Feminism and the Subversion of Identity* (London: Routledge, 1999).

— *Giving an Account of Oneself* (New York: Fordham University Press, 2005).

Camus, Albert, *Camus at Combat: Writing 1944–1947*, Arthur Goldhammer (trans.) (Princeton: Princeton University Press, 2007).

Chapman, Rowena, 'The Great Pretender: Variations on the New Man Theme', in *Male Order: Unwrapping Masculinity*, Rowena Chapman and Jonathan Rutherford (eds) (London: Lawrence & Wishart, 1988), pp. 225–48.

Chiesa, Lorenzo, *Subjectivity and Otherness: A Philosophical Reading of Lacan* (Cambridge, MA: MIT Press, 2007).

Connell, R. W., *Masculinities* (Cambridge: Polity, 1995).

Connor, Steven, 'Rewriting Wrong: On the Ethics of Literary Reversion', in *Postmodern Literary Theory: An Anthology*, Niall Lucy (ed.) (Oxford: Blackwell, 2000), pp. 123–39.

Cunningham, David, 'Obituary: J.G. Ballard, 1930–2009', *Radical Philosophy* (2009) 156, 66–8.

Dann, Graham, *The Language of Tourism* (London: CAB International, 1996).

Davidson, Julia O'Connell, *Prostitution, Power and Freedom* (Cambridge: Polity, 1998).

Dean, Tim, *Beyond Sexuality* (Chicago: University of Chicago Press, 2000).

Deleuze, Gilles, and Felix Guattari, *Anti-Oedipus*, Robert Hurley, Mark Seem and Helen R. Lane (trans.) (London: Continuum, 1984).

— *A Thousand Plateaus*, Brian Massumi (trans.) (London: Continuum, 1987).

Derrida, Jacques, *Writing and Difference*, Alan Bass (trans.) (London: Routledge, 1978).

— 'Sending: on Representation', Peter and Mary Ann Caws (trans.), *Social Research* (1982) 49 (2), 294–326.

— *Positions*, Alan Bass (trans.) (London: Continuum, 2004).

Dews, Peter, *Logics of Disintegration: Post-Structuralist Thought and the Claims of Critical Theory* (London: Verso, 1987).

Dickens, Charles, *Bleak House* (London: Penguin, 2003).

Diken, Bülent, *Nihilism* (London: Routledge, 2009).

Dolar, Mladen, '"I Shall Be with You on Your Wedding-Night": Lacan and the Uncanny', *October* (1991) 58: Rendering the Real, 5–23.

— *A Voice and Nothing More* (London: MIT Press, 2006).

— 'Hegel as the Other Side of Psychoanalysis', in *Jacques Lacan and the Other Side of Psychoanalysis: Reflections on Seminar XVII,* Justin Clemens and Russell Grigg (eds) (London: Duke University Press, 2006), pp. 129–54.

Downing, Lisa and Libby Saxton, *Film and Ethics: Foreclosed Encounters* (London: Routledge, 2010).

Durand, Alain-Philippe and Naomi Mandel, *Novels of the Contemporary Extreme* (London: Continuum, 2006).

Dyer, Gary, *British Satire and the Politics of Style, 1789–1832* (Cambridge: Cambridge University Press, 1997).

Dyer, Richard, *White: Essays on Race and Culture* (London: Routledge, 1997).

Ellis, Bret Easton, *Less Than Zero* (London: Picador, 1985).

— *American Psycho* (London: Picador, 1991).

— *Glamorama* (London: Picador, 1998).

— *Lunar Park* (London: Picador, 2005).

Epps, Brad, 'The Fetish of Fluidity', in *Homosexuality and Psychoanalysis*, Tim Dean and Christopher Lane (eds) (Chicago: University of Chicago Press, 2001), pp. 412–31.

Evans, Dylan, *An Introductory Dictionary of Lacanian Psychoanalysis* (London: Routledge, 1996).

Fink, Bruce, *The Lacanian Subject: Between Language and Jouissance* (Princeton: Princeton University Press, 1995).

— 'Knowledge and Jouissance', in *Reading Seminar XX: Lacan's Major Work on Love, Knowledge, and Feminine Sexuality*, Suzanne Barnard and Bruce Fink (eds) (New York: SUNY Press, 2002), pp. 21–46.

— 'Perversion', in *Perversion and the Social Relation*, Molly Anne Rothenberg, Dennis A. Foster and Slavoj Žižek (eds) (London: Duke University Press, 2003), pp. 38–67.

— *Lacan to the Letter: Reading Écrits Closely* (Minnesota: University of Minnesota Press, 2004).

Flieger, Jerry, *Is Oedipus Online? Siting Freud After Freud* (Cambridge, MA: MIT Press, 2005).

Fontana, David, *Psychology, Religion, and Spirituality* (Oxford: Blackwell, 2003).

Foucault, Michel, 'The Birth of Biopolitics', in *Ethics: Essential Works of Foucault 1954–1984*, Paul Rabinow (trans.) (London: Penguin, 1997), pp. 73–81.

Freud, Sigmund, 'Jokes and Their Relation to the Unconscious', in *The Standard Edition of the Complete Psychological Works of Sigmund Freud: Vol. 8,* James Strachey (trans.) (London: Vintage, 1905).

— 'The Antithetical Meaning of Primal Words', in *The Standard Edition of the Complete Psychological Works of Sigmund Freud: Vol. 11,* James Strachey (trans.) (London: Vintage, 1910), pp. 153–62.

— 'Totem and Taboo', in *The Standard Edition of the Complete Psychological Works of Sigmund Freud: Vol. 13,* James Strachey (trans.) (London: Vintage, 1913), pp. 1–161.

— 'On Narcissism: An Introduction', in *The Standard Edition of the Complete Psychological Works of Sigmund Freud: Vol. 14,* James Strachey (ed.) (London: Vintage, 1914), pp. 67–104.

— 'The Uncanny', in *The Standard Edition of the Complete Psychological Works of Sigmund Freud: Vol. 17*, James Strachey (trans.) (London: Vintage, 1919), pp. 217–52.

— 'Group Psychology and the Analysis of the Ego', in *The Standard Edition of the Complete Psychological Works of Sigmund Freud: Vol. 18*, James Strachey (trans.) (London: Vintage, 1921), pp. 65–144.

— 'Fetishism', in *The Standard Edition of the Complete Psychological Works of Sigmund Freud: Vol. 21*, James Strachey (trans.) (London: Vintage, 1927), pp. 147–58.

— 'Civilisation and Its Discontents', in *The Standard Edition of the Complete Psychological Works of Sigmund Freud: Vol. 21*, James Strachey (trans.) (London: Vintage, 1930), pp. 57–146.

— 'Humour', in *The Standard Edition of the Complete Psychological Works of Sigmund Freud: Vol. 21*, James Strachey (trans.) (London: Vintage, 1927), pp. 159–66.

— 'Moses and Monotheism', in *The Standard Edition of the Complete Psychological Works of Sigmund Freud: Vol. 23*, James Strachey (ed.) (London: Vintage, 1939), pp. 1–138.

— 'Splitting of the Ego in the Process of Defence', in *The Standard Edition of the Complete Psychological Works of Sigmund Freud: Vol. 23*, James Strachey (trans.) (London: Vintage, 1940), pp. 271–8.

Frye, Northrop, 'The Nature of Satire', *University of Toronto Quarterly* (1944) 14, 75–89.

Gantz, Katherine, 'Strolling with Houellebecq: The Textual Terrain of Postmodern *Flânerie*', *Journal of Modern Literature* (2005) 28 (3), 149–61.

Gasiorek, Andrzej, *J.G. Ballard* (Manchester: Manchester University Press, 2005).

Genz, Stéphanie, and Benjamin A. Brabon, *Postfeminism: Cultural Texts and Theories* (Edinburgh: Edinburgh University Press, 2009).

Geuss, Raymond, 'Review of Alain Badiou's *Ethics*', *The European Journal of Philosophy* (2001) 9 (3), 408–12.

Gilbert, S. M. and Susan Gubar, *The Madwoman in the Attic: The Woman Writer and the Nineteenth-Century Literary Imagination* (New Haven: Yale University Press, 2000).

Gillis, Stacy, Gillian Howie and Rebecca Munford, 'Introduction', in *Third Wave Feminism: A Critical Exploration*, Stacy Gillis, Gillian Howie and Rebecca Munford (eds) (Basingstoke: Palgrave Macmillan, 2007), pp. 283–92.

Goodrich, Peter, *The Laws of Love: A Brief Historical and Practical Manual* (Basingstoke: Palgrave Macmillan, 2006).

Gregson, Ian, *Character and Satire in Postwar Fiction* (London: Continuum, 2006).

Griffin, Dustin, *Satire: A Critical Reintroduction* (Lexington: University Press of Kentucky, 1994).

Grigg, Russell, *Lacan, Language and Philosophy* (New York: SUNY Press, 2008).

Harbord, Janet, 'Performing Parts: Gender and Sexuality in Recent Fiction and Theory', *Women: A Cultural Review* (1996) 7 (1), 39–47.

Hardt, Michael, and Antonio Negri, *Empire* (Cambridge, MA: Harvard University Press, 2000).

— *Multitude: War and Democracy in the Age of Empire* (London: Penguin, 2006).

Harris, Charles, 'PoMo's Wake I', *American Book Review* (2002) 23 (2), 1–3.

Harvey, David, *A Brief History of Neoliberalism* (Oxford: Oxford University Press, 2005).

Hawkes, David, *Ideology* (London: Routledge, 2003).

Hayes, M. H., *Understanding Will Self* (Columbia: University of South Carolina Press, 2007).

Hewlett, Nick, *Badiou, Balibar, Rancière: Re-thinking Emancipation* (London: Continuum, 2007).

Higgins, Lynn and Brenda Silver, *Rape and Representation* (New York: Columbia University Press, 1991).

Home, Stewart, *Down & Out in Shoreditch and Hoxton* (London: Do-Not Press, 2004).

Horace and Persius, *The Satires of Horace and Persius*, Niall Rudd (trans.) (Harmondsworth: Penguin, 1973).

Houellebecq, Michel, *Atomised*, Frank Wynne (trans.) (London: Vintage, 2001).

— *Platform*, Frank Wynne (trans.) (London: Vintage, 2003).

— *Lanzarote*, Frank Wynne (trans.) (London: Vintage, 2004).

— *The Possibility of an Island*, Gavin Bowd (trans.) (London: Phoenix, 2006).

Hoven, Gabriela van den, 'A Child Through the Mirror', in *The Later Lacan: An Introduction*, Véronique Voruz and Bogdan Wolf (eds) (New York: SUNY Press, 2007), pp. 128–36.

Howie, Gillian, 'Interview with Luce Irigaray', in *Third Wave Feminism: A Critical Exploration*. Stacy Gillis, Gillian Howie and Rebecca Munford (eds) (Basingstoke: Palgrave Macmillan, 2007), pp. 283–92.

Hutcheon, Linda, *The Politics of Postmodernism* (London: Routledge, 2002).

Huyssen, Andreas, *After the Great Divide* (Bloomington: Indiana University Press, 1987).

Irigaray, Luce, *This Sex Which is Not One*, Catherine Porter and Carolyn Burke (trans.) (New York: Cornell University Press, 1985).

— 'The Three Genres', in *Postmodern Literary Theory: An Anthology*, Niall Lucy (ed.) (Oxford: Blackwell, 2000), pp. 149–61.

— *An Ethics of Sexual Difference*, Carolyn Burke and Gillian C. Gill (trans.) (London: Continuum, 2004).

James, Henry, *The Turn of the Screw* (New York: Norton, 1999).

Jameson, Fredric, *Postmodernism, or the Cultural Logic of Late Capitalism* (London: Verso, 1991).

— *The Cultural Turn: Selected Writings on the Postmodern 1983–1998* (London: Verso, 1998).

Janowitz, Tama, *The Male Cross-Dresser Support Group* (Basingstoke: Picador, 1992).

— *A Certain Age* (London: Bloomsbury, 1999).

— *Area Code 212: New York Days, New York Nights* (London: Bloomsbury, 2002).

— *Peyton Amberg* (London: Bloomsbury, 2003).

Joyce, James, *Ulysses* (Oxford: Oxford University Press, 1993).

Kavka, Misha, 'Introduction', in *Feminist Consequences: Theory for the New Century*, Elisabeth Bronfen and Misha Kavka (eds) (New York: Columbia University Press, 2001), pp. ix–xxvi.

Kearney, Richard, 'Dialogue with Jacques Derrida', in *Dialogues with Contemporary Continental Thinkers* (Manchester: Manchester University Press, 1986), pp. 113–35.

Klein, Richard, 'Gender and Sexuation', *Lacanian Ink* (2001) 18, 30–41.

Kordela, A. Kiarina, *Surplus: Spinoza, Lacan* (New York: SUNY Press, 2007).

Lacan, Jacques, *The Language of the Self: The Function of Language in Psychoanalysis*, Anthony Wilden (trans.) (Baltimore: John Hopkins University Press, 1968).
— *Écrits: A Selection*, Alan Sheridan (trans.) (London: Routledge, 1977).
— *Seminar XI: The Four Fundamental Concepts of Psychoanalysis*, Alan Sheridan (trans.) (London: Norton, 1981).
— *Seminar I: Freud's Papers on Technique*, John Forrester (trans.) (London: Norton, 1988).
— *Seminar VII: The Ethics of Psychoanalysis*, Dennis Porter (trans.) (London: Norton, 1992).
— *Seminar III: The Psychoses*, Russell Grigg (trans.) (London: Norton, 1993).
— *Seminar XX: Encore: On Feminine Sexuality* (London: Norton, 1998).
— *Écrits*, Bruce Fink (trans.) (London: Norton, 2006).
— *Seminar XVII: The Other Side of Psychoanalysis*, Russell Grigg (trans.) (London: Norton, 2007).
— *My Teaching*, David Macey (trans.) (London: Verso, 2008).
Leavis, F. R., *The Great Tradition* (London: Chatto and Windus, 1948).
Leonard, Suzanne, ' "I Hate My Job, I Hate Everybody Here" Adultery, Boredom, and the "Working Girl" in Twenty-First-Century American Cinema', in *Interrogating Postfeminism: Gender and the Politics of Popular Culture*, Yvonne Tasker and Diane Negra (eds) (London: Duke University Press, 2007), pp. 100–31.
Lyotard, Jean-François, *The Postmodern Condition: A Report on Knowledge*, Geoff Bennington and Brian Massumi (trans.) (Minneapolis: University of Minneapolis Press, 1984).
Mannoni, Octave, 'I Know Well but All the Same . . .', in *Perversion and the Social Relation*, Molly Anne Rothenberg, Dennis A. Foster and Slavoj Žižek (eds) (London: Duke University Press, 2003), pp. 68–92.
McLaughlin, Robert, 'Post-Postmodern Discontent: Contemporary Fiction and the Social World', *Symploke* (2004) 12 (1–2), 53–64.
McRobbie, Angela, 'Postfeminism and Popular Culture: Bridget Jones and the New Gender Regime', in *Interrogating Postfeminism: Gender and the Politics of Popular Culture*, Yvonne Tasker and Diane Negra (eds) (London: Duke University Press, 2007), pp. 27–39.
Miller, Jacques-Alain, 'Extimité', in *Lacanian Theory of Discourse: Subject, Structure and Society*, Mark Bracher, Marshall W. Alcorn, Jr., Ronald J. Corthell and Françoise Massardier-Kenney (eds) (New York: New York University Press, 1994), pp. 74–87.
Morel, Geneviève, 'Psychoanalytical Anatomy', in *Sexuation*, Renata Salecl (ed.) (London: Duke University Press, 2000), pp. 28–38.
Mulvey, Laura, *Visual and Other Pleasures* (Basingstoke: Palgrave Macmillan, 2009).
Nancy, Jean-Luc, *The Birth to Presence*, Brian Holmes et al. (trans.) (Stanford: Standford University Press, 1993).
Negra, Diane, *What a Girl Wants? Fantasizing the Reclamation of Self in Postfeminism* (London: Routledge, 2009).
Negra, Diane, and Yvonne Tasker, 'Feminist Politics and Postfeminist Culture', in *Interrogating Postfeminism: Gender and the Politics of Popular Culture*, Yvonne

Tasker and Diane Negra (eds) (London: Duke University Press, 2007), pp. 1–26.

Negri, Antonio, *The Porcelain Workshop: For a New Grammar of Politics*, Noura Wedell (trans.) (Los Angeles: Semiotext(e), 2008).

— *Goodbye Mr. Socialism: Radical Politics in the 21st Century*, Peter Thomas (trans.) (London: Seven Stories Press, 2008).

Nemser, Cindy, 'A Conversation with Eva Hesse', in *Eva Hesse*, Mignon Nixon (ed.) (Cambridge, MA: MIT Press, 2002), pp. 1–27.

Nietzsche, Friedrich, *Thus Spoke Zarathustra*, R. J. Hollingdale (trans.) (London: Penguin, 1961).

— *On the Genealogy of Morality*, Carol Diethe (trans.) (Cambridge: Cambridge University Press, 1994).

— *The Anti-Christ, Ecce Homo, Twilight of the Idols and Other Writings*, Judith Norman (trans.) (Cambridge: Cambridge University Press, 2005).

Oppermann, Martin, *Sex Tourism and Prostitution: Aspects of Leisure, Recreation, and Work* (New York: Cognizant Communication, 1998).

Palahniuk, Chuck, *Fight Club* (London: Vintage, 1997).

— *Invisible Monsters* (London: Vintage, 2000).

— *Choke* (London: Vintage, 2002).

— *Lullaby* (London: Vintage, 2003).

Pater, Walter, *The Renaissance: Studies in Art and Poetry* (Oxford: Oxford University Press, 1986).

Plato, *The Symposium*, Christopher Gill (trans.) (London: Penguin, 1999).

Pluth, Ed, *Signifiers and Acts: Freedom in Lacan's Theory of the Subject* (New York: SUNY Press, 2007).

Rancière, Jacques, *The Emancipated Spectator*, Gregory Elliot (trans.) (London: Verso, 2009).

Rochet, Jean-Charles, and Jean Tirole, 'Platform Competition in Two-Sided Markets', *Journal of the European Economic Association* (2001) 1 (4), 990–1029.

Rose, Jacqueline, *Sexuality in the Field of Vision* (London: Verso, 2005).

Royle, Nicholas, *The Uncanny* (Manchester: Manchester University Press, 2003).

Said, Edward, *The Politics of Dispossession: The Struggle for Palestinian Self-Determination 1969–1994* (London: Vintage, 1995).

Salecl, Renata, *Perversions of Love and Hate* (London: Verso, 1998).

— *Sexuation* (London: Duke University Press, 2000).

Sedgwick, Eve Kosofsky, *Tendencies* (London: Duke University Press, 1993).

Self, Will, *Cock and Bull* (London: Penguin, 1993).

— *Feeding Frenzy* (London: Viking, 2001).

— *Dorian: An Imitation* (London: Penguin, 2002).

— *Junk Mail* (London: Bloomsbury, 2006).

Shaw, Philip, *The Sublime* (London: Routledge, 2006).

Simms, Eva-Maria, 'Uncanny Dolls: Images of Death in Rilke and Freud', *New Literary History* (1996) 27 (4), 663–77.

Simpson, Mark, *Male Impersonators* (London: Cassell, 1994).

Sloane, Ethel, *Biology of Women* (London: Virago, 1999).

Sloterdijk, Peter, *Critique of Cynical Reason*, Michael Eldred (trans.) (Minnesota: University of Minnesota Press, 1987).

Sophocles, *The Theban Plays*, E. F. Watling (trans.) (London: Penguin, 1947).

Stone, Alison, 'On the Genealogy of Women: A Defence of Anti-Essentialism', in *Third Wave Feminism: A Critical Exploration*, Stacy Gillis, Gillian Howie and Rebecca Munford (eds) (Basingstoke: Palgrave Macmillan, 2007), pp. 16–30.

Swift, Jonathan, *Poems* (London: Everyman, 1998).

Tew, Philip, 'Situating the Violence of J.G. Ballard's Postmillennial Fiction: The Possibilities of Sacrifice, the Certainties of Trauma', in *J.G. Ballard: Contemporary Critical Perspectives*, Jeanette Baxter (ed.) (London: Continuum, 2008), pp. 107–19.

Verhaeghe, Paul, 'The Collapse of the Function of the Father and Its Effect on Gender Roles', in *Sexuation*, Renata Salecl (ed.) (London: Duke University Press, 2000), pp. 131–56.

Vidler, Anthony, *The Architectural Uncanny: Essays in the Modern Unhomely* (Cambridge, MA: MIT Press, 1992).

Virilio, Paul, *Desert Screen: War at the Speed of Light*, Michael Degener (trans.) (London: Continuum, 2002).

— *Art and Fear*, Julie Rose (trans.) (London: Continuum, 2003).

Virno, Paolo, *A Grammar of the Multitude: For an Analysis of Contemporary Forms of Life*, Isabella Bertoletti, James Cascaito, and Andrea Casson (trans.) (Los Angeles: Semiotext(e), 2004).

Wells, H. G., 'James Joyce's *Portrait of the Artist as a Young Man*', *New Republic* (1917) X, 158–60.

Widdowson, Peter, '"Writing Back": Contemporary Re-visionary Fiction', *Textual Practice* (2006) 20 (3), 491–508.

Wilson, Lisa, 'British Women Writing Satirical Novels in the Romantic Period: Gendering Authorship and Narrative Voice', *Romantic Textualities: Literature and Print Culture, 1780–1840* (2007) 17, 17–24.

Wilson, Scott, *The Order of Joy: Beyond the Cultural Politics of Enjoyment* (New York: SUNY Press, 2008).

Woolf, Virginia, *Between the Acts* (London: Vintage, 1990).

Wright, Elizabeth, *Lacan and Postfeminism* (Cambridge: Icon, 2000).

Žižek, Slavoj, *The Sublime Object of Ideology* (London: Verso, 1989).

— *The Plague of Fantasies* (London: Verso, 1997).

— 'A Plea for Leninist Intolerance', *Critical Inquiry* (2000) 28 (2), 542–66.

— *For They Know Not What They Do: Enjoyment as a Political Factor* (London: Verso, 2002).

— *The Puppet and the Dwarf: The Perverse Core of Christianity* (Cambridge, MA: MIT Press, 2003).

— '*Objet a* in Social Links', in *Reflections on Seminar XVII: Jacques Lacan and the Other Side of Psychoanalysis*, Justin Clemens and Russell Grigg (eds) (London: Duke University Press, 2006), pp. 107–28.

— *The Parallax View* (Cambridge, MA: MIT Press, 2006).

— *Violence: Six Sideways Reflections* (London: Profile, 2008).

— *In Defense of Lost Causes* (London: Verso, 2008).

Zupančič, Alenka, *Ethics of the Real: Kant, Lacan* (London: Verso, 2000).

— *The Shortest Shadow: Nietzsche's Philosophy of the Two* (Cambridge, MA: MIT Press, 2003).

— 'When Surplus Enjoyment Meets Surplus Value', in *Reflections on Seminar XVII: Jacques Lacan and the Other Side of Psychoanalysis*, Justin Clemens and Russell Grigg (eds) (London: Duke University Press, 2006), pp. 155–78.

— *The Odd One In: On Comedy* (Cambridge, MA: MIT Press, 2008).

Index

nostalgia 47, 87, 90, 103, 165, 173
  text 107

Oedipus Complex 50, 51, 91, 101–2
One, fantasy of *see* wholeness, fantasy of
ontology 7, 97, 120
Oppermann, Martin 180n. 21
oppression 8, 11, 72, 74, 76, 89, 119,
    122, 128, 129, 144, 163, 166
  consumer culture and 71
  economic 167
  patriarchal 161
  of population 85
  social 90
  of women 37, 152, 157, 163, 170
ordinary and exceptional knowledge
    realms 119
Oriental Other 139, 145, 148
Other *see* Otherness
Otherness 35, 53, 55–6, 58, 118, 120,
    126, 128, 131, 132, 139–41,
    145–9, 156

Pac Man (videogame) 26–7
Palahniuk, Chuck 2, 34, 64, 175n. 37,
    177n. 3
  Choke 59
  Fight Club 35, 58, 59, 100, 102, 106,
    121 *see also* nihilism
  Haunted 59
  Invisible Monsters 29
  Lullaby 59
  Pygmy 59
  Rant 59
parody 20, 43, 44, 77, 107, 109, 129,
    151, 157
pastiche 105, 107
Pater, Walter 118, 122, 179n. 23
  The Renaissance 117
paternal function 35, 39, 48, 49–53, 56,
    58, 84, 101, 102, 103
patriarchy 21, 36, 103, 155–6, 161, 172
  authority and 51, 154, 169
  Great Chain of Being and 166
  hegemony 166
  ideology of 107, 151, 152, 166–70,
    173

norms 160, 163, 173
postfeminism 152, 154, 155, 157,
    161–2
power 29, 43, 50, 56, 63, 88, 91, 98,
    116, 153, 159
  capitalist 90
  decline of 52
  deconstructing position of 125
  diffusion of 73
  discourse 8, 21, 31, 42, 65, 114
  of fictions 95
  financial 21
  global 12
  and moral superiority 119
  sovereignty and 89
  structure 6, 9, 61, 64, 85, 163
  truth process and 122, 124, 125,
    126
  see also empowerment
pragmatism
  and language 7
praxis 1, 2, 34, 87
Project Mayhem and nihilism 62,
    77–80
psyche 45, 48, 53, 57, 63, 80, 94
psychoanalysis 22–7, 29, 31, 36, 39, 40,
    42, 50, 53, 57, 59, 60, 63, 64, 69,
    72, 74, 84, 91, 101, 102, 129, 131,
    133, 136, 137, 150
pure reason 40

racism 37, 113, 128, 131, 145, 149,
    156–7
Rancière, Jacques 1, 174n. 12
  The Emancipated Spectator 11
Real 23–4, 25, 27, 60, 65, 67, 69, 70, 71,
    72, 73, 74, 75, 77, 78, 122, 125
reality 11, 23, 24, 50, 68, 72, 101–2,
    109, 110, 111, 115, 119, 121,
    124–5, 126
  social 96
repression 14, 23, 25, 30, 42, 43,
    61, 63, 73, 75, 76, 87, 118,
    149, 157
re-visionary fictions 106–8
revolution and multitude 82–4
  empire and 88–93